The
Management
Tactician

The Management Tactician

EXECUTIVE TACTICS FOR GETTING RESULTS

EDWARD C. SCHLEH

President, Schleh Associates, Inc.
Palo Alto, California

McGRAW-HILL BOOK COMPANY

New York St. Louis San Francisco Düsseldorf Johannesburg
Kuala Lumpur London Mexico Montreal New Delhi
Panama Paris São Paulo Singapore
Sydney Toronto Tokyo

Library of Congress Cataloging in Publication Data:

Schleh, Edward C.
   The management tactician.

   1.   Industrial management.   I.   Title.
HD31.S334   658.4   74-9610
ISBN 0-07-055293-2

1234567890   BPBP   7987654

*The editors for this book were William H. Mogan and Patricia A. Allen,
the designer was Naomi Auerbach, and its production was supervised
by George E. Oechsner. It was set in Alphatype by John C. Meyer
& Son, Inc.*

It was printed and bound by The Book Press.

To my wife

Contents

Preface

The management literature of the past several years has been replete with simplified theories that purport to solve all management problems. All the theories sound good, but managers find them confusing and hard to apply when trying to solve concrete, complex management problems. Even when the theories are sound, there is no carry-through to teach the manager how to apply them effectively. A basic difficulty is that these theories all too frequently cover only a segment of each management problem. They cannot be applied effectively without covering the other segments.

My previous book, *Management by Results* (McGraw-Hill), was an attempt to take an overall approach to the solution of management problems and to cover all facets by principle. In effect, it was a systems approach. Although executives appeared to accept the principles presented, I was disappointed to find when I went into their firms that their application indicated a very poor understanding of the meaning of those principles. An entire change in approach was necessary if the principles were to be applied effectively. It was clear that executives would have to understand the "why" for each principle and that the background reasons and implications were critical to the application.

This book is an attempt to correct that deficiency. While some new principles are introduced, the main purpose of this book is to teach an executive how to apply management principles in practice to get a better operation. During the past twenty-five years, I have had the opportunity to help solve management problems in a wide variety of organizations in business and government at all functions and all levels. Since my work, unlike that of most similar practitioners, almost invariably included applying the recommendations and making them work, I developed a much better comprehension of the implications of the principles. In this book, I have tried to point up those implications by a series of real life examples. It is my hope that this approach will give every executive or manager a much more realistic perspective on the implications of the principles in practice.

For reasons that will be obvious to the reader, all examples used throughout the book have been camouflaged and, of course, all data refer to both women and men. The company, the function, or even the department, are often changed in the presentation. The examples have, of course, been simplified so that the reader will not be confused by extraneous material that does not apply to the principle being discussed. However, I am sure any sophisticated reader recognizes that many management problems have additional complexities beyond those that I might mention in any particular case.

Because of the way this philosophy has evolved, many other people besides myself have contributed to its development. I am, therefore, deeply indebted to the many friends, clients, and associates whose experience has contributed to the solutions of particular management problems and, therefore, to the insight that resulted from them. I am particularly indebted to my associate Edwin R. Hodges for his perceptive application and critical evaluation of the principles which have helped so much to broaden the philosophy. I am especially indebted to my associate Ardath Bierlein for her great help in research, planning, and editing the manuscript. I alone, of course, must assume full responsibility for any errors or mistaken conclusions in the book which may later be pointed up.

Edward C. Schleh

chapter one

Only the Right Tactics Get Results

Both sound overall strategy and good management tactics are necessary if an executive is to be successful. Strategy includes the planning needed to set broad direction and goals, the broad decisions on action to be taken, and the broad policies needed to maintain the direction that has been set. Strategy covers all the functions of the business—sales, production, product line, administration, personnel, and finance.

The frustrating thing is that even the best-laid plans and policies go awry in application. Sometimes it appears as though people down the line simply did not get the word and therefore the program was not carried through. At other times they seem to have received the word but misunderstood it. It is amazing how varied the interpretations can be of apparently clean-cut decisions or policies. Sometimes people simply work on other things besides those that lead in the direction of the goals set by the executive. At other times programs miss because little urgency is attached to the problem, so the timing is off. An executive is then hit with too many unpleasant surprises. The action does not come up to the plan. It seems that people have not developed a full sense of responsibility for contribution to the overall goals of the institution and do not exhibit aggressive initiative in pursuing expected results.

All these problems point up a basic need to have a sound system of management tactics by which all plans can be smoothly carried out down through the organization. Tactics get each management person in the organization to carry out his part of the plan efficiently. Too frequently tactics are merely assumed, but without a perceptive approach to tactics, strategy is often just wishful thinking, not a practical reality.

Why do tactics fail? A major factor is the tendency of management to focus on symptoms rather than on basic causes. For example, if costs are out of line, it seems natural to focus on the correction of the apparent cause of cost deviations. It would be better to place the emphasis on finding out the underlying reasons why the deviation occurred. It might have been poorly trained people, a poor tie-in with scheduling, or the lack of a thorough cost accountability system down the line.

An evidence of the tendency to focus on symptoms is the frequent comment "It is all a matter of communications." The implication is that people simply do not understand the policy or program. The cause is usually much deeper.

An executive needs tactics that emphasize basic causes. The tactics must solve the fundamental problems involved in carrying through on strategy. Without such a system of executive tactics, strategy will usually be disappointing.

Good management tactics are people-oriented. They

should encourage people to use all their energies in the best direction of the institution. Many modern management systems, encouraged by the increased sophistication of the computer, are often antagonistic to sound tactics. There is an increasing trend toward people control by figures. The underlying rationale is to assume that people "ought to" do something and a check is simply needed to see if they did it. This is poor tactics. Sound tactics would try to create a climate that encourages people to do the best job.

PRESSURE—THE KEY TO MANAGEMENT

How can you develop sound tactics that lead to an invigorating management climate? The starting point is to recognize that people do what they do in response to pressures. Most people would like to do a good job, provided they are encouraged to do it, but many of the pressures within an organization act as obstacles.

Any management man is subjected to many pressures. These pressures result from the way the organization is designed—the effect of policies, the impact of procedures, the limitations of control systems, the emphasis of accountability systems, the uncertainty of incomplete delegation, etc. In most organizations there seem to be just about as many pressures working against the direction of the company results as for them. As a consequence, a firm is lucky if it gets as much as 50 percent value from the talents of its management people.

Sound tactics aim at removing those obstacles that tend to prevent a person from driving toward the goals of the organization and increasing the positive pressures that will work toward those goals. A creative management climate strongly encourages each person to work in the best direction of the achievements of the institution.

Sound tactics is the most effective way to increase radically the productivity of all the management people in an organization. In the following chapters we will explore the way good management tactics get results in any organization.

chapter two

Focus the Whole Team
in the Right Direction

The purpose of tactics is to get people to carry out their work so that the overall ends of the organization are most effectively achieved. The starting point is to make sure that each person knows what results he should be aiming at in his job. There must be a delegation of a responsibility to get certain results, and the person must understand this delegation.

What is a result? It is any accomplishment that has a positive effect on the goals of the institution. In a corporation the profit and loss statement must usually be affected either currently or in the future.

The first error of delegation comes from the popular belief that if people carry through on the right activities, they will get the right results. As a consequence, managers will often delegate by activity, particularly where it is hard to trace a result to one person. A firm making control systems evaluated their methods engineers by the projected savings shown on cost sheets for new methods. To put emphasis on the sheets, bonuses were even paid on these projected savings. The savings often did not materialize, however, when the methods actually got into production. There always seemed to be off-setting activities that threw off costs. Projected savings on cost sheets were not results. The true result that should have been delegated to these methods engineers was the net improvement in cost per unit that showed up in production after the methods were in.

The typical job description is a prime example of the error of delegating by activity. It is primarily a catalog list of the duties and activities of a position. Frequently the person on the job (and his manager) feels that if he carries through on all the activities on the job description, he has done a good job. The prime results toward which the job should have been directed, however, may not have been achieved. Job descriptions, therefore, are a poor method of delegation.

Sometimes managers delegate by results, but they try to cover every small or large result that the job could possibly affect. In effect, this process subordinates major results. A person has only a certain amount of energy. Management is far better off picking the three to five major results toward which the job should be directed and having the individual concentrate on these. He will usually do the necessary work on the other items, anyway. By focusing on the few big items, total achievement is normally greater. This approach permits a broader delegation of authority. The person on the job has leeway to sacrifice what is less important.

The contact representatives in a wholesale grocery firm were constantly called on to make surveys, carry out special supplies, make reports on credit, etc. — all activity. This work took 50 to 60 percent of their time. As a consequence, they did not have enough time to spend with each supermarket helping the manager on merchandising and training so that he would give more effective service to customers and increase sales. In this case the basic job should have been to help the supermarkets merchandise and to make them profitable, with a minimum emphasis on reports and surveys.

Paper work can detract from results. It seems logical to have foremen fill out voluminous reports because the data is needed for computer analysis. After all, a computer is ineffective without adequate data. Foremen then become deskbound because of all the paper work they have to do. Their basic job is to train and supervise their people so that they produce well. Paper emphasis detracts from this job. It is usually far better to minimize this paper work or pull it back into an office to be done for the foreman so that he has time to direct himself to his basic result, good production from his people.

EVERYTHING MEASURED IS NOT A RESULT

A common fallacy of delegation is to assume that if an item can be measured, it is a result, or at least it is suitable for delegation. This is not true. In a farm equipment company, engineers were held accountable for turning out their designs by release dates. They did, but within a week they put "holds" on eight or ten parts of the design, which, in effect, held up the whole process in manufacturing until these items could be redesigned and put into production. The dates were definite and the percent release of designs was measurable, but results were still in doubt.

A similar kind of problem occurred with a group of sales representatives. Great emphasis was placed on the number of new customer calls made per month. The emphasis was fortified by a requirement for voluminous call reports. But new customer business lagged. The result should have been the number of new customer accounts put on the books or the volume of new customer orders received. As an aside, they had a beautiful file of "kitchen table" reports which no one used.

An airline was concerned about the service its reservation agents gave customers. They therefore had auditors plug in on the agents' telephone conversations and evaluate them by checking a standard list of items that were to be covered in a discussion with a customer. One agent came up with a rating of 60 when 90 was considered good. She sold a $400 complicated ticket to the customer and satisfied him, but still she was rated down. The system allowed no leeway for coping with the problem of the customer. It resulted in a measurement of activity, not of results.

Another error is to delegate a result that does not necessarily affect the goals of the institution (profit, if it is a corporation). A large research department of a company had carried on some fine research in a number of promising directions. Unfortunately, little of this research had resulted in profitable products. The argument given was that some excellent knowledge had been acquired. In this corporation the research director should have been aiming at only one result, profit on new products that comes from his research. In the long run it was the only result that could have justified the expense, even though certain knowledge might help crack a problem along the way.

The very nature of delegation itself presents a problem in delegating by results. Delegation is a downward process from the superior to the subordinate. At each level above the first level there seems to be a greatly reduced knowledge of the problems as they exist at the first level, where the action is. In order to meet this problem, it is better to have the expected results built up bit by bit from the bottom all through the management chain. They should then be approved or changed and delegated downward from the executive to the appropriate managers, and so on down the line. In effect, the best approach to effective delegation is to ask each manager down the line to build his own delegation and propose it. His boss then confirms or changes it as a delegation downward. This approach gets much greater commitment toward the direction in which the executive is aiming. The subordinate has planned for his contribution.

The first step in delegation in any organization is to determine the overall results of the organization. In a corporation, a profit level, percent growth, diversification of product lines, foreign expansion, or a general retrenchment costwise may be overall goals. In a state highway department one of the goals was to provide service in the form of maximum traffic movement per hour on certain highways. Another was to maintain these roads at a minimum cost per ton-mile.

The overall goals of the organization come from the broad strategy. The better the strategy, the better it is directed toward sound goals. Therefore, the more practical the ensuing tactics will be. Tactics should push everyone most effectively toward these goals. In effect, it gets the segments of the goals down to each job and develops a spirit or enthusiasm toward their accomplishment, so that they are more likely to be achieved—the purpose of tactics. If the strategy is impractical, tactics will be disappointing in achieving expected results.

ASK, "WHY THE JOB?"

How do you get the overall goals down to each management person in the management chain? The best process is what we call job purpose. It is a process whereby the manager and his subordinate clarify the results toward which the person should be striving. It is usually unwise to allow numbers to get into this discussion. The idea is to point the direction, not to develop objectives with figures.

The first questions you might ask are: "Why is the job here?" "What is supposed to happen in results because it is here?" "What should its contribution be to results?" In a paint company the sales representatives wound up with the purpose of helping their dealers move merchandise. Although the dealer was, in essence, the customer on the books of the company, the important job of the sales representatives was not simply to sell the dealer, but to develop merchandising and other methods so that the dealer, in turn, would sell. Only then would he repurchase and the representatives sell more. This is a common problem with almost all sales departments working through secondary distribution. They operate as though the dealer or the jobber is the customer instead of a further merchandiser to an eventual consumer.

In a state department of education a mathematics consultant initially felt that the purpose of her job was to develop training programs for mathematics teachers in high schools. After discussing why her job was there and what was supposed to happen because she was there, she agreed that a better purpose would be to maximize the mathematics knowledge assimilated by students by the time they left high school. One practical way to check this was to find out how well these students did later in mathematics-related courses in college.

In many manufacturing companies the job of machine maintenance is looked at as that of doing the required maintenance at the lowest cost. When the question arises, "Why is the job here?" it often becomes plain that the primary job should be to reduce machine downtime due to mechanical problems. More emphasis on preventive maintenance and scheduling of the work usually results from this approach.

In a bank, an experienced officer had gone downhill,

looking at his job as primarily that of handling customers who came into the bank. He did not aggressively try to increase bank income. After a discussion of the purpose of his job, it became clear to him that he was supposed to increase loan income as well as insurance income. (This bank could sell insurance.) Within a year he doubled his loan income and increased his insurance referrals.

A good question to ask in clarifying the purpose of the job is, "What would be lost if the job were not here?" The advertising department of a consumer service company favored large advertising outlays for slick magazine ads. The main consideration seemed to be image. When they considered the implications of eliminating the job, it became obvious that the major purpose was to increase revenue. A review of customer characteristics made it clear that if a portion of the advertising money were spent locally, it would have more effect on potential customers.

In a traffic department the question of the effect if the job were eliminated led to a surprising answer. This department had been focusing heavily on cutting traffic costs. As a consequence, many shipments were late, causing problems in the various plants and with customers. When the question was asked, "What would happen if the job were not here?" it immediately was apparent that plants would use different traffic approaches so that shipments would be on time, since this was the principal contribution of traffic as envisaged by the plants. The whole outlook of the traffic department changed. They balanced cost with service.

In digging deeper into the purpose of the job you should always ask, "How can this job affect other people's results?" Very frequently, the impact on other people is more important than the direct results from the job, and this impact must be emphasized. In a metal-fabricating company, the way the machining was done had a considerable effect on the cost and timing of the assembly department. In some cases it could affect it as much as 30 percent, even though the machining was apparently within specifications. Little problems of timing, nibs, stacking, and so on, all could affect assembly. The impact on the assembly had to be an important result for machining. The impact on others can be greater than the direct results if the second department has heavy equipment with perhaps $200 or $300 per hour overhead. Then the cost impact of something done in the first department may be much greater in the subsequent department than in its own. The printing industry is a good example of this. A prior department may have a heavy impact on press operation.

A sales department sometimes has greater profit impact by its effect on plants than by a reasonable increase in volume. When the general sales manager of a job shop company was asked how his job affected other people's results, it became clear that there could be a considerable effect on manufacturing cost of specials. To get the order a sales representative would agree to special parts or special handling for the same price. He could not believe the extra costs these caused. A principal purpose of his job was, therefore, the reduction of special parts orders and special handling.

CHECK FUTURE IMPACT

A common failing of delegation is to focus only on the current. Before finally deciding on the purpose of the job, you should always ask, "What are the important future results that this job should affect?" In many companies it is important to get maximum impact of new products the year they come out. Focusing the sales managers on volume alone will not get adequate concentration on new products. It usually takes a great deal of missionary work to launch new products with little showing on the order pad for the time spent. A separate result has to be set up for orders on new products. In this way sales managers and sales representatives build their territories for the future.

Only after there is a clear understanding of the results toward which a person should work should objectives be set with figures to formalize them for accountability purposes for a period, like a year. The prime benefit comes from defining the results toward which a manager should be working. After this definition it does help to solidify these results into measurable objectives.

Once objectives have been established for a job, there is a strong tendency to be locked in and to keep these objectives (perhaps with different figures) for a long time thereafter. Any system of defining objectives expected of a person must be flexible. If you have defined objectives that fit one period and hold them over to another when they do not fit, the setup may actually result in more losses than gains, even though you are apparently measuring results. You should go through a job purpose analysis each period to keep up to date on the results expected at this time. Only then should new objectives be set.

In an airline it seemed that sales cost per dollar of sales was a good objective for the sales department and, therefore, for each district. However, the airline had a high seasonal in its sales. A number of planes might run in October at 20 or 30 percent load factor. Obviously, it was hard to get people to ride in these periods and required more sales expense per seat to get them to go. There were certain ethnic groups who might want to go in this period, but it might take more sales expense or some concession to get them to travel at this time. Obviously, it was worth a great deal of sales expense to fill an otherwise empty seat. In the normal period, however, it was worthwhile for the sales department to focus on sales cost per dollar of sales.

Any objective that you set for a job should require a careful review for change for any major period, say a year. A plant may have a suitable objective in terms of costs in one period. If you then put in a new manufacturing line, this objective no longer holds. The plant manager should focus on getting that new line operating efficiently as quickly as possible. Too much emphasis on overall cost at that point may be detrimental.

Any delegation of objectives should always build in improvement. In most plants managers should have some responsibility each year to improve methods that reduce cost so that the firm will improve in the future. Improvement may be on a particular machine, it may be in certain methods, it may be on a particular product, or it may be on a series of products. However, this work usually costs money this year and affects this year's budget. Unless a separate objective is set up to encourage managers to do this work for the future, it will lag. Budget pressure is against it.

The improvement requirement should not be confined to line departments. Staff positions should have it, too. Even though accounting departments keep records on cost deviations of all the other people in the organization, they often direct little attention to the cost of their own methods. The time-consuming check and double-check, and sometimes triple-check, that is prevalent in many accounting departments is mute evidence of this. A cost improvement objective in these departments can often be more effective than in line departments.

chapter three

Avoid Crisis Management

Crises in management do not usually come from failure to focus on results. They are primarily due to failure to focus on *all* the important results. Gains in one result cause greater losses in other results, leading to imbalance. The final accomplishment may actually be negative.

THE GREAT PITFALL—IMBALANCE

What is imbalance? It means that one result is achieved but others lag. It is caused by excessive drive toward one result to the detriment of several other important results. It is the failure to recognize the optimum principle: For every result there is an optimum accomplishment in any one period of time beyond which pressure on that result will not get more accomplishment but will in most cases actually detract from

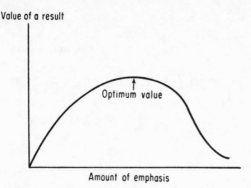

Value of a result

Optimum value ↑

Amount of emphasis

FIGURE 1 Optimum value of a result.

the overall accomplishment. Beyond the optimum point either a better result has no value or other results are affected negatively (see Figure 1) and crises develop.

The most common type of imbalance occurs in a typical sales department where the pressure is on volume of sales. This emphasis seems perfectly logical. Isn't it the reason for the existence of the sales department—to get sales? Because of this emphasis new accounts do not move, especially in outlying areas. It takes a great deal more missionary work to sell the same volume to new accounts than it does to sell it to old customers. Therefore, the field force tends to put little effort into the new-account drive. In three or four years overall volume does not increase because the new accounts were not added and attrition reduces the number of old accounts. There is then a frantic and constant crisis in trying to get increases in volume. This problem hits small companies particularly. They grow initially with pressure on volume. After volume has reached a reasonable level, the company finds that their sales tend to even off because they have not changed to a balanced approach to sales accountability.

Lack of balance, more than any other item, can lead to failure of a division or of a company. A sales-minded president pushes sales but does not put adequate emphasis on costs. His company is costed out of the market, and no matter what the sales effort, they have to struggle to maintain their position. In another company, a manufacturing-minded chief executive emphasizes low cost. He does not put adequate pressure on new-product development or on sales effectiveness, however. He then finds himself with a low-cost product which is somewhat obsolete and with a lagging sales force. His company does not show the profit that it should, considering its low-cost operation. He must put drive into all areas. Imbalance is critical at the top and remains critical in every management job in the organization.

Banks must put a great deal of weight on audits of branches because they are regulated and handle other people's money. Unfortunately, bank executives tend to expand this audit far beyond the actual governmental control requirement. A typical operations manager becomes almost a senior clerk trying to meet all the requirements of the audit. If she gets a few negative comments on the audit, the roof falls in on her. On the other hand, if she does not train her tellers very well and does not give good service to customers, there is little negative pressure. She usually has high turnover in her teller group, which adds to her problem of giving service to her customers. In this case a careful review of the absolute necessity for audit items is in order so that additional emphasis can be placed on the development of teller service. This is the old law of moderation: Something good carried too far tends to be negative.

Imbalance can be caused by an apparently logical procedure. A job shop sales representative was paid on straight commission. Whenever he got the estimator's price, he usually cut it, pointing out that he needed to in order to meet competition. It seemed logical to go along with him because he apparently knew the competitive situation best. The plant was always in a profit crisis, however, trying to maintain margins on orders. The error of the emphasis was pointed up when the estimator mistakenly estimated 20 percent too low and the sales representative cut even this price. Because the sales representative had such an influence on price, he should have been made accountable for total profit on his orders to encourage him toward a sound business decision of price versus volume. Having prices approved by the home office is an illusion of control. Who in the home office knows whether competition would have permitted a higher price in a particular case? Set it up to the individual's advantage to make a balanced price decision.

PLAN FOR COOPERATION

People do not work in isolation. A good management setup should, therefore, encourage cooperation. The Detroit sales manager of a railroad received credit only for sales originating in Detroit, the sales manager in New York only for those originating in New York, and so on. But the decision on the carrier might have been made by either the vendor or the purchaser. It was not in the interest of each sales manager to make a sale of a shipment that terminated in his area but originated with a vendor in another city. The plan encouraged unbalanced emphasis. A simple change in recognition solved the problem. Each sales manager was given one-half the credit for all sales originating or ending in his area. It was now to his advantage to cooperate with other sales managers to get all the sales possible.

The paper-treating department of a tape plant caused problems in the coating department by sending them treated rolls that were slightly off-grade, taking a chance that they might go through. Their own costs therefore looked good, but the procedure caused a great deal of trouble in the coating department. The plant manager was constantly arbitrating conflicts between the two departments. He then changed the system to charge back a penalty of three times the credit against the treating department when a roll sent to the coating department proved to be defective. The treating department then cut out a much higher percentage of poor rolls. It was to their advantage to make balanced decisions. A single charge was not enough to get them to do it.

Any good result, even improvement, can be carried too far and lead to a crisis. A vice president of manufacturing appointed a very creative engineer as plant manager to jog a lagging plant. The new plant manager put in one new idea after another, causing a great deal of turmoil. Strangely enough, costs steadily went up even though most of the ideas were good. He was then replaced with a new plant manager who simply put a six-month moratorium on new ideas and let everything settle in. He capitalized on the new ideas of his predecessor. By the end of six months his costs went down 25 percent. After that, he put a balanced emphasis on new ideas. In order to hit the optimum level on each result, you must devitalize the negative effect of going too far on one result, even on improvement.

To avoid a crisis in the future, an executive should weigh in future results. Even budget and management-by-objective programs often cause future crises. Frequently, both of these are aimed only at current results. Over a period of time a short-run stamping company showed a fine increase in sales, but with a constantly decreasing profit margin. Why? Very little of this was repeat business, which is where the profit was—no new dies were required. The vice president of sales was pressured for current volume, and budgets stressed current cost coverage in pricing. The vice president of sales was then made accountable for repeat business. This meant that first orders that had high potential for reorders might even be priced at a loss because the repeat business would be profitable. The result was a considerable increase in profitable business, even though some of the nonrepeat business was lost.

Executive pressure on a central engineering department to produce designs for low capital costs can cause future operating crises. If the cost of the subsequent maintenance or downtime is not charged back against the project, it is not the engineer's responsibility. Engineers make a greater company contribution when maintenance and downtime on machines they designed are considered part of the cost of the project. It is then worthwhile for the engineer to develop a balanced design. A longer term evaluation is required, however, instead of just a current cost evaluation.

In most companies long-range results are sacrificed because the short range is immediately measurable. Typical information systems are not geared to balance long-term with short-term. A well-managed company had excellent records on each of its machines, including maintenance. They therefore established bonuses for maintenance superintendents based on a percent decrease in maintenance costs per year. Over a period of years all maintenance superintendents consistently decreased their maintenance costs and earned good bonuses. It was then discovered that machines that should have lasted twelve years were replaced in nine; machines that should have lasted ten were replaced in seven years. When a machine was worn out, the plant manager simply called in a representative from the home office engineering department who agreed, "That's a piece of junk," and OK'd the form for capital approval. The maintenance saving was an illusion. The increased cost of equipment far outweighed the savings in maintenance cost. Always ask, "What's the long-range loss?" of any short-range measured objective. Put a hedge on the short-range.

In long-range development work a change in the evaluation of time can prevent expensive crises. There is ordinarily no push in the early part of a three-year project because there seems to be no urgency. It appears foolish to approve overtime at the beginning of the project or break-ins into schedule to complete testing. As a consequence, there is considerable waiting time on the part of engineers and an increased cost. Dates are missed later on, so it may require an extra year to go to market. Most long-term projects should be approached with an air of strong urgency once they are approved. It is almost always worthwhile in the accomplishment obtained and in the lower cost of the project.

CLARIFY ALL THE EFFECTS OF THE JOB

In order to maintain balance in every job, all its major effects on the organization must be clarified and accountability established for each of them. The pressure from home office staff must also be put into perspective. Inventories seemed high in a company, so the home office inventory specialists applied pressure to reduce local maintenance inventories. Machine downtime increased in one plant because maintenance men often waited for parts, even after they had torn down a machine. Since the plant was 70 miles from a major town, the parts manager cut his inventories, assuming he could depend upon suppliers' inventories in the city. However, it took a four-hour round trip to pick up a piece, so a crew would lose the four hours waiting for a part. More important, expensive machinery would be idle for four hours. The parts manager was tops with the home office, however, because he kept his inventories low. He had to be made accountable for waiting time for any part as well as for inventory levels in order to get him attuned to balanced plant effectiveness.

A different type of inventory emphasis caused imbalance in a supermarket chain. The treasurer's department highlighted inventory turnover in order to cut cash needs. Each store manager felt the pressure and got in tune. A number of stores had a whole series of empty shelves. What would this mean to you as a customer? It would mean that you had little choice, so you would go to another store. The managers were chasing sales away, but they had terrific inventory turnover. In the home office these managers were considered outstanding even though their stores were selling $40,000 per week and should have been hitting $60,000.

Even where inventory turnover is helpful in one place, it may be inappropriate throughout the system. A department store established a high-grade men's shop. In the first years it was perfectly logical that the major emphasis be placed on getting customers. After that, however, a more balanced approach had to include volume, inventory control, and profit on the investment. It seemed logical to use the same stock-control approaches that had worked so well in other departments. These were inappropriate. Inventory turnover had to be approached differently. Customers in a high-grade men's shop must be given choice, even though the volume is not high on any one item. Inventory turnover might be lower, but the higher margins would compensate.

Strangely enough, the computer is a status quo pressure and can therefore precipitate crises—it is against the setting of balanced results to meet changing conditions. There is a natural inclination for systems and program people to resist changes in the routines to meet changed requirements. Measurements exert pressure. If the same measurements are used as before, there is a tendency to exert pressure the same as before, whether it is in tune with the new conditions or not. The problem is apparent in trying to get new records to reflect improvement in methods. Computers must fit the problem. It is unrealistic to expect the problem to change to meet the needs of the computer.

Executives often deemphasize an important result because measurements seem difficult. The superintendents of an oil refinery were held accountable by number of barrels processed. Essentially the same credit was given if the barrels were diverted to a lower-level product. This change in yield, however, could make a considerable difference in value of output. It was difficult to keep a running record of yield value by department, since both the crude and the product expected from it varied frequently. As a consequence, central planning had to specify heats, pressures, and settings with the expectation that best yields would result. When a computer record was developed sensitive to the many changes in requirement, the value of yields increased. The foremen and superintendents could then be encouraged to make finer adjustments and recommend operating variations to optimize yield values.

In many operations, conditions change weekly or monthly, so executives feel they cannot set firm objectives in advance. Plants do not know what their volume will be in the subsequent year. The cost goals for the plant managers or their people are, therefore, hard to set in advance because they are usually affected by volume produced. A vice president of manufacturing then feels that he must exercise judgment in reviewing the performance of those people at the end of the period. Such a review can destroy commitment because managers will not know where they stand.

THE FLOATING STANDARD

A good way to approach this problem is to develop a floating standard (see Figure 2). Set one line for reasonable cost expected under different projected volumes. Then draw another line for the cost expected for the same projected

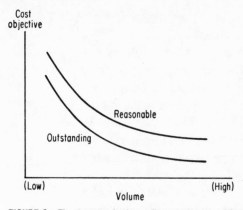

Cost
objective

Reasonable

Outstanding

(Low) (High)
Volume

FIGURE 2 Floating standard to reflect changing conditions.

volumes if it were an outstanding job. You have then set goals
that are flexible and yet fixed in concept at the beginning
of the period. The plant manager knows what he is shooting
at every month. He can check his volume on the chart and
see what his costs should be. Under such a setup a plant
manager takes more aggressive action in getting his costs
and crew in line as his output varies. An executive, in turn,
can delegate much greater authority to the manager under
these circumstances.

The floating standard approach can be applied to many
operations. For instance, a chief executive of a residential
construction business used a floating-goal setup to evaluate
a vice president of marketing by tying his goals to building
starts. Trying to anticipate building starts a year ahead may
be quite a chancy thing. The key to an accountability system
is that *the basis* on which the measurement will be made is
known in advance, even though the measurement itself may
not be known. A floating standard still meets that requirement.

A critical, but subtle, problem in balance occurs in the
way managers give their people recognition for accomplishment. Let's suppose an executive has delegated results well,

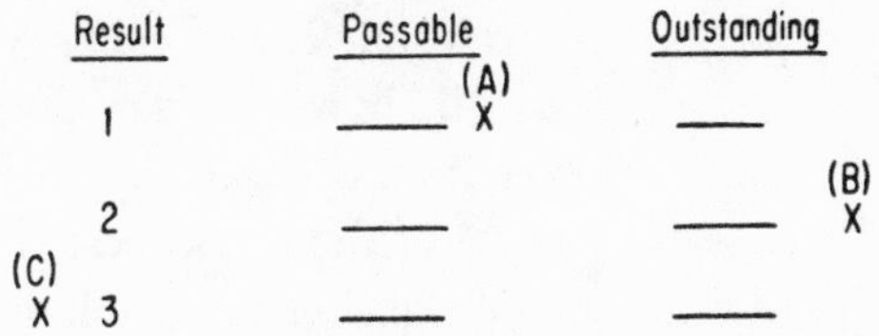

Result	Passable	Outstanding
1	___ (A) X	___
2	___	___ (B) X
(C) X 3	___	___

FIGURE 3 Unbalanced results.

perhaps three results (1, 2, and 3 in Figure 3), to a subordinate, and he has set a range for each result indicating passable results and outstanding results on each. On the first result the man has passable performance (A). He decides to stress one result (2) and gets far more than outstanding (B) on that result. He puts less effort on one of the other results (3), however, and gets less than passable accomplishment (C). He does not have time for that result. The normal inclination of the executive is to weigh the excess on one result (B) against the deficiency on the other (C). This is a mistake. When he has delegated three results, it means that they are all important and each requires at least reasonable accomplishment. For that matter, one may affect the results of another department. It should not be the option of the subordinate to decide not to emphasize any one of these results, at least not below an acceptable point; otherwise, he changes his delegation. If it is allowed, he will then feel free to do it again. His superior will never know what he can depend on.

WEIGH THE RESULTS

A good way to counter imbalance is to put weights on individual results expected of a person. Let's suppose that you set up three results for a man. He might feel that they are all of equal weight, or, what is more likely, he might pick or choose those that are appealing or those that are easiest and concentrate on them, feeling you will evaluate on an overall basis. If, however, you put weights on them, let's say 33 percent on each, this tells him that no matter what he does on two of them, the best that can be done is a 66 percent job. Weights encourage him to do a reasonable job on each of the items. They force balance.

In a container company most of the sales were consummated by higher-level executives. The sales people in the field did mainly servicing of the orders. As a consequence, few "closers" were developed, even though each sales representative was told to make a certain number of calls on prospective accounts each month. Only when new-account orders were given a 30 percent weight in the evaluation of the sales representative did they start to get new business. Some good closers developed in the process. Before that, new business-ended calls had been merely token calls. The emphasis had been only on servicing existing accounts.

Short-range goals can overshadow long-range goals. When a company is small, several functions are often combined and assigned to one person. A long-term function is often combined with a short-term function. Product development might be combined with engineering sales service and plant engineering. The latter two are short-range and always seem to have hot problems. The natural tendency of the chief engineer is to spend a great deal of time on them because they seem urgent. The long-range product development lags. When each of the three functions is given weight in the personal evaluation of the chief engineer, product development also moves.

Even if the results expected of a person are balanced in one period, they must be considered for change in a subsequent period. Conditions may have changed, requiring a change in results expected in order to maintain balance. Typical of this problem was a growing company that broke into the market by hiring sales representatives on a commission basis. They got a good foothold in the market. They then poured money into product development and customer service. Sales started to level off, however, because sales representatives tended to service existing business and did not push new accounts or new products. They could still easily earn high incomes. Their sales setup and compensation should have been changed. As the company got a better product line, they should have cut territories and put more intensive new-customer effort into each small territory. In addition, straight commission should have been changed to emphasize new accounts and products more. Almost any open-ended bonus plan can cause imbalance. A ceiling on the bonus permits change to meet changing conditions.

Should sales departments always be rated as tops if they sell so much the plants cannot produce it? Not necessarily. In fact, doing so might destroy the aggressiveness of your sales force in periods of tight industry supply. At that time almost any firm can sell whatever it makes. A new emphasis on service, allocation to hold the best customers for the future, profit, etc., is necessary to keep the sales force virile. Ask job purpose questions: "Why is the job here today?" "What contribution should it make?" "Why not eliminate the job?" The previous direction of effort is not appropriate in this period.

COMPETITION IS POOR MANAGEMENT

Many executives feel it is good management to encourage competition among their men. Here is how one of these contests backfired. In order to encourage good quality, a company took a random jar of product from each plant each month and graded it for quality. It was a "best jar" contest between plants. Obviously, every plant manager tried to be at the top of this list, since the list was circulated among the home office executives. The average quality of all plants was, in their terms, 99. On checking with the sales department it was found that 96 was perfectly adequate for all the customers' needs. The pressure for additional quality raised the cost of operation of these plants considerably. When the contest was thrown out and quality of 96 allowed, plant costs dropped.

Fluctuating executive pressure can cause crisis management. The chief executive of an over-the-road trucking company put pressure on his terminal managers for a new program every two months. One period it would be on the cost of loading trailers. Then when the low-cost loading caused trouble for unloading, the emphasis shifted to the way the cars were loaded. About this time sales were going down, so the terminal managers were put into a volume contest. Everyone increased volume until it was discovered that much of it was lightweight items like bread where there was little profit. Of course, the next program was on profitable volume. In the course of all this, it was noted that quite a few trailers stayed on the lots overnight, a costly process. There was then a drive to cut down the trailers on the lots.

Over a period of three years, every program was an outstanding success—obviously, every terminal manager followed the president's direction. But the total operation was no better after three years of successful programs than it was when it was begun. The program approach pushed toward imbalance. Every terminal manager would emphasize the item that was highlighted and would gradually deemphasize the items that were not. Accomplishment in these situations is an illusion. For best development, a manager must be recognized for a blend of the total requirements all the time, as if he were in business for himself.

A big hangup in many companies is the cost syndrome.

Because costs are so measurable, they are often highlighted, but accomplishment goals are not stressed with them. No cost is important except in terms of what you get for it. An extreme example of this emphasis is a sales bonus plan that was set up so that each sales representative's bonus was based on his total expense each year compared with his sales. In some cases sales representatives ran out of expense money a month and a half before the end of the year and simply did not go out on the road. They still got good bonuses, but the company lost the effectiveness of this time.

NO STARS

The star approach to delegation can perpetuate crises. A manager may have four people working for him—three are poor and one is a star. He may even delegate responsibility to all four on the basis of results. If difficult problems occur in the areas of the weak employees, his natural inclination is to give these problems to the star. She can be depended on. If the star had a full job in the beginning, she becomes overloaded. She lets some of her regular work go by the board and develops a relaxed sense of accountability for it. After all, she is handling the tough problems of the other three. On the other hand, if she is not able to carry through completely on one of the tough problems, she cannot be blamed. Didn't she take them on in addition to her regular work? This results in poor development of the star because she is not truly accountable. What is more important, it makes the weak ones even weaker. They do not have to carry through on a full delegation. Instead, the manager should delegate the full job to the weaker people but spend time with them to help them work through their problems so that they will develop. That is one of the manager's jobs: to develop all his people.

chapter four

The First Level —
Where the Results Are

Where do you get results? The results that you can trace to the final objectives or goals of the organization usually occur at the first decision-making level. All other levels should be aimed at making this level most effective. Executives do not give enough thought to the problems of the first management level when making decisions.

What is the first decision-making level? In a plant, it would be a foreman. His people produce all or part of the product. In a sales department, it would be a sales representative. He is the one who actually signs up the order. In an engineering company, it would be each individual engineer who makes a direct contribution to the final design. In the Internal Revenue Service, it would be each individual agent who reviews the return of a taxpayer.

Firms that operate through secondary distribution have a special problem in gearing to the first level. For sound management it is wise to look at the first-level management as that which serves the final customer. For example, in a petroleum company or a paint company, the independent dealer or retail store should be considered the bottom level. If the dealer or store manager does not satisfy the customer and sell him, neither the petroleum company nor the paint company will do very well. In a food-processing company, the final supermarket department managers should be looked at as the first level. All programs should be geared in this direction. No matter what the product, if adequate facings and shelf space are not assigned, the chances are that sales will be poor. If the firm sells through brokers or distributors, they, too, should be looked at as part of the company's sales chain, rather than stopping with the company representative who calls on them.

Much of the misdirection in companies comes because of a failure to recognize that the first level gets the results. The foreman builds a product through his operators. The vice president of manufacturing and the plant managers do not build anything. In sales, it is the sales representative who gets the order. Ordinarily, sales managers, product managers, and market research men do not, except through the sales representative.

While top executives may and should spend much of their time on strategy, they still need tactics to make the strategy effective. In most cases, the results of both the strategy and the tactics finally end up being first-level results. In other words, you can maximize executive results only by creative first-level operation and attention. For example, a strategy to increase market penetration is usually possible only through the effective first-level contact of the sales representative and the support of these contacts.

EXECUTIVE EDICT CAN MISDIRECT

Many executives operate as though the first level is not important; that all results come from executive edict. In a steel plant the president decided that there should be a 10 percent cut in costs. The tendency was to apply this 10 percent uniformly to all departments. One plant department, however, had just put in new machinery and changed methods so that a 20 percent cut was possible. Another department was in the process of changing the line and would be lucky if they could simply maintain their present costs. It was their responsibility to spend their time making the new line work. A third department had grown rapidly so that half of the employees were new. It would take a considerable effort to attain a 5 percent cost reduction. Their big job was to train new employees. Many cost reduction programs are just not realistic in light of the problems of the first level.

Supervision, especially training, is most critical at the first supervisory level. That is usually where the new people are. In a garment company, foreladies spent much of their time getting material. This was changed and they were made full-time supervisors, taught how to train, and given a half-time utility clerk to get materials. Output went up 10 percent, while returns and transportation cost went down.

First-level area sales managers in the field tend to be deskbound, especially if they are given offices. Their basic job should be to upgrade their sales representatives in the field. Since this is done best face to face, they should be out in the field 60 to 80 percent of their time working with their people. One company eliminated the offices of area sales managers so that they were out working in the field over 80 percent of the time. Sales showed a dramatic increase. This decision was more effective than all the special merchandising programs that had been concocted during the year.

Executives often think they know the problems of the first level because they remember what it was like when they were there twenty years ago. But that was a different day. A manufacturing vice president pushed a series of impractical programs in cost, maintenance, and quality in his plants because he remembered what it was like when he was there. Plants were much smaller and the product line was much less complex when he worked in them. In addition, there were no big plants to act as swing plants to take overloads. This swing approach is a complicating factor in a large plant of a multiplant operation. An executive must constantly develop feedup on the problems of the first level as they exist today if his decisions are to be practical.

Policies and procedures should be geared to the first level. A company operating through independent stores with a common name began to set policies and procedures in light of the fact that the store owner (their first level) was an independent operator. The company tried to sell him, to load him up by plugging programs with special deals, but they watched his credit very carefully. They then changed this policy to one of making each store owner successful. The company representatives trained store managers and their personnel in the store to be more effective. In addition, they helped the stores merchandise better and coached them on profitable store management. The appearance of the stores improved, they gave better service, and sales went up.

POLICY UNIFORM—PROCEDURE NOT

If policy is uniform, should procedure be uniform too? No. If procedure is in tune with first-level problems, it must allow for differences, because day-to-day first-level problems are rarely the same from job to job. Broad policy intent can still be met.

A company grew up on a shelf line, then developed several other divisions, one of which sold systems to the construction industry. In a tight cost period the president issued an order that all division managers were to cut inventories 30 percent. Of course, the vice president in charge of the construction division objected (as did the others), so he was allowed a little leeway. He had to cut only 25 percent. However, in serving the construction business, a supplier may deliver 99 percent of an order on time to a contractor, but if one item is late, it may hold up a crew of 100 for several days. This may result in the company being cut out as a supplier. In one year the loss in profit in this one division from the cut in inventory was greater than all the gains made in inventory in all the other divisions. A different approach to inventory reduction was needed for this division.

The chronic problem with procedure is that it becomes so detailed that it straps the first level. Procedures should always be checked at the first level in the different parts of the operation to be sure that they do not unduly restrict action. Whoever sets up the procedure should be accountable for any excessive losses that he causes in restraint at the first level. Some employee relations policies practically force almost all grievances up the line. It is usually far better to set them up so the foremen can handle grievances directly. Detailed sales call reports can get managers into the act so much that the sales representative cannot carry through and close a sale. He is too busy explaining what happened.

It seems very easy for skilled staff to operate in a rarefied atmosphere of independence. But staff, too, can be effective only through its impact on the first level (see Figure 4). It should be their goal to help the first level to be more effective in some way. A market research analyst may develop comprehensive studies of markets, but these studies must help the sales representatives make more sales. Otherwise, the information is merely academic.

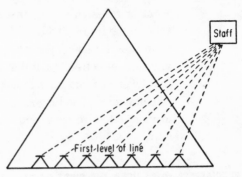

FIGURE 4 Impact of staff on first level.

Improving the organization setup can often get staff functions to increase their contribution to the first level. In a small plant, time study incentive and personnel were both aimed at getting more productivity from the operators. Dissimilar though these functions may seem, they were combined in one person. She had the total job of getting accurate time studies, selling them to employees, and getting the union to go along with fair standards. The setup simplified the organization to get results—motivating employees to higher productivity.

Computer installations often fail to give data that fit first-level problems. The computer group of a branch operation grew larger and larger and still wanted to expand further. The branches were asked what data were needed to help them get results. The branches could specify what they needed but would have to assume the cost. As a result, many reports were eliminated so that instead of requiring a larger installation, the computer installation developed idle time. A common reason for the unexpected high cost of computer installations is that they are not asked to gear to the solid first-level needs of the firm.

Long-range work should also be based on the first level, but it is the first level of the future. New-product development or research is effective only if it results in profitable sales in the future. To be able to do this three to eight years from now it should tie into first-level manufacturing costs and sales effectiveness at that time. The need to tie in to the first level is often also overlooked in the long-range planning of companies. The long-range planner should aim his plans at more effective operation of the first level at some future date.

SPECIALISTS MUST HELP THE FIRST LEVEL

It is more difficult to concentrate on first-level line problems in a functional organization, particularly when functional groups are redivided into more and more specialties. Specialists seem to have trouble looking at their jobs from the point of view of the first level, particularly if they are guided by high-level functional people.

A vice president of a large technical company was set up over all technical people, all the way down to the bottom. Wherever there was a plant manager, there was also a technical plant manager. Wherever there was a superintendent, there was a technical superintendent. Wherever there was a foreman, there was a technical foreman. But all these technical people reported up the chain finally to the technical vice president, not to any line people en route. At the bottom level, the quality foremen had the right to shut down machinery. They were typically inexperienced technical men right out of college who did not know the operation. They were not accountable for cost or for waste and were not, therefore, in tune with first-level operating requirements. Obviously, the line foremen and superintendents were not anxious to help them. In some cases the setup almost brought operations to a standstill.

A branch bank had a similar problem with an accounts receivable specialist. He set up policies and restrictions on accounts receivable loans to reduce losses. It was difficult for local branch managers to meet their customers' problems and build business. In many cases, accounts receivable borrowers could be substantial customers for the future, but this did not concern the accounts receivable specialist, who was mainly worried about maintaining a low loss ratio.

Each specialist focuses on his function, too frequently to the detriment of other functions when the effect gets down to the first level. This happened in a sales department with 400 sales representatives selling to the construction industry. With the multiplicity of products, they had nineteen product managers. The programs of these product managers all impinged on each sales representative. No sales representative could do an adequate job on all the programs of nineteen product managers, so the programs were lagging. In addition, a program might be inappropriate to a particular territory or inappropriate because of the timing, but there was home office pressure on each sales representative to carry through on it. The answer was to determine the number of programs a sales representative could work. It took only four product managers to develop this number of programs. The number of product managers was reduced to four and all products distributed among them. The timing of programs to the field was stretched out so the sales representatives could handle them. They had fewer but much more effective programs.

Information systems, too, should be based on the first level. Because they are usually an offshoot of financial systems, they are more often aimed at top-level executives. They lose their realism in terms of bottom-level problems. A department store chain set up a complete system of reports for every department. These were cross-compared from one store to another and from one branch to another. This comparison caused more harm than good because it assumed that customers and customer problems were the same in all localities. This assumption was not realistic. The problems of a store that sold in a semirural area were different from those of one that operated in a high-income area, or those of a store in a blue-collar area.

ORGANIZE BY THE FIRST LEVEL

At a certain stage of development almost all companies face a decision as to whether they should divisionalize or not. The key to the decision is the first-level problems. If the first-level sales and manufacturing problems are different in two major product lines, you will get greater impetus if you separate them into two independent divisions. Otherwise, one line tends to be overshadowed by the first-level approaches needed for the other.

In an airline, freight sales were combined with passenger sales in districts. But passenger sales managers had usually come up through passenger sales. There was a natural tendency to try the same approaches for selling freight as those used for selling seats to passengers. There was also a tendency to deemphasize freight sales. As a result, freight sales did not advance as rapidly as they should have.

On the other hand, an original equipment supplier for the automotive industry developed a lawn-care product. The selling and manufacturing problems were entirely different. They separated the lawn-care product entirely and put it under a division manager who had full control of manufacturing, sales, and development. This turned out to be a very profitable item very quickly. It would have been smothered if it had been kept in the established marketing and manufacturing departments. The first-level problems were different.

Many firms find that new products do not develop the way they should because management does not recognize the first-level differences. A firm that had been quite successful making and selling large generators developed a line of home standby generators. It was assumed that the marketing department would handle the marketing of the standby generators, the manufacturing department the manufacturing, and the engineering department the engineering. It did not work. Selling to a home is entirely different from selling to a utility. In their large generator business they were used to building in longevity and strength. Home standbys needed neither, and if you built this in, they would be too costly. The engineers who worked on large generators could not get themselves to accept the low quality, as they saw it, that was perfectly acceptable on standby generators. Sales of the home standbys did not take off until they were put under a division manager who had complete control of marketing, manufacturing, and engineering and was not bound by past practice. In most cases new products should be placed under a new product manager with complete control until the first-level marketing, manufacturing, and engineering problems become clear.

In deciding organizational combinations, the first-level problems should usually be considered first. For example, a firm marketing both food and nonfood products found that they could very effectively put these in one division because the consumer problems for both were the same. In the insurance business, an agent could sell health insurance, life insurance, and investment funds even though they were different items, because they were all sold to the same kinds of customers. They merely broadened the line.

There is an interesting corollary to the emphasis on the first level when you consider management development. If it is important to make sure that programs, policies, and procedures are realistic in terms of the first level, the most important experience that any top executive should have had is first-level experience. Some of the best management development programs I have seen are quite informal. They take a young college graduate and make him or her a foreman for a year and a half, a laboratory assistant for another year and a half, a cost accountant for another year and a half, and finally a sales representative for a year and a half. The combined experience gives the trainee a balanced feeling of the various facets of the business at the first level. It is excellent management training, because it teaches the basic problems of the business. Unfortunately, it is sometimes hard to sell a good man on going through this sequence, but it is one of the best ways to develop basic understanding for future executive decision making.

chapter five

Uniformity Is Poor Management

In the management of any enterprise there seems to be an inexorable march toward uniformity—a natural tendency to want to put things and people into categories. It is essential to learning and is the only way most of us can make sense out of complex problems. Besides, executives need an overall way to evaluate people, functions, and expenditures. The process, however, leads to poor management. For example, if an executive tries to evaluate an old plant on the same basis as a new, up-to-date one, he can easily be too tough on the old plant and too easy on the new one. Results are not achieved by classification. The classification approach leads to control rather than to stimulation in a specific direction.

JOBS ARE NOT ALL THE SAME

How does uniformity show up? First of all, there is a tendency to treat all jobs the same. This starts with a natural requirement of financial accounting. Since the final financial reports must be the same for the firm, the application to individual areas usually follows the same approach, i.e., the same chart of accounts. Budgets, which are an outgrowth of financial theory, reflect the same tendency. To get the best stimulation toward results of the organization, it must be recognized that the requirements of one job are not the same as those of another job.

Overall programs, like compensation, suffer from the uniformity approach. The philosophy of compensation may be the same for technical, sales, and manufacturing. If you want an incentive toward the greatest possible achievement in each area, however, the administration of merit pay systems for technical people should be different from that for sales people. Administration for manufacturing people would be different from that for each of these. Uniform appraisal systems do not recognize the different problems of different jobs.

A common error of uniformity is to treat all jobs of a type as though they had the same problems. It seems so logical. For example, department store branches in a working-class neighborhood and those in a high-income neighborhood may sell high-priced shirts. Different kinds of shirts may appeal in the two areas. One vice president is in charge of a growing electronics division which has a low capital-per-employee ratio with plants in Malaysia. Another vice president directs an established chemical division which is capital-intensive with plants in the United States. The problems in sales, return on investment, personnel, etc., are entirely different. The world's record for running 220 yards is 19.5 seconds. However, the record for the 220-yard hurdle is 21.9 seconds. The problems are different.

There is an executive fallacy in the assumption that cross-comparison leads to more accomplishment. It does not, necessarily. One large engineering project is not easily compared with another. It may even be hard to compare the schedules. There may be different imponderables in one case versus another. If you are comparing the achievements of a division selling original equipment to manufacturers with another division selling shelf items to retail stores, the comparisons in inventory control, advertising, and individual cost deviations are almost impossible.

The same problem occurs in government. The welfare problems in the city of New York, with its high immigration, can be entirely different from those of Minneapolis. The problems of a Department of Education providing education for disadvantaged students of minorities who have great difficulty even learning to read would be far different from those of one educating students in a literate middle-class neighborhood.

The desire to cross-compare seems to be fortified by the idea that internal competition is good. It stems from our free enterprise approach that stresses competition between companies. Sales contests reflect this tendency. In our experience much more is accomplished in getting individual drive and spirit by having every man work against objectives for his territory so each one can be a winner instead of fighting his peers.

PROBLEMS ARE NOT STATIC

When managers have determined what the problems of a job are, they like to feel that they have settled the situation. This is almost never true, because jobs have a habit of changing their problems all the time. For example, the cost problems of a plant manager working with stable products and a stable crew may focus heavily on cost reduction. Should the product line double or triple quickly, he may have to double the size of his crews so that half of them are trainees. His basic problem, then, is not cost, but training in the new people as quickly as possible.

An extreme example of this training problem occurred with an aircraft company that had planned for a total overall market of 600 planes a year for the kind of plane they were manufacturing. They felt that with their good marketing techniques they could corral sales for 200 of these planes. In the first year alone they sold 675, more than their anticipated total potential of the market. This meant they had to put on second- and third-shift crews, for which they had not planned. As a consequence, plant supervision had to be increased rapidly. They assumed the normal complement of employees per supervisor for the additional crews. They failed to recognize that their training and coordination problems had multiplied, and costs skyrocketed. Even for the same work, the problems were different because of untrained crews and supervisors.

Credit departments may have to operate differently in a tight money market with high business activity as against a loose money market with average business activity. In the first period, customers lag in paying their bills when money is at a premium. In the second period, the danger of losses may be much greater. Assuming that jobs have the same problems from year to year is poor management.

A subtle error of uniformity occurs in the common assumption that the problems of similar jobs change similarly. It is reasonable to expect that one industrial sales territory of a mill supply business would change like another, but that is not the case. One might lose a big arms plant one year. A firm that had been a previous customer of the company might build a new plant in another territory. This plant is, therefore, an easy sell for the sales representative in that territory. In the one case the potential goes down substantially and in the other it goes up in the same period.

Bank branches also reflect differences in territory. One branch is in an area that grows substantially in wealthy retirees. Another branch grows because more industry moves into the area. The first has an influx of deposits but few loan requests. The second has a lower deposit increase but a substantial increase in good loan business. A corporate analytical approach that presupposes similar changes in problems in similar jobs is laying the foundation for poor management.

With the advent of sophisticated information systems, there has been a tendency to look at people as interchangeable units. This tendency develops because every action seems to be recorded somewhere on a printout. Scheduling in a large food plant put maintenance men on assignments day by day. A man was often put on another assignment before finishing the present one, and someone else would finish the job he had started. There was an implied assumption that one maintenance man was the same as another; that you could plug each in and out at will. This assumption just did not hold true, and the procedure resulted in very high maintenance cost. Too much time was lost in the switches.

The evidence of the "unit tendency" can be seen in any operation where employees are referred to impersonally as "bodies." The process is encouraged by computers. People then tend to be treated as numbers. "Number 707 should not be assigned to Department X." The whole process does not recognize that employees are people and accomplish the most if they are encouraged to work in a direction as individuals. The failure to recognize this is poor management.

Because of the high cost of the computer, there seems to be a natural tendency to manage for the computer instead of having the computer operate to help you manage. The computer, therefore, promotes uniformity by the mere fact that it encourages uniformity in reporting and in programming. It is not usually geared to the uniqueness of a job. Progress is being made to meet this difficulty through the developments of tie-in equipment and small computers.

A multiplant company had a requirement that all weekly plant reports be in to the central computer by the end of the day on Friday. One plant had a 24-hour operation six days a week. They had to close their books at noon on Friday in order to meet this requirement. They therefore estimated Friday afternoon and Saturday. The process led to inaccurate reporting.

There is a natural tendency for computer people to want to reduce changes in programming. They resist the development of specific sales data by territory, even though it helps in working the territory. For example, the product impact of competition by customer could be very important to one particular territory but not to another.

In a government unemployment office the computer data may show the cost of processing problems by activity. An activity could be entirely different, however, in a Detroit industrial area versus a South Dakota agricultural area.

In a railroad even the uniform accounting reports on track maintenance could be misleading, because the interpretations to be made from figures on rural track would not be the same as those on main line. Additional information is necessary to interpret the data.

ARE ACCOUNTING REPORTS TRUE?

Accounting reports do not report true accomplishment in all cases because they report costs on a uniform basis from department to department. In a printing company, the department that did the layout and planning of the plates was on a $20 per hour overhead basis, there being no equipment in the department. Monthly records always emphasized the actual cost compared to estimated cost. However, this department had a considerable impact on the presses, which had a $300 per hour overhead. This impact, however, did not appear in the accounting reports. It was hard to get the layout department to go all out to save time in the press, because that would hurt their own cost showing.

What does the fetish for uniformity cause? First of all, it seems to feed the delusion that grand designs at the top will do everything. Unfortunately, it is good for an executive ego trip. Underlying the philosophy of uniformity is the idea that you can push buttons and people will do the right things. It leads to voluminous reports to people at higher levels so that they know what is happening and can spot deviations. It is an illusion of executive control. It detracts from creative action down the line and leads instead to attempts to prevent deviations from appearing on a report, sometimes to falsification of reports. The overall process leads to less risk taking and less aggressive management down the line, a don't-rock-the-boat type of philosophy.

A serious result of a strong emphasis on uniformity is a lack of management confidence in the bottom-level people, as well as in the middle management. In a consumer business, product managers often assume by their plans that a uniform approach should be taken in every territory. This standard planning almost always results in lower sales from each territory because buying habits vary by area. Executives, of course, assume that the territory representatives and district managers are to blame for the lack of achievement and cannot be depended on to grasp the potential of the plans.

A romance with uniformity usually develops an excessive amount of time on long-term planning, three, five, and ten years out. Before long, the amount of time spent on planning is so great there is little time for doing, so accomplishment wanes. There is an assumption that with the right figures everything can be planned ahead perfectly. The figures are almost always based on a concept of uniform evaluation, because central staff usually reviews them on a uniform basis.

The typical job description form exerts strong pressure toward uniformity. Descriptions are often written for a type of job, like district manager, regional controller, sales manager, research director, and so on. Many of the managerial responsibilities appear the same in all the descriptions. The process presupposes that the managerial action in each of these jobs is the same. The fallacy lies in the presumption that a description of a job (usually of the duties) is a description of the problems.

As a case in point, the job descriptions of two plant managers stated that they were to handle their own employee relations problems. In the one case a very militant union had just been certified. In the other case the industrial engineers were engaged in a wholesale changing of jobs throughout the plant, with all the attendant disruption. A cross-comparison of the work of these two plant managers is just not valid.

In a research department of a pharmaceutical house the typical description of a research man said that it was his job to carry on appropriate research leading to a product. One research man was on a product that was an extension of a current product while another man was on a problem that was well ahead of the state of the art. Direct comparisons of the work were meaningless. Different timetables, different testing, and different check points were required.

Appraisal systems encourage uniform analysis. The typical appraisal system that uniformly applies factors like judgment, initiative, and cooperation to superintendents, controllers, employee relations managers, and sales managers forces all jobs into a mold. Personnel departments often do a great disservice to management by striving for uniform appraisal systems. The main objective of an appraisal system should be an accountability plan that encourages a person toward best accomplishment. Accomplishments expected are different from job to job and in different periods. The argument that it is too much trouble to have different systems for different jobs does not hold water. Appraisal systems are too important as a stimulus in direction to let this argument hold.

Executives often argue that if they did not have a uniform appraisal system, they could not cross-compare. There is an assumption here that direct cross-comparison is the major requirement in stimulating and promoting people. It is time that this hoary fetish be shot down. It comes from an anachronistic philosophy that the problems of one job are similar to those of another. In our complex society this reasoning does not hold true. This philosophy can only lead to a control approach that is restrictive rather than stimulating.

Policies, of course, tend toward uniformity. That is their intent. This is all the more reason why they should be very carefully scrutinized to set limitations on them. It may be necessary to have some uniformity in salary policy so that the general treatment of all employees is equally fair. It detracts from the system to then insist that every pay raise follow a definite pattern instead of leaving administration open for best use by the manager.

A similar problem occurs with a policy of strict adherence to a budget. The conditions may change in a department or special problems may occur which were not predictable.

Strict adherence to budget leads to a drive to get as much as possible into the budget to be on the safe side. We do not mean to detract from the overall value of a budget in planning the financial requirements of a business. Using the budget as a strict control, however, is a bastardized approach to management.

Budget systems tend to assume that all deviations are the same no matter where they occur. They make little differentiation between those that occur in a developing division, for example, and those that occur in a stable one, even though you would expect more deviations in a developing division. There are likely to be more imponderables and therefore more deviations. Excessive attention to deviations could result in a stagnating division.

PROCEDURE – THE UNIFORMITY QUAGMIRE

Of course, procedures extend the uniformity effect of policy even farther. Procedures tend toward tighter control than that envisaged by the policy. They encourage operation to be similar throughout the organization. For example, a bank had a requirement that all personal loans should be secured. If they were secured with an over-the-counter stock, it should be at the ratio of three to one. In addition, the bank required a financial statement. A business executive with a AA credit history who had been a good customer of the bank for some years wanted to get a small personal loan. The branch manager insisted on the same requirement; the loan manual allowed no room for local initiative. Of course, the bank lost her accounts.

Procedure manuals imply that the same procedures are important for all jobs at all times. For example, a purchasing procedure set up by a home-office purchasing department of a technical company required that all requisitions over $100 be checked in the home office. The typical requisition went through four engineering hands plus eight other people before it was approved. Not only was the cost excessive, but the time required to give service to the field was too great. When the procedure was loosened so all items up to $10,000 were purchased in the field, the whole cost of purchasing went down, and the service was considerably improved. The bogey of potential losses just did not materialize.

The fundamental error of the procedure approach is that it assumes that you will get greater results if you have less deviation. Show me the man with no deviations and you will show me the man who does not accomplish anything. All management is a gamble. If a man makes many decisions, some will go wrong, even though his average is excellent.

One of the debilitating examples of deviation control occurs when there is a requirement to PI (profit improvement) every new idea in detail. A supervisor or manager who wants to do something capitalwise must fill out the whole PI form. He gives up because he would have to spend more time proving that the idea was good than in actually carrying it out. It is a major clamper on initiative. But, of course, the losses from good ideas that die are unrecorded.

WHY UNIFORMITY?

If uniformity exerts such a strong pressure against the stimulation of management people, why the strong tendency toward it? First of all, it seems to simplify things. Even in a hospital it simplifies the work of a dietetic department if all patients are given the same menu. The fact that individual patients eat a very small amount of food does not make any difference, even though the process leads to excessive food costs.

In justification, uniformity occurs because many operations

are now more complex than they once were. There is a constant march toward higher technology in most firms. Many firms have developed far in foreign activities. A firm selling commerical gauges develops an electronic control system for industrial buildings and then enters the computer business — each a complex business by itself. Governmental insinuation and control have grown steadily stronger. Note the long-term trend in labor relations control, safety control, environmental control, pricing control, and trust control. An executive, therefore, wants an easier way to put all these factors into perspective. The whole situation encourages some system of categorization.

Uniformity is also the natural result of increased size. Executives are so removed from the first-line problems that they want a remedy for lack of communication. The number of echelons militate against the proper feedup. They therefore leap to a mass of figures that gives them cross-comparisons, but results are still dependent on first-line problems. The management complexity that accompanies large size is an often-forgotten argument against growth.

Executives often lean toward uniformity in desperation because the science of organization has not yet developed to the point where they can confidently delegate all the way down the line. They are frustrated by the numerous unexpected deviations that seem to occur. The president of a centralized company changed his management setup and delegated broadly to regional managers. He could not tell how they, in turn, delegated below them nor how they trained their people. In two-thirds of the cases the results were disappointing. The managers did not know how to redelegate with assurance.

Making the regional vice presidents profit centers did not teach them how to delegate. An example of their poor organization was an accounting department head who had two subdepartments under his control. It seemed natural to him to set up a supervisor for each part. This was excessive delegation. It would have been more efficient to delegate half of his people to a supervisor and have the other half report to him directly.

chapter six

A Design for Cooperation

Almost all human enterprise gets results through cooperation. Paradoxically, most management systems have a built-in design against cooperation. As a consequence, most middle managers and executives waste a great deal of time on coordination. Much of this is unnecessary and wastes high-caliber talent. It comes from a failure to recognize that an executive edict to cooperate is limited in its effect if internal pressures work against cooperation. For example, an executive may want line to check with staff specialists on problems in their area. If the staff has been trained to look at its job as that of reporting line deficiencies to top executives, it will not work. Who wants to cooperate with the Gestapo? By the same token, an edict to plant managers to give customers service loses its effect if they feel extreme pressure on budgets which encourage long runs in order to get costs down.

Why are most management systems antagonistic to coopera-tion? There is a slavish adherence to unique accountability, which says that you may delegate a responsibility to one man, A (Figure 5), but if you do, you cannot then delegate it to B also and hold A accountable for it. As the comment goes, "If you want to give me the responsibility, give it to me; then give me the authority and let me alone."

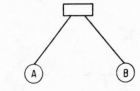

FIGURE 5 Unique accountability.

Accounting practices are based on unique accountability. You may charge a dollar to one account but then not to another account. It has to be one or the other. For example, in a plant, break-in costs for new equipment have to be charged either to the plant manager or to the plant engineer, but not to both. In a job shop, the manufacturing cost of specials has to be charged either to the plant or to the sales department, but not to both.

Budgets, being a reflection of accounting, follow the same principles. There is an attempt to affix accountability for any particular cost to a department or to an individual.

Appraisals also follow unique accountability. What are managers usually trying to appraise? Isn't it the contribution that the individual person has made to the organization? This, too, is unique accountability.

In our opinion, the principle of unique accountability is fallacious. The premises underlying it are not true to life. They presuppose that any result comes from only one person.

In the vast majority of cases, more than one person has an important contribution to make to a result. A further fallacy in unique accountability is the implication that if each person contributes his own unique part, the sum total of all the parts will lead to the overall result. This is not true. It is like building a brick wall. We have given too much attention to the individual bricks. The mortar in between is also important and overcomes the irregularities in the brick to make a sound overall wall.

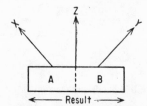

FIGURE 6   Joint accountability.

Suppose two people, A and B (Figure 6), have an important contribution to make to a result. Following unique accountability, A would be held only for his part of the result, usually for activity. He might feel, quite conscientiously, that he should work in the direction X. B, in turn, would be held only for his part, probably also activity. He, in turn, feels, equally conscientiously, that he should work in direction Y. The manager has direction Z in mind. He must then spend a considerable amount of time "coordinating" to get all to work in the same direction. Much of this coordination is wasted time.

Unique accountability seems to be fortified by moral rectitude. In the free enterprise system it seems "right" to give a man a job to do and hold only him for it. But administration is amoral.

In practice, unique accountability carried to an extreme discourages cooperation toward real results. It encourages each person to go along his own track. It is not to his interest to focus on others' results even though he affects them. The social climate in most operations suggests that he should not freely stick his nose into their business. The whole theory of staff exemplifies the thinking when it says that a staff person should help line only when asked, but the line is always accountable and the line has full authority. In engineering departments unique accountability encourages the NIH factor (not invented here). As projects move along from one person to another, each one must add his bit and practically reinvent. The problem is especially evident between research, product development, and product application engineering departments.

Unique accountability can be antagonistic to best accomplishment by encouraging the adversary approach. Executives equate the value of companies competing to give service to customers with that of people competing with each other in a company. The latter can prevent accomplishment. A chief executive encouraged the vice presidents of manufacturing and sales to compete with each other for the job of executive vice president. Instead of working together, each tried subtly to show the other up, and costs and service suffered. The whole organization was torn apart into two camps.

MANAGEMENT BY OBJECTIVES—AGAINST COOPERATION

Most management-by-objective programs follow traditional management theory and therefore unique accountability. There is an assumption that you will get impetus toward overall results by setting objectives. You will get impetus, all right, but you may very well get imbalance. A company that made floor-cleaning equipment had strong objectives on volume for their sales people. They had a large number of back orders at the same time that two major machines in the plant were idle because the firm had no business for the product they made. Volume objectives did not encourage balanced selling. In a plastics plant the maintenance department had tough objectives on maintenance costs. They met them, but there was an increase in downtime. They met their current cost objectives well, but they soft-pedalled preventive maintenance and prompt repairs in the process.

Unique accountability violates another basic principle. One should not depend on another to get one's results if the other person does not have the same interest in the outcome. The market research department of a company was supposed to make long-range market studies to guide technical research. The pressure from the vice president of sales was for current market studies to help the sales force. They therefore did little to guide long-range technical research.

It is usually good organization to first combine those functions that should work together. Try to get one person in control of a result, if possible. At a bottom level, a short-run stampings company combined the jobs of press operator and setup. Eliminating the setup job resulted in a cut of 10 percent in staff with an additional 5 percent improvement in output.

An engineering department of a large farm equipment company organized projects with a number of specialists on various parts of a vehicle. Many engineers were often involved in the design of any one major component. Projects were then reanalyzed and for every component or subcomponent the question was asked, "Could an experienced engineer cover the various specialties involved?" In many cases it was found that he could. Fewer engineers, then, got into each individual act; more time was spent on designing and less time on conferring.

The fundamental thinking underlying unique accountability is erroneous. Many results do not come from just one person. True commitment toward those results must be commitment of several people toward each result. Most management theory, therefore, is based on the wrong premise. As a consequence, pay systems, appraisal systems, and budget systems are often disappointing.

When cooperation fails, executives often jump to the conclusion that it is all a matter of communications. The problem is not communications. If you want people who affect a result to cooperate, the result must be of mutual interest to each of them. What is needed is a design to make cooperation of mutual interest rather than a design against cooperation.

A NEW THEORY—JOINT ACCOUNTABILITY

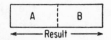

FIGURE 7   Joint accountability.

Let's suppose that two people, A and B (Figure 7), have an important contribution to make to a result. Instead of recognizing A for only his share and B for only his share, we would give each recognition only for the joint result—joint accountability. If one is a superintendent and the other a scheduler, both would be given recognition for improvement in the cost resulting from schedule changes.

In a petroleum company both the international division and the United States divisions were given full credit for all international sales to encourage cooperation between them. In a supermarket chain both the home-office produce merchandiser-buyer, as well as the local produce department heads, were recognized for the net produce profit achieved. Both of them were then interested in fresher, better-presented displays, as well as in lower costs.

Joint accountability makes it advantageous to the people involved in a result to cooperate. You can see this operate in a good restaurant where both the busboys and the waiters participate in the tips. The two cooperate better to give good service.

In a soap company, special promotion men had been given credit for their special sales, and sales representatives received credit only for normal sales. There was a sharp increase in promotion sales when both the special promotion men and the sales representatives in the territory got full credit for all promotion sales. It was then advantageous to the territory men to help the promotion men.

Most recognition systems try to evaluate each person's contribution. Strangely enough, these systems often militate against most effective management. To be most effective, they should be directed toward the result of the relationships with others. In a large air-conditioning company that sold systems for industrial buildings, it was advantageous to get the architect to specify their product. The consulting engineer who cooperated with the architect also should have favored it. In addition, the owner could have quite an influence on the specifications, so it was helpful to sell him. Finally, the contractor who installed the system might have some options, so he had to be sold. Each of these four could have been in different cities and, therefore, in different sales territories. It was effective to give one-fourth of the credit to the territory representative in the area of any one of the four (the architect, the consulting engineer, the owner, and the contractor). The system encouraged the four to cooperate with each other to get the most effective sales impact. The important point is that no attempt was made to measure who did the most.

In an architectural firm, the architect, the structural engineer, and the electrical engineer all had to be accountable for a functional building at reasonable cost. If the architect overemphasized aesthetics so that it was difficult to build, cost would be affected. The structural engineer might design in such a way that there was inadequate room left for the electrical work, and so on. All three had to be tied in to the cost of the building in order to give service to the client.

THE RULE OF INFLUENCE

Joint accountability leads to a new rule, the rule of influence, which states that if a person has a strong influence on a result, even though he only contributes part, he must be made accountable for the effect of that influence. In a large equipment company, design engineers were recognized for any subsequent profit the company made on the products they developed. They had an influence on cost, saleability, and price. They were therefore encouraged, first of all, to make sure of the saleability of the item; second, to make certain that it was designed so it could be easy to produce at low cost without excessive equipment installation; and finally, to give the sales force data on the new machines that would be helpful in selling them. It was to their advantage to take the broad company view.

A small firm often pays manufacturing representatives a commission based on volume. There seems to be a give-up attitude that nothing more can be done to redirect them toward best corporate emphasis. This is not true. If new products need push, extra commissions can be paid for new-product orders. If broader distribution is needed, extra pay can focus on new accounts. If emphasis is needed on profit, more commissions can be paid for profitable products.

It is common to believe that foremen have no effect on many of the costs of the plant, particularly various overhead costs. Only the plant manager and the engineers could affect these. The foremen of a machine shop as well as the engineers were then made accountable for all the space and equipment costs of their departments. At the time, everyone felt that the plant was overcrowded. As a consequence of the change, foremen eliminated several machines, consolidated space, and used it more effectively. Within a couple of years they were producing in the same space 120 percent of the volume they had produced before.

Applying joint accountability requires a major overhaul of recognition systems. In order to encourage cooperation, two or more people must be recognized for the same result. Supervisors of a planning department of a plant were paid bonuses based on the number of plans they completed. After all, that was their work—to turn out plans efficiently. No credit was given for their impact on the large manufacturing machines for which they planned. This was the job of the superintendents. Efficiency increased when the bonus plan of the planners was changed so that half of their bonus was based on the effectiveness of the manufacturing machines. At the same time, the efficiency of those machines also remained a major factor in recognition of the superintendents. There was a complete overlap.

The bonuses of the vice president of sales and of the account executives of a job shop had been based on volume. This basis was then changed to one of profit on accounts. The cost of all specials and break-ins into schedule was charged against their profits and therefore affected their bonuses. At the same time, the cost of these specials and the cost of break-ins into schedule were still kept in the plant budget. Account executives became concerned about plant costs. The cost of specials and break-ins was cut in half with no loss in volume. They worked out other ways to satisfy their customers. There was less argument with the plant about the cost of specials.

At the top level, executives who exert a strong influence on policy and overall strategy should probably have a substantial part of their bonuses based on overall achievement of the company. The other part should be based on their individual responsibilities. This principle could carry right down into the various divisions of a multidivisional company.

Business increased in a bank when the appraisal of tellers was changed so that a part of it was based on the amount of business obtained from customers whom the tellers referred to the officers. The officers, of course, got full credit for all the business they wrote up. It was to the tellers' interest to watch for additional opportunity to increase bank revenues.

RESULTS MUST BE MUTUALLY ADVANTAGEOUS

The purpose of joint accountability is to make it advantageous for two people to cooperate. Both need not be measured by the same figures. For example, a safety engineer may be accountable for severity and frequency rates. What do these mean to a foreman who has a minor accident every two months? A more effective way might be to charge the cost of the foreman's accidents against his budget. In addition, safety is obviously weighted at 100 percent of the safety engineer's job. It may be weighted at only 10 percent of the foreman's job because he must get other results as well in order to maintain balance.

A product manager may be held 100 percent for the market effectiveness of his product. A district manager includes this product with other products in his volume objectives. He may also have objectives on both new accounts and account retention.

A major change must occur in accounting philosophy, because charges must be made to two or more people. A design engineer may have to be charged with break-in costs of machinery, and later of maintenance, even though these costs will also be in manufacturing. A firm selling control systems found that both the home-office marketing people and the field sales people had to get credit and absorb charges on sales of individual products. The accounting rule of no more than 100 percent charge must be changed. Clearing double charges out of your financial statements can be done through washout accounts.

THE ERROR OF COMMITTEES—NO ACCOUNTABILITY

Joint accountability is not the same as committee operation. In most committees, the members are not truly accountable for the results of the committee's work. In fact, each one is colored more by his own personal responsibility than by the committee operation. In joint accountability each one is recognized for the result, or lack of it, as though he alone had control.

Occasionally task forces are set up in such a way that each member has a vested interest in the result. Unintentionally, they have been set up following the principle of joint accountability. These task forces may work quite well.

Because some task forces do well in solving a problem, many people have been attracted to group dynamics. They assume that groups, not individuals, accomplish things. Even if two or three people work together, their result is the summation of the results of the effort of individuals working together.

In the Japanese culture the social system exerts strong pressure toward cooperation. The system encourages a spirit of joint commitment. Joint accountability helps build this spirit, and recognition systems should be changed to fortify it.

AUTHORITY NOT EQUAL TO RESPONSIBILITY

If you accept joint accountability, a hallowed organization principle must now go by the board—the idea that authority must be commensurate with responsibility. This principle no longer holds. If both a systems engineer and a line manager are to be recognized for a cost reduction, each works toward this cost reduction without full authority. The systems engineer could not be given authority over the manager, nor, in turn, could the line manager have authority over the systems engineer. Neither has authority over the other.

The principle of commensurate authority has been one reason why executives have found it difficult to delegate. Since most results are joint, executives have hesitated to delegate responsibility for a result because they felt they could not give the person full authority. The problem is especially acute in interlaced operations like a railroad, where traffic, transportation, mechanical maintenance, track maintenance, and business development must all pull together. As a consequence, an executive tends to centralize.

Since a chief executive does not feel that he can give line divisions full authority, he forces the requirement that the line consult with the staff heads as the right arm of the executive. He then feels that neither can be held full accountable for the result. This attitude is then reflected all the way down the organization.

MEASURE THE RESULTS, NOT THE INDIVIDUAL

Another misconception of many executives is that the purpose of measurement is to measure the performance of a person. On the contrary, the purpose of measurement should be to stimulate the individual toward the results you want to accomplish. It should point the direction and give the basis for a recognition system that encourages him in that direction. Such a system is not the same as measuring the results that an individual accomplishes by himself. In many cases, measuring what the man accomplishes by himself is antagonistic to good results. A prime purpose of measurement is to stimulate cooperation between the various people who must work together to get results.

The research head is better directed to company results if he is measured by the profit achieved on the products that he develops. It does not seem that way, because he does not control manufacturing costs or sell any products directly. He tries much harder, however, to develop products that are practical to produce and that satisfy customers.

Most management-by-objective approaches, as well as executive approaches, err because they are trying to measure the individual. It is a natural outgrowth of basing them on unique accountability. A whole new vista opens up in the field of measurement once it is recognized that people are best stimulated in the most profitable direction by measurements of overall results instead of by measurements of the individual.

If you accept the principle of measuring the result instead of the individual, there are other ramifications, however. Most of us accept the concept that new ideas should be rewarded. Isn't this the way to encourage improvement? Not necessarily. Let's suppose that two men in the same kind of job have been delegated a very similar result. One does an excellent job, burning the midnight oil and solving the problem. The other has trouble, but he talks to his friend, takes his idea, and puts it into effect. Both of them get a fine result. Who should receive the most credit? Under the old theory of unique accountability, of course the one who thought of the idea should get the most credit. From a good tactical point of view, however, both should receive exactly the same credit. If you want to give something extra to the person with the idea, this would be all right, but above all things, do not detract from the other man who copies an idea. There are millions of ideas available in this world.

Isn't it a sign of a good executive when he goes out and reaches for them, puts them into effect, and makes them work? The thought of not rewarding for original ideas seems antagonistic to the American system, however.

But how do you finally measure a man? You do it by the effect of his projects on the organization. What you are really measuring is this: if he is involved in a project, does it work? Isn't this the only true measurement of his work? This approach develops a much broader person. He has to make his work worthwhile within the context of the organization.

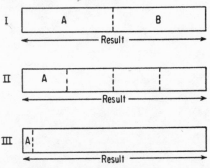

FIGURE 8 Limit to joint accountability with decreasing impact.

There is a distinct limit to joint accountability, however. Let's assume that you (A) and I (B) (Figure 8) have to work together to get a result and you contribute about half of it (Figure 8, I). You would probably accept some accountability for it. What if more people are involved and your effect is only one-quarter (Figure 8, II)? You are probably more reluctant to accept accountability now, because three people could affect you negatively. But suppose the result has so many people involved in it that your part seems almost infinitesimal (Figure 8, III). It is very hard for you to accept accountability for that result. In other words, if a person feels his effect is too small, joint accountability is weakened. Most profit-sharing plans suffer from this problem. Executive bonus plans that put considerable weight on company profit lack credibility for the same reason when applied to people several steps down the line. These people see their effect on overall profit as being very small. Joint accountability works better the greater the person's impact on the result that is measured. Unique accountability is best, but the difficulty is that most results come from the work of more than one person.

chapter seven

The Highest Type of Management— Self-Coordination

There is a tendency to coordinate by directive, partly because of the feeling of power in a managerial or executive job and partly because of the difficulty in coordinating complex operations. It is unrealistic management to assume that if an executive issues a statement as to what people should do, they will do it. The highest type of management is that which spends a great deal of time setting the climate, the organization plan, the policies, the accountability system, and the reporting systems so that people tend to coordinate themselves. Most people want to do a good job, and they will if the climate is right. All management pressure should work in the direction of cooperation toward the overall results of the organization. It should be advantageous to each individual person to coordinate himself in this direction, or at least not be disadvantageous to him.

REALIZE THE VALUE FROM STAFF

A common coordination problem is staff-line conflict. Much of this is caused by the erroneous historical concept that it is staff's job to work with the line when it is asked to carry out certain specialized activities, but not to be accountable for any results. To the contrary, the basic purpose of any staff is to improve line results, not to give them reports or simply carry out certain activities. The first step in getting an improved climate, therefore, is to change the whole concept of staff from that of carrying through on activity to one of being committed to an improvement of the line results that staff affects. This raises the whole level of staff from that of being second-class citizens to that of contributing on a par with the line in getting worthwhile results. The old concept of staff as merely assisting the line has been a great misfortune for staff and has reduced its value in many organizations.

Product design and research departments have often been criticized for lack of accomplishment for the money spent. The lack of accomplishment has usually resulted from too much concentration on design and research activity instead of a requirement to get a satisfactory number of profitable products for the money spent. The latter emphasis encourages each technical man to make sound business decisions on technical problems with less control needed from technical directors and executives.

The staff should be organized so that they are accountable for line results and are on the same team with the line. In one company, the purpose of market research was to help the individual sales areas be more effective. The individual market research analysts, however, felt that they had done a high-grade professional job when they had developed fine reports. When they were evaluated only on sales improvement resulting from their studies, they became much more effective. They now were on the same team with the district managers and required less coordination by the vice president of marketing.

Training functions are often inadequate because their goals are not clear. Ask, "Why are we training?" The answer should always be stated in terms of improvement in the work of those people trained, not improvement of knowledge. When the objective of a training function is stated in this way, it becomes harder hitting, whether it is in terms of productivity, sales increases, or greater profitability. It is unfortunate that so many training men are not held accountable for the results of their training in terms of line improvement. Wherever this is done, we have noted that training men become stronger and make greater contributions to the operation. They coordinate their work with line results and find that it is more challenging and rewarding.

A common problem between staff and line is that the line feels that if a staff plan works, staff takes all the credit, and if it does not work, all the negatives redound to the line. Too often this belief turns out to be true, but it does not have to be.

In a multiplant company the home-office labor negotiator had only recently been made accountable for the labor cost per unit in the plants for which he negotiated. This meant that any cost of fringes, time wasted, or increased base rate would affect him. He had always had only one concern before—to prevent a strike. He got down to the wire on a negotiation, called the general manager of the division, and told him that the contract could be settled for a certain wage increase plus two or three special work clauses. The general manager pointed up the negotiator's objective of labor cost per unit and that these clauses alone would cost approximately 15 cents an hour. The manager told him that if this was the best settlement that could be worked out, it would be very tough for both the negotiator and him to meet their objectives. The negotiator went back and negotiated two more weeks and changed the clauses so that they cost only 1½ cents an hour. The setup made him coordinate himself with the needs of the line.

Sometimes a staff function has to satisfy two groups or balance between them. An estimator in a printing company was in this position. Because of executive pressure, he was excessively sensitive about any estimate he made that proved to be too low. He would therefore tend to overestimate, making it difficult for sales to price so that they were competitive in the market. He was then made accountable for volume, so it was to his advantage to give the lowest estimate. He was also made accountable for any actual cost over or under his estimate. Either was considered to be equally negative. If he was too low or if he was too high, he would be looked at as having done a poorer job. In this way he had to balance between sales and the plant without executive pressure to do so. His estimate could then be used as a good basis for pricing and the firm could be in a good competitive position. At the same time, he had a realistic estimate and the plant people could be expected to meet estimated costs.

CENTRAL STAFF TIED TO LONG-TERM RESULTS

It is more difficult to tie in central staff to results, because its work is aimed at long-term line results, not short-term. The designs of a research and development department of an aeronautical firm were often impractical when they were carried over into hardware. The cost of redesigning for production was excessive. The general manager had to continually arbitrate arguments between manufacturing and R&D. Research and development was then made accountable for the total cost of design plus redesign to make it producible. In addition, plant engineering was also made accountable for reducing break-in time. Research then brought plant engineering into design early so that as the development was carried on, it was done in a far more practical way. In addition, a system was worked out where a number of the research engineers would transfer over with the product to the local engineering as the product was produced. In this way, the developmental know-how was carried over into the application. Some of the manufacturing break-in costs were cut as much as 50 percent. The engineers tied their work more effectively into plant operations.

At times, it is hard to use long-term results effectively for short-term stimulation. Short-term milestones should be set up, then, but they should be based on some kind of accomplishment that looks reasonable in arriving at the final result. For example, in a long-term development plan of a machine, six primary component developments may be necessary. Each could be carried out in a shorter period. It should be clear that they are not final results, but technical men can direct their efforts more effectively with these milestones than they can by merely evaluating the professional excellence of their activities up to that point.

Every specialty must be fitted into the overall line results. Self-coordination can be established by combining functions. For example, purchasing and production scheduling departments should often be combined so that they can jointly be made accountable for downtime, due either to lack of materials or lack of proper scheduling. They closely affect each other in this impact on the line. Combined, they are often much more effective in helping the line do its work better.

ORGANIZE BY RESULT

It is always easier to get accomplishment if you organize so that all parts of a result are under one manager. A plant making floor-cleaning equipment was originally organized by specialty—machining, drill press, assembly, electrical. They then developed balanced lines by products and all work on a product was done on a line under one superintendent. There was much less conferring and quicker correction of any problems that occurred, because the superintendent was in charge of the whole unit, and did not have to coordinate with three other superintendents.

The same analysis applies to specialization of work, even relatively unskilled work. In a packing unit each package went through five operations with five different people before it was finished. Productivity immediately went up when the work stations were changed so that one person did all the work on a package and did not need to coordinate with others. Very often complicated computer systems have paid off in large offices only because the work had been poorly organized and broken down into so many fragments that a great deal of time was lost in paper shuffling. If they had merely combined work better, a simpler system might have been adequate. Combining the work eliminates handling.

There has been a great deal of confusion about job enrichment. Too frequently, behaviorists suggest that the great value comes from the increased morale when people are given several tasks, thereby reducing the monotony. In our experience, the main value comes from combining all the tasks toward a result so that one person can be accountable. There is then less wasted effort, and less coordination is required between people handling related work.

We have verified this conclusion in carrying the same idea over to more complex jobs. An engineering department was broken down into sections, design and production engineering (whose job it was to make the design practical for production). There was always a great deal of controversy between the design and the production engineers, frequently causing redesign. The setup was then changed so that every designer had to carry through on production design as well. The designers then became much more practical and more aware of production problems. The total output of the department increased substantially. One person was now responsible for the total design and for its practicality.

A similar problem occurred one level higher in the same engineering department. There were project directors who had money control but no supervision of people. In addition, there were supervisors of the engineers, but the engineers were assigned to different projects under the project directors —a loose supervisory setup at best. The supervisors were then also given money control and the project directors were eliminated. In addition to reducing total supervision about 30 percent, projects moved ahead much better.

LINE, TOO, SHOULD HELP LINE

A common error is to evaluate line departments as though they were independent of each other. The plant manager then spends a great deal of time straightening out inter-departmental problems. In a paper company, poor quality of paper off the paper machine could slow up the converting department and make it more difficult for them to turn out good product. The paper mill was held for tonnage. It appeared that they were properly accountable because any poor rolls sent to converting were charged against the paper mill as waste. It would count the same as though the paper mill had rejected it in the first place. Their natural inclination, however, was to run all questionable rolls through to the converting department, hoping that they might get by. Converting, in turn, could run up to one-third of a roll without being charged for the roll. If the roll was reasonably good but not tops, they might then find it advantageous to send it back after running one-third of it. The system was changed so that the waste from paper rolls was charged to both the paper mill and the converting department. It was then advantageous for both of them to work together to get the optimum paper usage without getting the plant manager into the problem. Waste was considerably reduced and output increased because the two departments coordinated themselves.

Since almost all operation is cooperative enterprise, prime attention should be given to a setup that encourages cooperation between major functions. One way is to base part of the compensation of all policy officers, whether they are function or division heads, on overall profit.

One major operating division of a heavy equipment company sold to the same customers as another operating division but often through different distributors. The managers of each division were recognized by the volume and profit of their divisions. In many cases, one division would actually cooperate with the distributors against the sales of the other division. To make it advantageous for each division to help the other, a partial cross-credit of sales for the two operating divisions was established. The president was called into fewer complaint meetings between the two division heads.

In the federal government, there is often a failure of one department to capitalize on the work of another. It is not to their advantage. An example was a study of a part of the economy laid out by the Department of Agricultural Economics. The job was to take sixty people six months. It provided key jobs for the various supervisors needed. Although the Department of Commerce had made an almost identical study some time previously, there was practically no interest on the part of the first department to use the work of the Department of Commerce and eliminate their own study. This would have cut out budget and jobs from the department and given them no recognition.

Sometimes sales can make its greatest contribution to the

company by helping in plant efficiency. A vice president of sales was evaluated by volume. His department would frequently sell large orders, but deliveries were made in relatively small amounts, causing a large number of runs in the plant. The manufacturing head was constantly objecting to the president about the practice. By careful selling, he was able to reduce considerably the number of deliveries per order, greatly increasing the length of runs in the plant and substantially increasing the profit of the firm. The change only occurred when part of his accountability was based on the average dollar value per delivery.

A salesman of a printing company was selling about 30 percent below the average for his territory. The firm had made a study and found that sales people should make five calls per day; therefore, each one was required to report his five calls every day. If he did not do it, he was reprimanded by his supervisor. This salesman was creative. He could go to a customer on a small printing problem and talk about the whole printing requirement of the firm, go back and develop a plan, and probably get all the business of the firm. The analysis might require two days, however.

In addition, the salesman would require help from the plant manager on estimates of different ways to do the work. The plant manager, however, was recognized for his costs compared to estimates. Can you visualize him giving the salesman the rock bottom estimate by which he himself would later be evaluated? He had to be evaluated partly by the amount of sales the company obtained on orders where he gave estimates to tie him in to the salesman.

The art director looked at her job as that of creating good art for printing. The viewpoint sounds logical, doesn't it? Note the error: she did not feel accountable for art that *sold a customer* on giving the order to this company. The art director, too, had to be given credit for any sales obtained where she developed the art work. She was then tied to the salesman.

Finally, the whole call report system had to be thrown out. This salesman could now use his creativity and he could get the help of both the plant manager and the art director. Within a year and a half he increased his sales 80 percent with the same customers. He also increased his margins from 6 to 8 percent, not because he was gouging the customer, but because he was giving much more valuable service. He was now considered an outstanding salesman.

THE VALUE OF THE PLANNING IS IN THE DOING

Every executive wants to be sure that his planning results in creative doing. Because of the apparent difficulty in coordinating, a common practice of managers at various levels in the organization is to hold a planning meeting of all their immediate subordinates every week, sometimes every day. The rationale is that this helps coordinate, informs people, and keeps the manager on top of problems as they occur. Although it seems to do this, in most cases it leads to a poor delegation and poor accountability. It is too easy to throw individual problems to the group.

For example, a plant manager may get all his subordinates together every day or every week to plan production. In this way he can be sure that they are all together on current orders. It is usually an evidence of poor delegation in the operation and a substitute for individual accountability. For instance, if scheduling and purchasing are not tying into production, a far better way is to make them accountable for their impact on production in downtime, costs, or (in the case of purchasing) quality. They then coordinate themselves.

In a large aluminum plant, maintenance was under pressure to cut costs, so six of the top foremen were pulled out and made planners. The planners did not supervise the crews. The crews were organized by crafts, so there was no accountability for a problem involving several crafts, including no responsibility for downtime. After two years of operation, both the number of failures of equipment and the cost of maintenance were up. Reliance on planning was not a good way to solve a basic operating problem. What was needed was area maintenance supervisors who were accountable for all maintenance work and downtime in their areas.

It is difficult enough to have accountability on long-range projects, but if the planning on them becomes divorced from the responsibility for carrying through, the situation can be even worse. That is the way it was in a large laboratory where all projects in any area of the laboratory had to be approved in detail by each of the five assistant directors. The director felt that he could better coordinate the work of the laboratory in this way. In many cases an assistant director was unfamiliar with the technology of the particular project. It took a long time to get a project approved. The procedure required a great deal of time to prepare the proposals so that they would be approved. It resulted in great frustration on the part of the chemists and project leaders. In addition, it took the assistant directors partly off the hook for the success or failure of their own projects.

Because the essence of management is to get commitment to results, it is wise to force much of the planning down as low as possible. People tend to be much more committed to a result if they have a hand in the planning. Less executive time is needed to tie the planning and doing together. A medium-sized firm had a great deal of trouble with quality. The firm was up to 8 percent waste when the average of the industry was about 4 percent. The president, therefore, formed a committee consisting of the chief engineer, the controller, himself, and the head of manufacturing to police quality on a weekly basis. They developed quite a few records and issued corrective orders so that over a period of three years they cut their waste down to 3 percent, well below the average. The setup solved the problem. The difficulty was that foremen and superintendents became mere robots following orders rather than assuming responsibility themselves. In addition, the top people spent a great deal of time on the activity.

The system was changed, then, to get the responsibility for all quality planning and doing down into the foreman and superintendent levels. They were given training and staff help in doing the work. Within six months, waste dropped to 1½ percent. In this case, as in most when the doers were made responsible for planning, much less coordination was necessary. Higher management people could spend their time on broader creative problems.

DON'T ISOLATE THE SPECIALISTS

One of the reasons for the increasing need for coordination is the phenomenal increase in specialization, and, as a consequence, fragmentation of work leading to any particular result. With higher technology we have many more disciplines and subdisciplines, very often a number of these working on one particular result. The danger is that each is committed to his particular part of the work, which is usually activity. There are then gaps between the work of the specialists, so a great deal of the management time must be spent pulling them together. This time is usually wasted time. It is far better to set up a plan whereby people are encouraged by accountability to work effectively with others to accomplish the result.

An employment man, a trainer, and a personnel supervisor may all have a staff impact on a new employee. It is well to make them all accountable for the best return in productivity and quality of work from the new employees hired. The trainer should then work with the employment man and both, in turn, should be working with the personnel supervisor handling the personal problems through the supervisor so that their systems work together to get an effective employee on the job. When this is the case, they look at their jobs differently.

The same problem occurs in a marketing department between an economist, a market research man, and a statistician. Each one should feel a responsibility for an improvement in sales results, but each one contributes only a part. If you try to set up a way to measure each one's part, you will end up measuring the kinds of reports they turn out, and the manager must then tie them together to get sales results. Each should be accountable for sales results so that he coordinates his work with that of the others.

One of the best ways to induce self-coordination is to set broad objectives for perhaps a year for each job. These should cover the major results toward which the person should be working. They should include those results to which he should contribute with other people (joint accountability) and, also, those places where he should make long-range contributions. These results should therefore include those dependent upon the relationships between line and line or between staff and line.

A person's goals should always include some area of improvement in his job. In the New England territory the weakest penetration might be in Maine. A separate goal may, therefore, be set for improved penetration in Maine. Let the person police his own time during the year to accomplish the goals that are set.

DISCOURAGE ALIBI-ITIS

To make such an approach to self-coordination work, though, small results should not be reported to management above. Otherwise, managers cannot avoid nit-picking—focusing on errors. In too many cases this focus takes an undue amount of time of the manager and contributes very little to the stimulation of his people. As a case in point, one president felt he should be able to ask his vice president of manufacturing detailed questions regarding anything that was happening in the plants. To be on the safe side, this vice president set up a separate record group outside the controller's division to keep him informed on all the details. This involved an extra cost of around $50,000 a year. The president was coordinating by detail. It resulted in a strapping of authority all the way from the vice president down to the foremen.

In a large multilocation company, any variations in budget figures each month had to be explained to the home office. Everyone, of course, became quite adept at giving explanations. It got to a point where alibis were almost as good as results. This tightened control gave a great deal of satisfaction to the executives in the home office but gradually reduced the drive out in the field toward worthwhile company results. Such detail approaches lead away from management by exception. They lead to executive coordination rather than to self-coordination and reduce overall results.

chapter eight

Mining the Gold of Staff

The effective use of skilled staff offers a great opportunity for any organization to be more effective. What is staff? First of all, let's look at line. A line person is anyone who accomplishes some result that is part of the overall objectives of the organization. He does this either directly or through someone who reports to him. In a manufacturing company a sales representative, a sales manager, a foreman, a plant manager, and a vice president of manufacturing are all line.

On the other hand, a staff person is anyone who contributes to a result through someone else who does not report to him. Typical staff jobs are personnel managers, accountants, engineers, market research men, and lawyers.

It has been popular to question any definition of line or staff. Shouldn't they all be aiming at the results of the organization? Yes, but it is significant that they contribute to these results in a different way. Staff does it through someone who is not a subordinate.

Part of the confusion comes from assuming that there is staff work as such, and that staff work for some reason or other is less important than the line. Neither is true. There is no such thing as staff work. All work is line work. There are simply staff jobs. This can be seen clearly in a small company. A plant manager does his own methods and scheduling work. As the firm gets larger, the methods and scheduling work is pulled out and staff men are set up to handle it. A sales manager may do his own product development or market study work in addition to laying out his own advertising. Each of these functions may later be set up as a staff job as the company grows larger.

The same job may be line in one company and staff in another. In an architectural firm the jobs of engineers and architects are line. The firm is in the business of selling plans. The construction department of a department store chain, however, may also employ architects and engineers, but in that case they are staff. The firm is not in the business of selling plans. The stores that are built are used to merchandise other products.

THERE ARE ONLY LINE RESULTS

A staff result is always a line result. In other words, every staff job an executive sets up should improve line results. A product manager who does not help the sales representatives sell more profitably contributes nothing. It is true that the sales representatives may have difficulty selling without the work of the product manager in product planning, packaging, and promotion. A sharp product manager can make a substantial contribution to sales effectiveness, in many cases greater than that of some line managers.

In order to capitalize on staff it helps to define the various types. The first type we would call manipulative. These are the people who provide a service to actually change the mode of operating of the line people. This is the touchiest type of staff service. Methods engineers who try to get people to change methods are in this category. Training people are also in this category. If training is to be effective, supervisors and other people being trained must change their modes of operation. These staffs should be geared to help the line solve their problems better.

A key to success of manipulative staff jobs is a sound personal relationship with the line people they serve. It is especially important that the concept of joint accountability be used here. It is then advantageous for staff to get line results. Line, in turn, knows that staff is in tune with them.

A manipulative staff can serve another staff. The same setup holds. A research department had engineers developing simulated models to reduce testing. The development engineers did not think that the models fit their needs. In addition, the simulating staff did not assume the responsibility for teaching the engineers how to use the models. They were not pushed to do this, either, because the cost of the simulation development was allocated to the user groups even if they did not use the models. Simulation was much more effective when simulation specialists were allocated to individual project groups and made accountable for helping the groups cut engineering costs through simulation.

The second type of staff we would call autonomous staff. This type includes staff functions that are essentially separate services. They provide something for, not to, individual line supervision. Employment and recruiting are in this category. They can operate somewhat independently of the normal line operation. Purchasing may be in the same category. They must provide materials of good quality on time but do not usually have to change the line's mode of operation.

It is essential, of course, that the service must fit the line and not retard it. The work is set up separately because it can be done better by concentrating a specialist on it. Purchasing may buy materials at low cost, but if the quality is slightly off or they are not delivered on time, it may hold up the line. They must have an obligation to fit into the timing and quality requirements of the line operation.

Some service functions can be controlled by setting up a plan where the line may accept or reject them or go outside the company. This can often be done with central computer operations. If they do not give a reasonable service at a cost, the line divisions may buy them from outside. This acts as a good discipline to the inside computer service.

The third kind of staff is control staff. Its purpose is to correct some kind of aberration. Ordinarily a controller is in this category. He should be reporting deviations on costs to line people so that they correct them. The same is true of a quality control man. He should turn down off-quality and point out where quality is slipping so that the line corrects it.

The error of most control staffs is that they tend to be a sort of collective spy trying to ferret out deviations but assuming no other obligation. They, too, should be set up to help the line. After all, there is nothing constructive about control per se. It is too easy to get overcontrol. Typical was a quality control manager who set up a fine statistical quality control system. Three-sigma deviation would have been satisfactory for their customers. Just to be sure that nothing slipped through, he turned down everything beyond two-sigma variation. Of course, costs went up, as did waste. When he was made accountable for both quality and waste, he became more realistic in his evaluation of quality. He was then in tune with the line operation. He even began to let them know ahead of time when the quality was starting to go off so they could correct it before a deviation occurred.

Too many control staffs report small deviations up the line. An executive should set them up so they report only excessive deviation up the line. In other words, management by exception must be enforced to keep the control staffs from curtailing initiative. Budget reporting often errs in this way. People up the line get too much detail on deviations.

Because control staffs have the information, they often want to tell the line what to do. Solutions are not usually their function and problem solving is usually not in their area of competency. Controllers or cost accountants may develop some excellent ideas on costs, but they should not propose ways of operating to reduce these costs. In most cases they are not capable of doing this.

GEAR STAFF TO THE FIRST LEVEL

In most cases, staff's work is finally accomplished through the first line level. In a plant, no one produces except an operator. All the staff people should aim at helping the foreman operate better through his crews. A basic value of an actuary's work in an insurance company is realized only through the sales representatives of the company. It is the actuary's job to prepare a profitable product that they can sell. The company gets value only when it receives profit from the sale of the policies resulting from actuarial studies.

We all saw the line-focus in relief in the space program. The whole program, consisting of all the various specialists, was focused on the action of the astronauts when they went up in the space ships. That is where the payoff was.

The payoff of even intricate staff problems is finally realized at the first line level. Computerized instrumentation in a refinery is aimed at the final control exercised by the operators on the shifts. The value of a capital planning group in a retail chain is realized only through the sales of the clerks in the new store locations.

Many firms become staff-heavy because they do not approach the staff problem correctly. A staff job should not be set up if the line can be trained to do the work reasonably well. Note, I said reasonably well. Even if a staff man could do a superb job versus an average job by the line, the gamble is almost always with the line man. The line man does not have anyone else to go through; he is directly committed to the result.

A growing three-shift operation gradually added five extra day foremen on special planning and quality work. But costs and waste were increasing. The condition was reversed only when three extra supervisors were put on the night shifts and the five day-shift staff men were eliminated. The solution came in getting the work done through direct supervision—a line job, not a staff job.

Line people, even first-level line people, can often do things well if given the chance. A foreman of an automatic screw machine department had never done any methods work. He was then given an assistant foreman to whom he delegated the supervision of two-thirds of his crew. He was given some basic training in work simplification and was then given the responsibility for improving methods. He now had time to work on methods, and was able to reduce the cost on almost every operation in the department. He had not had time before.

There are slippages when staff does the work, because the payoff is in the doing and the line does the doing. It is often better to have the foreman do his own quality inspection if he can be made accountable for the quality as well as the cost. Management training is usually much more effective when the regional sales manager or the plant manager trains his own managers rather than having trainers train them. He is committed to their training, they are *his* men, and he will follow up.

THE COST OF STAFF

One of the reasons for being overstaffed comes from a failure to recognize the practicalities of the cost return. Let's suppose a manipulative staff man costs $20,000 a year. He will probably cost another $20,000 in fringes, office space, travel, secretarial help, supervision, and so on. This makes $40,000. To be effective, he usually has to take quite a bit of time from both line people and other staff people to get information in the first place. In addition, he needs a great deal of time and effort on the part of the line people to put his methods into effect once they have been developed. In our experience this is about a fifty-fifty proposition. It takes about as much line effort as original staff work to make the idea pay off in practice. The staff man, therefore, should produce about $80,000 in value per year to break even. In order to make a good profit on him $120,000 per year would be required.

This cost-return formula for staff is only a rule of thumb, but we have found it extremely helpful when analyzing staff operations. It highlights staff jobs that cannot possibly make an adequate contribution. It is actually unfair to put a good staff man in that position. He can only become frustrated.

The work of a staff job might have been needed and might actually have paid off at first. The work then declines, but the staff man is kept on. This setup is also unfair to the staff man. An insurance company hired four industrial engineers to go all through the company and make complete analyses of all methods. They were very effective. After the first time through all four men were kept on, but there was enough major work on a continuing basis for only two men. They started working on minor projects and were costing more than they were contributing. They became a source of irritation to department heads. Government departments often suffer from this problem. Staff men are used for initial development and installation, but the same crew is kept on after the major work has been done. The staff group should then be cut down.

HAVE STAFF REPORT TO LOWEST LEVEL

Staff can usually make its greatest contribution at the lowest line level. If a staff man can report to a lower level and still do all his work, he will usually contribute more. A market research department was broken up and individual analysts were put into each marketing region reporting to the line regional manager. They were then part of the team of that region and made a greater contribution because they became more familiar with its problems.

In one firm there was a 30 to 50 percent increase in the efficiency of a very touchy tower operation when the planning and engineering expense was shifted from central engineering to the plant. The engineers were then closer to the problems and could be made more firmly accountable for the results.

Even at one location it is worthwhile pushing staff to its lowest level. A large chemical plant was made up of four major manufacturing units each under a superintendent with plant staff reporting to the resident manager. The organization was changed to a modular form and, in effect, each superintendent was made a small plant manager reporting to the resident manager. Plant staff services, like industrial engineering, technical service, planning, and maintenance were broken up and assigned appropriately to the individual module head. The total number of staff people was then reduced by 35 percent and yet the total contribution from those remaining was greater because they were now directly assigned to the team they were serving. This setup also turned out to be an excellent development device for future resident managers.

You might question whether the individual module head would have the skill to train these staff people. A senior staff man in each function was retained and reported to the overall resident manager. It was this senior man's job to train and upgrade each of the modular staff people. This form of organization is touchy, but it can work quite well when people are trained in the way it would be used. The senior staff man must be made accountable for the total achievement of his counterparts in each of the modules— joint accountability.

LINE DEDICATED TO STAFF RESULTS

We said that the staff should be geared to line results. Executives often forget that in fairness to good staff people line also must be dedicated to the results toward which staff is working or else staff will not be effective. In other words, staff needs a strong line vehicle to be effective. It is the obligation of the line manager to approve the setup whereby his men use staff, not a setup whereby they cut them out.

A market research man in an airline developed a fine packaged program for California business. He cleared the project beforehand with the line district managers and at the time they felt the package was needed. When the plan was put in, however, it was a flop because all the regional managers were pushing their district managers to sell overseas business. They were not interested in California business. It is unfair to put a staff man on a study when the executives are not prepared to make the line accountable for the results at which the project is directed.

In a state department of education it was a mathematics

consultant's job to develop improved mathematics courses for the public schools. It was very difficult for her to do this for grade schools, because the teachers had not been taught how to teach mathematics and did not view it as their job. She therefore tended to concentrate on high school teaching because that is where the mathematics teachers were, even though many mathematics fundamentals could be taught very well in grade school.

COMBINE STAFFS

Since the line is where the results are, it is usually wise for a manager to have as many line functions as possible report directly to him. If necessary, combine staffs under one staff head and have the staff head report to the line executive. It would be better for a president to have various line divisions report to him directly and have a director of staff services who supervises all staff functions also report to him. He is then closer to the line and can actually be more effective in deciding how to use his staff. There is a tendency for the vice president of marketing to have all the central sales and marketing staff people report to him and have all his sales people report to his general sales manager. It is usually better to have regional or district sales managers report to the vice president of marketing and have one head of all the staff services also report to him. This thinking also carries down into a plant. A plant manager usually has various staffs reporting to him along with a general superintendent over all the line operations. The plant manager should have the superintendents report directly to him and have an assistant plant manager over all the staffs. While it looks as though you are deemphasizing staff this way, in our experience the setup results in a far better utilization of staff.

Larger companies usually have too many staff men impinging on the line people. In one company selling through dealers there were so many merchandisers' programs impinging on the individual district sales managers and sales representatives that they did not have time to do their basic job, to help the dealers merchandise.

In a plant, superintendents and foremen often have to cope with methods men, engineers, quality men, schedule men, personnel people, training men, budget men, maintenance engineers, maintenance foremen, and safety engineers. Foremen begin to feel that they are not accountable for each of these specialized areas, that the staff men are.

Foremen feel no accountability to make machines work; that is the engineer's job. Quality, in turn, is the quality man's job. Labor relations is the personnel man's job, and so on. There are too many gaps between these various staff jobs, so efficiency goes down. The line must always be made to feel accountable for the total operation.

The attitude always reduces the effectiveness of the organization. Ordinarily, a line man can work effectively with only two to four staff people at a time. It is often better to combine various staff jobs as they impinge on a line man, so that he has to deal with only a limited number of people.

Government has a special problem because often many different planning sections impinge on the various district offices. Line must always be committed to total results. Too many staff people detract from this commitment.

There seems to be a conflict between working on long-range staff problems and also on short-range. In one company it was helpful to separate central engineering on overall facilities planning from plant engineering where the current maintenance work was done. A plastics firm sharply increased their business from new-product lines by separating current product improvement from research. Product development problems were short-range and hot, and when the two groups were together, product development problems got all the attention and new-product research lagged. Within five years after they were separated, 40 percent of the firm's business and 70 percent of their profit were from the new product lines developed by the research department.

It is important that long-range staff work be tied to the effectiveness of short-term line at some future date. If an executive does not provide for this relationship, long-range effort is less effective. Long-range staff, too, must have a line vehicle to carry through on its work.

If a staff's work can be autonomous, it may be set up as a central service for efficiency. Overflow pools sometimes are very helpful in keeping an organization slim. Routine office work may be put into a pool that can be used by anyone. However, the pool must have an obligation to give prompt service on request and to give the kind of service needed.

In engineering departments it is helpful to have a central pool of engineers who are not needed on current projects. Project budgets can be better held within limits because the supervisors do not have to lay off engineers. Available engineers are highlighted, and engineering supervisors are discouraged from hoarding engineers who are not needed at the time.

In plants, it is worthwhile to have a central pool where supervisors can put men even for a day to cut their costs. If supervisors are fully accountable for costs, they will do this. The system highlights surplus personnel, making it much easier to cut back when necessary. To be effective these pools must make help available whenever the supervisor needs it, or else he will still hoard people.

Central pools lose some of their effectiveness if a function has a high requirement for specialized knowledge compared with the average of the people in the pool. Legal typing does not work as well in a general typing pool as copy typing. In addition, some people do not want to be in a pool. They want a home department and a tie-in with other people. A special effort must be made to meet this natural objection.

RESIST OVERPROFESSIONALIZATION

With the great increase in specialization there has been a strong trend toward professionalization in various fields. Specialists often put their vocation above service to the organization. The attitude is really a "cop-out," an unwillingness to assume responsibility. An economist feels that he is doing his job when he presents fine professional economic studies but will not take a responsibility for forecasting so that decisions can be made. A personnel man is proud of the professional aspect of his appraisals, even though they do not help department heads motivate their people. An engineer is more impressed with the fine scientific paper he wrote for a journal reporting a careful analysis of what will not work than with whether he helped develop a new product in the company. A market research man, in turn, presents a fine analytical market study but does not help get more sales.

These people forget that the basic purpose of staff is to help the line. Everyone should have a professional attitude of service, integrity, and accomplishment, and these are not the prerogative of staff people. Assuming that staff people are more professional merely leads to divisiveness in the organization. Often colleges do a great disservice by encouraging graduates to feel that their profession comes ahead of giving service to the organization they work in.

chapter nine

Results Must Be
Personally Rewarding

If you wanted to put the objective of management into a concise statement, you might say that it is to get the personal commitment of every management person toward best results for the organization. Most executives would be in favor of this objective. There is a corollary to it, however. Human beings react to the pressure of the systems under which they work. An executive must make sure that all internal management systems make a results commitment personally rewarding to every management person. To the contrary, many management systems are actually at odds with a commitment toward best results for the organization.

A president of a small company had been trying for years to get the sales department to emphasize profitable volume. All the records were kept by total volume, and recognition and salary increases were based on volume. Because this company was not big enough to manufacture a full line, they sold a number of items as a distributor for other manufacturers. These items did not make any profit for the firm. Some of their own manufactured items made 10 percent and others 20 percent. The distributor items were kept because the sales representatives felt they were needed for a full line (a common request from sales departments).

The recognition system was then changed so that all volume at 20 percent profit was counted double — $200 of sales for every $100 actually sold. Ten percent profit volume was counted even — $100 for $100. Zero profit items were counted as zero. When the sales representatives objected, they were told they should not try to sell these items; these items were in the line merely to help sell the profit items. In one year the "necessary" zero profit items declined 85 percent at the same time that the profitable items went up 15 percent. Sales representatives had been expending sales effort on these items. The company then eliminated 80 percent of the nonprofit items from inventory with the full acquiescence of the sales department. Profit selling had been made personally rewarding for the sales representatives.

A manufacturer of control systems had maintained its position as a quality house for a long time. As a consequence, engineers and manufacturing people were less concerned about cost and schedule than they were about quality. When the cost and schedule went off, there was only mild pressure on either of these two groups. However, if any complaint came in on quality, there was a wholesale investigation. What do you suppose these people would emphasize? Quality. Quality standards were then established at an acceptable level and strong pressure was placed equally on cost control and on schedules. Both groups then made substantial progress in these two areas also. It was now personally rewarding to do so.

Sound management dictates that balanced direction in every job must be personally rewarding to the man. A plant manager had been getting an annual bonus amounting to 50 percent of his salary. Theoretically, the bonus was based on overall corporate profit, but, in fact, was paid almost every year regardless of profit levels. The costs in the plant, however, had not been decreasing. The plant manager seemed most concerned about good morale and gave little attention to costs. He was then told that 60 percent of his bonus was going to be based on achieving a 10 percent cut in costs in the plant. His reaction was, "You really want me to cut costs." He began to check his schedules much more closely to make sure that they were most effective; he worked on cost reduction programs and became greatly concerned about idle machine- and man-hours. He achieved his 10 percent cut in costs. The bonus plan now encouraged him toward a balanced approach to his problems. It made cost reduction personally rewarding.

A plant had a Scanlon plan that paid off on the basis of percentage of labor cost to value of goods produced. As a result, the plant frequently changed schedules in order to get higher-valued output. If they ran out of materials, they reverted to the most valuable product they could produce so it would look good at the end of the month on their bonus plan. As a consequence, they were often under-inventoried in some finished goods and had difficulty meeting schedules, with many deliveries being shipped by air freight. The plan did not make it personally rewarding to the employees in the plant to do the best possible job in arranging schedules and reducing costs.

A policy, too, may have an excellent intent but actually discourage best results. An insurance company had a rule that if a job were eliminated, the incumbent would retain his rate on a red-circle basis but would not be eligible for a raise until he got into a new job where the raise could be justified. One active young supervisor in the computer department worked out a new system of programming that practically eliminated his job. He was in the lower end of his bracket. His initiative was killed when he was told that he could not now get a raise even though he had done a substantial part of the work involved in the improvement. It would have been far better to have red-circled his range and given him an immediate raise for the achievement which he had made. Executives often sit back satisfied that they have done the right thing when they have merely red-circled the rate. The practice seems to tell a man, "It does not pay to participate in an improvement which may reduce the value of your job." Many salary policies suffer from this deficiency.

Specific executive programs may tear apart commitment. A bank instituted a special drive for more commercial-loan business in all the branches. Commercial loans did increase, but the small-loan business and collections went down. The kudos were for those who were successful in the program even though they had losses in the other two areas. The commercial-loan drive encouraged a poor commitment on the part of the branch managers for the total job. They waited for the next pressure.

MAKE COMMUNICATION ADVANTAGEOUS

Because of a need to get cooperation in an organization, many executives are concerned about communications. It is easy to assume that the reason why things go awry is that people just did not get the word. In many cases the management system does not encourage good communications.

The chief executive of a steel company was very proud of

the production achievements of his firm. He had a fixation about errors, however. He would not accept errors of his managers, and cataloged as unpromotable a manager who told him of any mistakes. Managers soon learned to cover up their errors and not report them if at all possible. The practice also led to a non-risk-taking management.

USE INTANGIBLE REWARDS

Some of the most rewarding activities may not come from a tangible reward. Many men in the military service have experienced a strong commitment to the work of their company or ship, especially not to let a buddy down.

We have all seen devotion to a cause, in crusades or in politics. Political parties can sometimes get a strong commitment to their work without any tangible rewards, and, of course, religious groups can attain a very strong commitment to their missionary activities. Over the years, crusades such as antislavery, ecology, peace, zero population, and so on all have attained a degree of devotion that has rarely been surpassed by work with only a tangible reward.

People in companies also feel work is very rewarding if they get a sense of contribution from doing it. They get a sense of satisfaction if they feel that their accomplishment is socially worthwhile. During a war, industry develops quite a bit of enthusiasm on the part of employees by the feeling that they are contributing to a worthwhile war effort. Many times employees in food companies feel that they are helping to feed the nation better. Employees of any organization have a greater commitment if they feel the product is making a contribution to our society. If not, very often an employee feels a sense of futility in his work. To develop enthusiasm, it is therefore worthwhile to explain to employees the value of the products or services they are working on.

New ventures have their own appeal. Almost all employees involved in launching a new product or division seem to develop a kind of group enthusiasm. They find the whole project personally rewarding. New companies sometimes have this spirit. In almost any old company a similar spirit seems to develop at a new location, a new area, or, perhaps, a new foreign subsidiary. Ordinarily, if an old organization is constantly sparked by some new activity or area, it seems to add spice to the operation. Almost every sales department seems to get added pep when there is a steady stream of new and interesting products coming into the line.

Employees also react very well to crises such as strikes, floods, or fires. It seems to be personally rewarding to almost everyone to feel that he is helping the organization pull itself up by its bootstraps. Ordinarily, employees react well when you can throw a challenge to them, a challenge to overcome a major hurdle to accomplishment.

SOCIAL PRESSURE CAN BE USEFUL

Social pressure can easily make any work personally rewarding or unrewarding. It puts a sort of group spirit behind the work. For example, employees in an ethnic group that has a strong work ethic find personal satisfaction in turning out more and more work.

On the other hand, if the social pressure is antagonistic to the work, it may overcome any personally rewarding factor. Incentive plans for hourly employees often slip into this difficulty. If an employee develops a more efficient way to do some work and gets an award, she may incur the social displeasure of all her associates, who must now speed up to get the same bonus as before. This peer pressure is often the reason why new ideas do not seem to come from such groups. The reaction can be turned around, however, to make new ideas acceptable. If the reward for any improvement is spread among all the employees in the group, new ideas can be socially acceptable. Some plans get group acceptance by dividing up the improvement award among all the employees on that job. By themselves, exhortations to improve will often not overcome this social negative pressure. The social pressure, too, should be personally rewarding to the person.

Executives are often unaware of the stimulating impact they can have on younger people in the organization. One farsighted executive had asked a younger man in the organization to analyze a contract the company was going to sign, basing the purchase price of a chemical on the commodity price index. When the young man presented his analysis to the executive, he was treated as though he were an executive vice president of the firm. The impact developed a strong spirit of cooperation on the part of this young man and full confidence in the wisdom of the executive group. The contact with the executive was personally rewarding.

It is usually flattering to a person if you make it clear that you are relying on him to get something done for you. The more a manager can use the "we" in discussing a target, the better. A regional sales manager was very dubious about a national marketing program. He was dragging his heels though it was supposed to be a test in his region. The vice president of marketing came into the region and taking this regional manager aside, said how interested he was in seeing this program get a trial, and that he was depending on this regional manager to carry it through for him. The regional manager dove into the problem and soon had the program working at top speed all through his region.

Of course, the opposite of relying on the person is to saddle him with a complicated system of checks and balances. This financial approach has unfortunately been encouraged in recent years by more sophisticated record and computing services. It implies that you do not trust the man. Before long, this lack of trust tends to destroy some of the trust the man has in himself and can subtly undermine much of his self-confidence. It is far better to set a goal for a man to imply that you trust him and then give him recognition for the accomplishment of that goal. In most cases the man rises to the occasion.

DON'T HAVE PEOPLE FIGHT EACH OTHER

Some executives give two people the same assignment so that they can check one against the other. It does not indicate confidence in either manager. Sometimes it develops politics in the organization, and at other times it develops super-conservatism. Rarely does it develop aggressive, risk-taking, cooperative management.

Many executives feel that competition between employees inspires them to greater achievement. In our experience, it is far better to encourage cooperation rather than competition. Sales departments often have sales contests which are aimed at stimulating accomplishment. You have the top dog in the contest all the way down to the bottom to the dirty dog of the group. Do you think it is inspiring to all those people who are halfway down or below to be constantly reminded that they are inadequate? Whenever we have seen these contests changed so that each salesman was working against objectives for his territories and every salesman could be a winner, the total achievement from the sales force was almost always greater. The management climate was then made personally rewarding to every salesman, not just to those few who won the contest.

An employee is usually stimulated when he participates in the planning part of his job. It indicates a reliance on his judgment and, therefore, greater prestige is attached to it. Most employees react very well to this reliance. They make contributions to the planning and, what is more important, feel much more committed to the plan so that they make it work. Note: a token request that an employee review a plan developed by someone else is not true participation in planning.

Most executives assume that their pay and appraisal systems reward for results. In many cases, however, these systems do not reward for the best achievement of company results. First of all, judgment often is used in evaluating an individual's performance. This kind of approach does not evaluate results but evaluates the way the man tried to get results. In other words, it evaluates activity. For example, design engineers are often evaluated on the professional completeness of their studies whether or not the designs resulted in profitable products or effective, low-cost, reliable machines. Some traffic policemen are rewarded for the number of arrests they make instead of for accident reduction on the roads they patrol, which is presumably the purpose of the arrests.

Both pay and appraisals often encourage imbalance. Printing sales representatives are usually paid on a percentage of the volume they get. Such a plan does not encourage them to sell better margins, to fill in idle press time, and to minimize rush orders that result in overtime. Sales representatives of many companies often put little effort into selling new products that are different from the older ones they have been selling. There is no extra recognition in pay or appraisals to cover the extra missionary work that new products usually require. The additional work is not worthwhile to the sales representatives.

PROFIT BONUSES REDUCE PROFIT

An executive or division bonus plan based entirely on current profit stresses short-term profit excessively, deemphasizing long-term growth, stability, and profitability of the business. Part of the plan should be directed toward sound long-range decisions.

A basic problem with most pay and appraisal systems is the tendency to treat all jobs the same. Although it is easier administratively and seems fair on the surface, it leads to poor management. The bonus of each sales representative of a paint company was based on the volume of sales sold through the dealers in his territory. The plan seemed logical until it was examined a little more deeply. One territory had four areas with no representation. The most important job of that representative was to get four good dealers set up in those areas. Another territory had four large dealers who took the line the previous year. The big job of the representative was to get these dealers up to expected performance on a balanced line. The same appraisal plan would not fit the two territories.

In a multiplant operation there is a great tendency to appraise one plant against another. If one plant was built twenty-five years ago and is essentially made up of old equipment, it is going to be a great deal more difficult to achieve the same results than it would be in a new plant with new equipment. The cross-comparison is not rewarding to the manager of the old plant. He will always be a loser.

One mail-order house had an excellent but simple appraisal system for appliance repair men. The day after they had gone to a home to repair an appliance, a self-addressed card was sent out asking the customer to check ratings on the neatness, efficiency, and satisfactoriness of the repair work of the service man. It was simple but focused on the essential, a satisfied customer. One of the best ways for any service organization to check its effectiveness is to ask the customer.

Many firms feel that they should separate appraisals from performance ratings. These appraisal systems, then, usually emphasize specific traits, such as judgment and initiative. They are usually aimed at evaluations for promotion. While they may have value, it should be clear that they pull away from results. There is an erroneous assumption that an individual can pulsate feverishly for results and at the same time, without any loss in results, pulsate feverishly in exhibiting various traits that are rated for promotion. People cannot be dichotomized for pulsation. At least if the rating is in terms of traits, it should be based on whether the traits resulted in accomplishment; otherwise, the very appraisal plan may not make results on the job rewarding to the ambitious man.

THE KEY RULE OF COMPENSATION—INCENTIVE

To put pay into results perspective, all compensation should be viewed with the overall objective of incentive:

1. Incentive to get competent people on the job—ordinarily if a firm is within 5 or 10 percent of an average of what is paid by other good firms, this requirement is usually met.

2. Incentive to produce more work.

3. Incentive to produce better quality work.

4. Incentive to produce more important or more valuable work to the organization—this requirement should help encourage the best men to take on the most important jobs. Note that the best contributions are not always made in supervisory jobs. From a results point of view contribution of other jobs may actually be greater.

5. Incentive to produce balanced results—that requirement is, on the one hand, perhaps the most valuable use of incentive, but, on the other hand, the most difficult to work out practically for each job.

If an executive applies these incentive principles to any

compensation decision, he is more likely to get value for his money. His pay system will encourage commitment toward the company results by making them personally rewarding to the manager.

Information systems often drive people in the wrong direction. Cost tends to be overemphasized because it is measurable, and imbalance results. It seems perfectly logical to keep a careful record of all supervision in a plant based on cost per unit. Such figures, however, do not show the long-run cost effect of poor labor relations precedents. These tend to be brushed off later as having been a natural result of negotiations and not traceable to action of supervisors pushing too hard on costs.

Most information systems deemphasize the future since it is harder to measure than current accomplishment. It seems perfectly logical to record the results of a sales territory by volume or by volume of major product line. The system does not record missionary work on new-account orders or on new products. Both of these might require a great deal of work today without much to show on the order pad. In both cases the results could be of great significance in future years.

Many chief executives feel that holding division heads accountable for return on investment encourages them to do the most valuable work for the company as a whole. This emphasis is also short-range and leads to imbalance. A chief executive of a packaging corporation did this with his major regional vice presidents. It did not work because he did not at the same time provide other important evaluations such as growth, new accounts, improved labor relations, and so on. Some of these regional vice presidents made substantial improvements in return on investment and therefore got large bonuses, only to have their regions fall into major difficulties in three or four years. The system rewarded imbalance.

Many management bonus systems suffer from return-on-investment problems in a little different way. Bonuses for executives two, three, or four levels down are based entirely on profit, which is really a return-on-investment concept. At best, these men affect only a small part of what is measured. For that matter, they are often quite removed from the investment decisions. A new district manager came into a men's clothing store chain after all of the stores had been built on locations chosen by someone else. Some locations were poor. A return-on-investment approach did not stimulate him to the best accomplishment in his district. He felt a good return was impossible from the poor locations.

chapter ten

Solving Problems
at Their Source

Many executives give too much attention to the selection
and development of "comers," the upper 10 percent. There
is a vast store of ability, however, in the other 90 percent.
A creative manager takes advantage of the abilities of all
his people, not just the upper 10 percent.

GIVE FREEDOM TO TAKE ACTION

How can an executive release the initiative of all his management people? Ordinarily, people will do what is most comfortable. If there are pressures against the correct action,
therefore, they will not take it. An executive must be sure
that at every level in his management chain employees feel
freedom to effect appropriate action. Authority is not set up
by simply writing it in a job description; it is what the

employee *feels*. A plant manager does not feel free to handle union relations if he must always clear with personnel first. Hardly any government manager feels that she is controlling her department if she is on the spot when she wants to fire an incompetent employee.

Authority is not a stimulator as such. It permits action, and people ordinarily want to take action if they are allowed to. The perceptive manager removes those obstacles that prevent it.

Many subtle things prevent action where the problem is. One executive was enthusiastic about improvement. Every meeting or memo mentioned it. He was disappointed, however, at the small amount of improvement that he got. Several years before, one of the employees down the management chain had taken him seriously and tried out a new idea of his own. It did not work, so he took it out. The executive heard about it, called him in and asked whether he had done this all by himself. The employee said, yes, he had. The executive said, "Well, that's fine. We like people with initiative, but you know some of us have had a little more experience than you have had, and we could have told you that it would not work." Just as surely as if he had told the man, his comment said, "You have no authority to try a new method." This story spread throughout the organization and killed improvement initiative.

A stumbling block to action comes from the fact that every management decision is a gamble. There is always a percentage chance that it will go wrong. If you want to encourage people to take initiative, you must reduce the fear of reprisal for an error. To the contrary, many executives operate by management by error. In other words, they focus on every deviation. In one firm every deviation from plan required a detailed explanation from the management man concerned.

It became clear that the ideal was to have no deviations, so no one took a chance. The same problem occurs when firms use detailed budgets with many copies to many different people. More attention is paid to deviations than to overall accomplishment. It does not pay to make an error. In one company there was a widespread feeling that above all things you should never be associated with an error. This meant, of course, that everyone meticulously avoided any risky proposition. Even for outstanding managers, errors must be looked at as normal.

ACCEPT ERRORS AS NORMAL

Many executives talk about management by exception without recognizing its true meaning. It can be realistic only if there is, first, a sound delegation of objectives and, second, adequate leeway or authority to meet these objectives. This means minimizing the control approach to authority and accepting errors as normal.

If errors are not accepted as normal, the result will be less overall accomplishment. A plant manager became sold on zero defects. Everyone in the plant got the word and every department had a chart showing a declining number of defects over a period of nine months. But the quality at the shipping dock was worse than it had ever been. Why? No engineer can set specifications so well that every eventuality is covered. Previously, foremen and operators would put aside a piece if it "didn't feel right," "didn't seem right," even though it was within specifications. One out of five of these turned out to be defective. Now the workers went by the book. The boss wanted a good defect chart. Within specifications, they would accept the part; outside of specifications, they would reject it. The company was no longer capitalizing on the abilities of the plant people.

Since all management decisions have some element of risk, it requires personal discipline on the part of an executive to delegate authority down the line. He has to accept a percentage of deviation as normal for even outstanding people. A good way to look at it is to assume that a certain percent of the budget will be wasted each year by different management people with the full confidence that the initiative released will get far more accomplishment. Even a first-level supervisor can often produce substantial savings if given a chance to experiment with different methods.

In one company known for the development of many new products, the history of the losers that had to be washed out would fill pages. This fact, however, did not restrain executives from always trying a new product. The problem of leeway is especially critical at the early stages of a product development project. The risk is much greater at that time than when the project is along the way. In the early phases of the project the objective is to reduce the gamble. As more and more time and money is spent on it, percentages should improve. If not, the project should be questioned.

If the delegation of authority is so great that the executive himself will be in severe trouble, then he must hold back and set a review or checkpoint along the way. Otherwise he has abdicated. The general manager of a seasonal recreational product felt he should delegate fully to his vice president of sales, including the leeway to set inventory levels for finished goods. In a downturn of the market the vice president of sales was, typically, optimistic and maintained high inventories. His boys told him that they were about to make a lot more sales. The sales did not materialize, and by the time the season ended the firm had six months' inventory in stock, much of which would deteriorate over a period of time. The division was almost sunk because of this error. There should have been a limit on the amount of inventory that the vice president of sales could build up (perhaps two months' inventory based on current sales).

AUTHORITY VARIES WITH THE OBJECTIVE

The amount of authority you can delegate to an individual varies with the objectives, and it is not the same for all jobs of the same level. To solve problems at their source, authority must be adequate to meet them as they occur. A superintendent who produces rush parts to keep the next department going has a different requirement from one who is building parts for stock. The requirements in a mental ward of a hospital are not the same as those in a maternity ward.

In one national sales department the word was out that no extra sales representatives were to be employed. When one district was told to increase its electrical sales substantially, the obvious answer was to increase the number of electrical sales representatives. They did not feel they had this leeway, however. As a consequence, there was very little increase in electrical sales. Other district managers did not need the authority to hire any additional men because they did not have the same objectives.

Time requirements will change authority. A product that must be developed within a year and a half does not require the same authority as one that must be ready in nine months.

Conditions may be different at different times. An engineering department was set up to construct new equipment in a number of new plants. Conditions changed so that the big bulk of the engineering work was to maintain and upgrade the machinery that was already in the plants. Their work did not require the same engineering experimentation or the same staffs that were needed in the new design phase. Most installation functions require more leeway than a continuing one. Otherwise, new functions stumble.

There may be greater difficulties facing one manager than those facing another with essentially the same objectives. In the tire business, Detroit may be an extremely competitive market; New England may not. The manager of Detroit, therefore, needs more price leeway in order to meet his competition. There is quite a contrast between the requirements of a superintendent who is in charge of a packing operation with known standards versus one in charge of a job shop machining operation where there are no standards. The latter needs more leeway if he is to meet problems as they occur.

The gamble goes up as the creativity requirement goes up. Decisions are usually less sure. Costs are therefore less important than achievement in product development or in research. In other words, more leeway must be allowed if each engineer is to make his contribution. The same might be true of an economist, who must be encouraged to make actionable predictions based on partial facts, knowing that errors will be common. The key factor is what you get out of the operation, not what you spend to get the result.

BUILD AUTHORITY FROM THE BOTTOM UP

Executives usually build authority from the top down. Authority should be built up from the lowest level to make sure that it is adequate to encourage action there. The bottom is where the action is required. In a plant the work gets done on the individual machines. The foreman is the manager who should take action. In a department store it is the individual sales clerk who deals with a customer. He or his manager should have enough authority to satisfy customers, if possible.

Many executives tend to look at authority down the line from a control point of view only. They want to prevent unpleasant deviations. This concern is valid, but the prime purpose of authority is to get something done down the line. It must, therefore, be realistic in terms of the problems to be solved down the line, not just the control needed at the top. To make authority realistic, therefore, ask each manager down the line to propose the authority he needs in light of his problems. In effect, ask the manager to tell you what is preventing his accomplishment of the objectives that he wants to achieve. Executives should try to delegate enough leeway to allow him to get his job done.

Authority is often most useful when it is expressed in terms of a special authority item, rather than just in dollars. Most job descriptions tend to emphasize authority in terms of dollar limits only. To the contrary, a superintendent may feel he cannot take aggressive action unless he can send someone home who is not doing a job, or unless he can demand maintenance whenever he needs it. Sales representatives may feel they must be able to vary some prices in order to sell effectively.

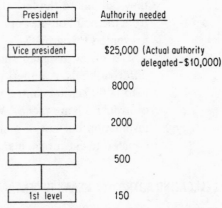

FIGURE 9 Authority needed at each level to redelegate adequately.

Chief executives often commit a major error of authority by delegating too little to other executives. As a consequence, there is not enough for redelegation to the bottom levels. These levels, then, do not seem to shoulder their responsibilities because they do not have enough authority. The total authority requirement looks so big to the chief executive. For example, if you are talking about dollars, a president may feel that he should not delegate authority to a vice president beyond $10,000 (see Figure 9). This vice president, however, has four management levels below him. By the time authority is parceled out downward there just is not enough left for the bottom manager to do his job. At each level a manager must have several times the authority that he delegates to an individual under him in order to delegate adequately to all of his subordinates. When you build the authority required from the bottom level all the way up to the vice-presidential level, the total can be substantial. The failure to recognize this requirement is often the reason why very little authority is delegated in large companies. What it means, in effect, is that the top executives (not bottom managers) have not really grown with the company. Although they talk about the lack of growth of people down the line, from the point of view of authority many top executives have prevented this growth.

It is often assumed that there are differences between different kinds of authority. Is there really any more value in a $50,000 capital control versus a $50,000 current expense control? Both are money. Why have close control of machine installation but not of maintenance cost? The two must be equated to encourage managers to make balanced decisions.

DELEGATING AUTHORITY MEANS DECENTRALIZATION

Building freedom to act as far as possible means pushing decentralization. Many executives debate centralization versus decentralization. There is nothing magical about it. Decentralization merely means delegation of authority. It should be carried out just as far as it is feasible to encourage everyone to shoulder his part of the load. When the authority to design and install touchy processing vats was pushed to the engineering department of the individual plant of a food company, efficiency increased 30 percent in the first year. It had been too hard to get action before in central engineering. There was too much paper work.

Before any authority is delegated to a person, there must be a setup which encourages a commitment on his or her part to accomplish results. Most decentralization programs err in this regard. Since decentralization is essentially an authority concept, executives delegate authority but fail to set up sound accountability first. Sound accountability must always precede authority. A plant manager who has the authority to cut costs but is not fully accountable for service will not do a balanced job. In order to have the right to cut costs he must also be accountable for the impact of that cost on service.

It is only with a setup that gets commitment to results, in other words uses authority soundly, that the centralization-decentralization cycle can be broken. Many executives have decentralized and lost control. They therefore centralize and see initiative being killed. The key item is not decentralization of authority but an accountability system that makes sure that people at each level are committed to accomplishment.

Often a chief executive decentralizes, but the executives who report to him do not decentralize in turn. There is merely a different level of centralization and initiative is still stifled. In most cases we have found that the executives who do not redelegate do not know how to delegate accountability. A chief executive who wishes to decentralize must at the same time set up a way whereby the executives below him can be taught a system to carry accountability all the way down. In other words, he needs a management mode of operation that he can teach other executives. Without this, decentralization plans fail.

INFLUENCE IS AUTHORITY

Whenever a manager has an influence on a result, he does, in effect, have authority. He must then be accountable in some way for the sound exercise of that influence. This thinking has special relevancy for staff people, because they often have the ear of the executive. In effect, they are influencing a decision, even though they do not make it. They must, therefore, be made accountable for that decision so the influence is appropriate. In many cases, joint accountability is the only way this can be done.

Many executives assume that there is only one type of

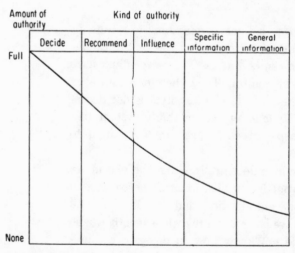

FIGURE 10   Levels of authority.

authority. In fact, there are many gradations of authority. It goes all the way from decision, to recommendation, to giving information (Figure 10).

DOUBLE-CHECKS REDUCE INITIATIVE

It is very tempting to an executive who wants control to establish checks and double-checks. For example, requisitions might require several signatures. Most checking is antagonistic to a sound stimulation of initiative, and it should be instituted only when there is a great deal at stake. The problem is that the loss of initiative does not show on the profit and loss statement as clearly as the expenditure.

A large consumer company established very careful checking on all credit requests that came in from the field. A number of credit men plus several levels of supervision worked on this. When district managers were made accountable for profit in their districts, they were given the credit responsibility to delegate to their sales representatives. The sales representatives were trained by the credit men. The work went on very well at about half the cost.

A woodworking company set up a quality man to make sure that good quality came out of a department with two foremen. The quality man was then eliminated and another foreman was added. All three were made fully accountable for quality. A great deal more output was achieved with a much better quality record. After all, quality men do not produce quality.

Checking often costs more than it saves. A vice president of manufacturing built up a duplicate set of records so that he would always be prepared to answer detailed questioning by the president. He had an additional staff of about ten people working on this. The procedure was not lost on the foremen and superintendents. All action was curtailed for fear an error would show up in the detail reported to the president.

Even down the line, checking can be overly expensive. In a grain company a comptometer operator worked on reports where an error might cause quite a bit of lost time in other departments. To avoid errors, the obvious answer was to have another comptometer operator do the same work over. It would be unlikely that both would make the same error. When the process was analyzed, it was found that an error might cause the loss of only one hour of time. The extra comptometer operator was then removed and the first operator told that the company was depending on her. Her average number of errors per month was about seven.

GOOD MANAGERS REPEAT ERRORS

A philosophy that assumes that anyone who makes the same error twice is stupid will unduly discourage initiative. If a manager handles sticky employee relations problems, there is a good chance that his solution will work two-thirds of the time. If he handles ten such problems, we should expect him to make an error three times. An executive might then assume that this manager just never learns, but he has actually done a good job. Most management decisions are repeated with about the same probability of error each time. Good management puts no weight whatsoever on the repetition of an error but only on the total losses from errors compared to the results achieved. All decisions have a percentage of risk. A district engineer of a railroad whose crews lay track would be expected to have an occasional derailment. That does not mean that he is doing a poor job.

chapter eleven

Policy and Procedure — A Positive Tool

Why are policy and procedure so often stultifying instead of invigorating to the organization? First, there is often a failure to differentiate between policy and procedure. Second, both of these are not worked out realistically in terms of the impact on the first level, the place where all policy and procedure finally has an impact.

POLICY GIVES INTENT

Policies should be a general guide for carrying out executive decisions. The fundamental purpose of policy is to give executive intent. Adjustment policy in a department store should be set up to satisfy customer complaints at a reasonable cost and hold customers, not to talk the customer out of his complaint. Policy, overall, should tell people the underlying basis for making a decision.

People need policy to remove doubt as to the direction they should take. In a bank, loan policy should help a loan officer decide how to approach a loan to a new business with experienced partners who have limited financial resources.

Policy often goes awry because of a misunderstanding of the way it should be developed. A chief executive should decide corporate policy, but this does not mean that he should develop it. He should insist that all the functional vice presidents be responsible for proposing adequate policy to him for approval. To the extent that problems occur later on because of inadequate policy, the function heads must then be responsible. One of the basic reasons for an expert in a function is to keep the chief executive free of trouble in that area.

Policies should give broad direction, because the purpose is to encourage employees in that direction. People need a signal from the chief executive. This is true even in educational institutions. If high school course consultants are to adequately consider vocational versus college emphasis in high school, it is helpful for them to know that their main purpose is to provide an education that prepares the student for his role in life.

There should be a stated purpose behind a policy so that the limitations of the policy can be clarified. Even a policy of good housekeeping in plants is weak unless it states the purpose so that people administering the policy know how far they should go. A firm that made precision gauges had a policy of high quality. When they entered the home thermometer business, however, the same high quality was not appropriate to those consumers. The quality policy had to be stated in terms of the needs of the final customer in order to fit the consumer business.

Policy is a help in setting the direction so recognition systems (pay, appraisals, etc.) can be geared properly. Recognition systems should reward the employee for taking action that carries out the intent of the policy. If the firm has a policy of growth in the number of its product lines, the recognition systems should be set up to reward those people or divisions that get a foothold for new product lines.

Policy is a form of authority definition. Its purpose is to prevent wide deviations from direction, really parameters. In a spark plug company, sales policy limited distribution to good-sized dealers with good territories. Sales representatives were, therefore, prevented from accepting a dealer who had a very limited territory. In an auto parts manufacturing plant it was the policy to meet shipping dates on all parts of an order. This policy was a limiting factor for plant managers because at times it could lead to extra costs.

Policy may be aimed at limiting an undesirable action. A pricing policy might be necessary in the sales department to prevent antitrust action.

Because policy is a limitation on authority, however, it should be minimal, set up only to the extent needed for broad corporate or division control. In order to ensure the wise application of capital in one firm, a policy was set up requiring a return of 13 percent on investment within two years and the capital replacement within the life of the investment. There were no further specifications because no more were needed.

UNDEFINED POLICY STOPS ACTION

Some executives, particularly those in small companies, pride themselves on having very few policies. This attitude is a mistake. Undefined policy actually stops action. Some people tend to be careful about every action because of uncertainty about policy. Others take unwarranted excursions in areas that are inappropriate. In a company that had no policy on inventory, procedures developed requiring detailed reports on all inventories to be sent into the home office. The detailed reporting system and questioning acted as a stronger limitation than any policy would have. It prevented the flexibility needed in inventories to meet customer needs in the field.

When do you need policy? The first major area is where you need continuity or consistency, so that the whole corporation looks at similar problems in the same way. An obvious place is where there are legal implications to consider. You may also need policies in order to satisfy customers. A broad personnel policy is needed so that people are treated fairly. Promotions and management development should be covered in overall policy so that they apply uniformly to all divisions of the company.

But consistency should always be limited to what is absolutely necessary for the company, region, or overall location. A sales policy might state that the firm will sell through secondary distribution but might very well leave open whether it will be through a dealer or a distributor in a particular district. Sales policy may also leave open the kind of district emphasis—product, type of individual incentives, promotions, and so on. A policy of giving the controller necessary information on deviations should not be abused by requiring line people to justify the deviation to him. The latter approach makes the controller the supervisor of the line without being accountable.

Policy may be necessary when one group unduly affects the work of another. As a matter of policy, manufacturing may be required to follow specifications and not develop their own "black books" on engineering requirements. In a multiplant operation it could be a wise policy to treat all interplant work as though the supplying plant were a customer so that the supplying plant must satisfy the receiving plant. The plant would then get the same profit credit that they would on a similar production order from a customer.

It was necessary in a multiplant corporation to have a purchasing policy that required all central purchases to fit the specifications and schedules of the receiving plants. Otherwise, there was a tendency to focus too much on prices.

POLICY MUST POINT FUTURE DIRECTION

Policy for future position is often the most important area that an executive must cover. He needs it to guide in a new direction, perhaps to diversify or to go international. In a department store chain a change of policy was needed to switch over to the discount business. Policy is essential to give the organization the signal of change. A small company that made only 6 to 8 percent on the investment for years set up a policy to arrive at 14 percent in five years. Immediately all action on products, product development, machine investment, and methods was geared to meet this goal. Even though many managers felt it could not be done, they made it in three years instead of five.

Policies should be reviewed for change periodically. A policy in growth in an industry could change when the industry matures or when the firm gets to be a major factor in that industry. With a policy of diversification a company may easily get to a point where the diversity of its businesses becomes unmanageable and the policy must be changed.

Policy almost inevitably seems to lead to procedure. Policy should give broad intent and direction. Procedure states specific ways that things should be done, ostensibly to carry out the policy. A policy usually needs some procedures on the way to carry out action to make the policy effective.

What is often lost sight of is that the reason for procedure is to effect the policy. In the federal government the reason for a civil service approach to employees was to provide better administration by minimizing the spoils system. Its purpose was not to give security to employees, particularly to incompetent ones. Unfortunately, the procedures have deviated from the original intent of the policy.

Procedures, even more than policy, are a specific limitation on authority. As such they should always be questioned by their impact on the first level where their effect finally settles in. Procedures should encourage people at the first level to take action in tune with the policy, not to prevent them from taking action. A sales policy on growth should lead to procedures that encourage first-level sales representatives to work toward growth.

PROCEDURES CAN VITIATE POLICY

It is frustrating to an executive to find that the application of procedures often seems to go in the opposite direction from the intent of his policy. A policy on reducing costs should encourage the first level to reduce costs and give service. It should not simply lead to a tight budget. A foreman on an expensive processing machine found that he could save ten machine hours per week if he could have two members of the crew come in two hours earlier on overtime to warm up the machines. The idea did not fit the overtime control system that was considered part of the cost reduction program. The overtime cost was minor compared with productivity from ten additional machine hours.

Procedures must be flexible enough to carry through on the policy in light of the different problems in different areas and different lines. A procedure trying to encourage sales growth that suggests that all territories spend x percent of their time on new accounts may be unrealistic. Some territories have no potential new accounts. In other territories the timing of these calls may be much more important than the number of them. The procedure would militate against sound achievement.

In effect, procedure must always include leeway so that the first level has adequate freedom to meet its problems. On most procedures ask, "What is helpful to the first level in getting achievement?" not, "What might be helpful to control?" The latter approach tends to be stultifying. A sales department required long call reports of each sales representative. These reports led to detailed questioning from the home office and to long "kitchen table" reports by the sales representatives. They did not reflect realism in the territory. They substituted writing skills for selling skills in the sales force.

Procedures should be as broad as possible. It is impossible to prevent every small aberration from a general norm. The problems in practice are almost always different. If a salary policy is aimed at providing incentive, the procedure for it would be different for technical people than for sales people. Even in sales departments incentive procedure for a consumer-sales group might be far different from that for a commercial-sales group. It may be different for sales service personnel versus sales representatives and different for plant foremen as against sales representatives. Procedures must be flexible to meet bottom-level needs.

EVERY MANAGER HAS POLICY RESPONSIBILITY

Many executives are frustrated by the lack of upward communication from people down the line. The situation often comes from an erroneous and dangerous philosophy that policy and procedure development are the exclusive domains of executive row. Any manager at any level in the organization down through the first level should be expected to question policy and procedure that are inappropriate. Surely, the purpose of policy and procedure is to help the operation. Executives need a feedback of deficiencies if they are to make policy and procedure virile. Managers down the line frequently hesitate to question a policy, especially when they get a quick reply, "You don't see the broad picture." Unfortunately, it is only people down the line who fully feel the negative effect of policies and procedures. An accounts receivable expert in a bank chain set up procedures that tightened down considerably on accounts receivable loans in order to reduce risks. Of course, the branch managers felt the impact because they were prevented from taking on as much business. This latter effect did not hit the accounts receivable expert, however. It was hard for branch managers to be heard in the home office.

Executives need a feedup from the bottom because they cannot be close to the effect of their policies and procedures. How can a president know whether an inventory policy is effective unless he gets a feedup from the first-level supervisors and sales representatives who are affected by it?

One of the best ways to get feedup is to make sure that there is a commitment to results in each job all the way down the line. The lack of this is often the reason for inadequate feedup. Many executives feel, for example, that it is important to set objectives for their top managers, but they are not as concerned about requiring this all the way down the line through every foreman and sales representative. When a man is solidly accountable for results objectives, he is more insistent in presenting inadequacies of policies and procedures. The good feedback on policies and procedures is one of the big advantages of a management-by-objective system carried all the way down. Then when managers down the line repeatedly question an employee appraisal procedure because it does not fit the results they should get, executives up the line tend to listen.

MAKE PROCEDURES VOLUNTARY

As the number of central staff people increases, so does the tendency to consider procedures to be required rather than optional. Specific procedures should be required only where uniformity throughout the organization is obsolutely necessary. There is a tendency, however, to look at any suggested procedure coming from a skilled staff as compulsory. In a chemical research department, for example, if an overall project approach is developed with normal steps, these steps are assumed to be followed even though inappropriate to the particular project. Ordinarily, many of them should be voluntary.

Required procedures should be constantly reviewed to see whether they should still be required. In a steel company maintenance inventories went way out of line, so the company set up very rigid temporary procedures to control them. After the inventories were back in line, however, the rigid procedures should have been loosened to allow more flexibility to meet current problems. In a drug company, sales representatives were frequently asked to make surveys and deliver merchandising and sales items to the customer. The saying was, "They were going, anyway." While a small amount of this work might have been done by the sales representatives without much of a problem, it soon developed to be standard practice, requiring 40 to 50 percent of the time of the sales representative. The procedure should have been reviewed earlier and questioned as to whether it was absolutely critical and worth the time spent on it.

Voluntary procedures can easily be made compulsory by

administrative action. A consumer company sold to drugstores and supermarkets for resale. The home-office marketing department was constantly developing product merchandising programs to help the sales department. Recognizing that territories could have different problems, all programs were made voluntary for the field sales force. The policy was sound. In order to make sure that the firm had a record as to how well the programs were doing, however, a listing was kept in the home office ranking each of the representatives and district managers on each program. Can you visualize any ambitious field man willing to be at the bottom of one of these lists with all of its home-office visibility? The listing made all programs compulsory. The effect was that many of these representatives and district managers were spending 30 and 40 percent of their time pushing programs which were inappropriate to their particular areas. To make them voluntary, all of these rankings had to be abolished.

chapter twelve

Make Information Systems
Solve Management Problems

With the advent of the computer, information problems were supposed to be solved. Many an executive, however, has been frustrated by the escalating costs of computer systems without comparable value in the management process. A prime difficulty is the failure to keep the major purpose of all information systems in mind: to help management make sound and timely decisions. The major purpose should not be, as it often seems to be, to record a mass of data or to report on someone so he can be held accountable.

To put information systems into perspective, it is helpful to recognize that there are different types. First, there is financial information which is necessary to record the financial status of the organization. Profit and loss statements and balance sheets must be prepared on a comprehensive basis so that broad corporate decisions can be made. Since these are usually the first records developed in a firm, the financial thinking involved in them tends to be applied to all other types of information. It is the first reason why executives often have poor information systems.

The second major type of information is that needed for long-term decisions. It is aimed at the planning of the organization for the long run. Usually, external economic data and general data are necessary, as well as internal data. Much of these internal data are financial; for example, information on expected return on a plant or outlet, or the analysis in a department store chain of the investment needed to go into a discount business and of the projected return. Most of this information is for strategic use for broad planning. The main error is that the long-term information is also used for tactical purposes. It is not designed to help management people meet their ever-changing problems. When it is used for tactics, it often contributes to the loss of initiative down the line.

There is a third set of information necessary for the evaluation of the performance of an individual or a function. The data must usually be pulled together on a broad basis for six months or a year. To be valuable, this kind of information should evaluate a result. In an aeronautical division of a company, the data on engineering projects were amassed only up to the time the prints were turned over to the plant. However, true engineering performance could be evaluated only if included were all the engineering costs of breaking into production, which in many cases were as great as the initial engineering cost. Above all, performance should be evaluated in terms of a result which is traceable to the over-all objectives of the organization. It should not stop at a measurement of activity, in this case, completed prints.

Because financial statements are usually prepared annually, there is a natural tendency to evaluate performance annually also. While a year is feasible in many cases, sometimes other periods are more appropriate. If a firm is selling large computers, it might take two or three years to get a result, the sale of a large system. In a two-seasonal recreation business, two six-month periods worked best.

It is a common misconception that measurement of performance should be a measurement of what the man personally contributed. If the purpose is to get him to do a better job, it is far better to measure the result of a project that he is connected with. In other words, ask the question, "When he is connected with a project, does it go well?" Approached in this way, for example, a credit manager can sometimes make a substantial contribution to sales by accepting border-line accounts and helping these accounts maintain an acceptable financial position. She does not make the sale, but she makes it economically feasible. She is on the team with the sales representatives. Performance records should be aimed at getting individual management people committed to broad results so that they take constructive action toward them.

KEY INFORMATION—ACTION REPORTS

The fourth area of information systems, and the most critical one for the encouragement of action, is what we call action records. Their purpose is to stimulate individual managers to take corrective action promptly on deviations. Current data systems often work the other way. A paper mill had a tight cost control system. Every slight cost deviation was reported to the plant manager, who would demand action. I asked the foreman of a crew whether he did not have more people than he needed, and he admitted that he had four extra. "But," he said, "We've got close cost control here. We also have a rule that every order that comes in during the week must be shipped out that week." This rule was necessary for good customer relationships. He went on: "If I have a tight crew and get a rush order on Thursday, I have to go to both my superintendent and the plant manager to get approval for overtime. They don't want any overtime. They always ask me pointed questions as to why I need overtime. They always end up giving me an OK, but I never look good." "Now," he continued, "I get myself ahead on Monday, Tuesday, and Wednesday. If a rush order comes in on Thursday, I tell them, 'I don't know if I can do it, but I will do my best.' They always say, 'Do your best, will you?' I always get my orders out on time. I don't have any overtime. I'm a hero in the front office. What would you do?" The same as he would. The whole control system was militating against sound action.

This foreman was then made accountable simply for his costs compared to standard with an allowance for the normal amount of overtime expected in a year's period. He was told he could have overtime any time he wanted to, but it was to his advantage to reduce his crew to minimum size. Within six months he cut off five people.

The action record system should also push toward additional opportunities. An estimator in a job shop was using average costing for much of his system. The effect of this was to undercost complex systems and overcost simple ones. As a consequence, the sales representatives were encouraged to take unprofitable business while they were passing up some very good profitable business. The system had to be changed so actual costing reflected the true cost of the particular order, even though it took more time.

Action records must cover much more than performance records. Action reporting should cover each little subsection of the work where action might be taken. In some plants, quality records are kept by department, not by run or shift.

Action is normally not taken by department but is taken by run and shift. If the records do not get down to this point, action will not be taken as promptly or as consistently.

REPORTS MUST BE TIMELY TO GET ACTION

At other times, performance records are not current enough to make decisions in time. In a paint company, a simple check each day of each tank with a ruler was necessary to get action taken on filling various tanks to fit runs. The normal machine run data were not adequate. Many executives assume that long-range financial data coupled with overall performance data on individuals will give action records. On the contrary, action records are very often different from financial and performance records.

One of the main differences is that action records must be very timely, but they may also be very crude. All they need to tell someone is that he is off enough so that he should do something about it. An engineering department in the space industry suffered because many of the projects were late. Data were kept on each project monthly and reported to the project leader two or three weeks later. He might get data seven weeks after a deviation.

Simple cost data were then amassed in a very rough way and reported weekly to each project leader. Within four months late projects dropped 50 percent. The project leaders now knew much sooner when a project was going off.

Computer data and much financial data often do not stimulate adequate action because it is too late. The accuracy required coupled with cutoff dates forces the data into such a straitjacket that they do not serve the current needs of the managers. The first law for computers should be that they give the manager the information that he wants *when* he wants it.

Constant changes in routines may be necessary in order for computer records to be current. In the department-store business, changes in the market may very well require changes in reporting to keep the managers abreast. In the petroleum industry different districts may have different goals at different times. The computer setup must be flexible enough to program data immediately to fit the changes. If it is not flexible, it is impractical.

Most information systems report too much data. If your purpose is to stimulate action, you should be focusing on significant data only. In many cases, deviations that are reported are random. You cannot "cry wolf" all the time and expect someone to take action. In the case cited earlier, for example, is there any value in pointing up overtime on a rush order that comes in on Thursday or Friday and has to be shipped out that week?

ACTION REPORTS MUST REFLECT AUTHORITY

Information systems managers must develop broad management know-how because the basis for action records is authority. If these records are to be effective in stimulating action, they must reflect authority as it is delegated down the line and fortify it. How should they do this? They should report deviations on any subpart to the man himself and not to his boss. In other words, the essence of authority is that the man himself makes the decision and takes corrective action, without information ever going to his superior. If information does go above, as it so frequently does in companies, a manager would not be human if he did not at least ask the question, "Why?" A manager cannot ask such a question without overtones—an implication of reprimand. The information itself, then, tends to restrict authority in practice, because it puts the man on the defensive. Instead, he should be encouraged to take action. In an airline, for example, the local district manager should know daily load factors on which he should take action. He does not need daily questions from his boss on his load factor, however, if he is accountable.

Executives often fail to realize that their information systems can easily vitiate the exception principle in the management flow. Computers may develop the idea among many people that they are merely numbers and are not being relied on to take action because data, even minute data, are reported up the line to inform executives. Too many copies of many of these reports go to too many people—it is too easy to run off another copy.

If all the key staff of an executive get copies of a report, each one feels that it is his job to analyze it and ask questions about it. His view of his function, therefore, becomes warped. To make an information system stimulate initiative, there should be fewer and grosser figures as you go up the line. In one plant, for example, the plant manager received only eight figures a month. The detail went to his superintendents and foremen. After all, they were the ones who should have taken action on it.

ACTION REPORTS DEPEND ON OBJECTIVES

Objectives of individual managers will change over different periods of time. Since action records should reflect individual objectives, the information system must also be flexible enough to change with them. The objectives for an industrial sales territory will change when a new plant comes in, changing the potential. A division has different objectives in a period of materials shortages as against a tough competitive period. Different objectives, and therefore different items of information, are important in the two periods.

Reports must also reflect changing conditions. A food plant put in a new unit that was much more sensitive than any they had ever had. New records were required to keep on top of it or it would be shut down 14 hours out of every 24. A petrochemical company needs different records, both for its plants and for its sales departments in periods of rapid industry growth as against a stable period. If the information system does not change at this time, it will be inappropriate.

There is a strong tendency for all information systems to pressure for standardization. Standardization in records appeals to an executive because it seems cheaper. It takes less programming for the computers if you can use the same routines for all similar jobs and if you do not have to change them over a period of time. An executive must resist this tendency, however, and keep in mind that the prime purpose of the information is to stimulate corrective action currently.

In order to develop a vital information system, systems people must know the needs of the line people. A good way to assure this is to train line people to do the programming and systems work. They already have an understanding of the line problems. It has usually been a mistake to have no one in the computer department who knows the actual line problems. The assumption that all that is needed is a specialist in the system misses the purpose of the system—to help the line. To get the most value from an information system an executive should establish as a standard rule that the control of records be in the line to be served, even with a central computer. The computer is merely serving the same function as a local information system would have. The field should decide when and what they want, and the computer should give it. You should be managing an information system to help you manage rather than managing to help you run an information system.

The basic purpose of a cost and allocation system is to present financial data, not to stimulate action. Therefore, the executive must insist on the action emphasis in addition to the financial data if he wants the information system to stimulate corrective action.

In a lawn equipment company, the cost data showed that purchased parts were less expensive than those made in the plant. The cost of extra inspection and handling of these purchased parts was not included in figuring the cost of purchased pieces, however. As a consequence, a plant manager could not make sound "make or buy" decisions. Meanwhile, purchasing was claiming savings on purchased parts.

In a supermarket chain, merchandisers did not bear any cost of handling the merchandise when it got to the store. In fact, they did not even know what the cost was. As a result, a produce merchandiser would often buy produce that was cheaper but took a great deal of the time of store personnel to make it presentable. The cost of this time was not charged back against him, so he was constantly in conflict with the stores who were on a profit basis.

For ease in keeping books, allocations are often made instead of direct charges, but allocations can push in the wrong direction. Allocations of sales cost and order handling in a company making air-conditioning systems were made simply by the sales dollar. The accounting department was constantly suggesting that the sales department emphasize small orders (in this case, about $500) as against large orders ($50,000 to $500,000), because the former provided a 40 percent margin and the latter only 20 percent. Small orders took extra sales calls, however. Small-order customers were less sophisticated, so more servicing was required afterward. Although the sales department knew that these orders were not as profitable, they had difficulty resisting the weight of the cost system as it reported up the line.

A small company almost went bankrupt because engineering and administrative expenses were allocated by the sales dollar to its three lines. One line took a great deal of engineering, and the orders were quite small. Another line took practically no engineering, and the orders were all large. The first line was underpriced; the latter was overpriced. The firm found that it was substantially increasing its business in the underpriced line and decreasing it in the overpriced line, with the consequence that they had a 20 percent increase in overall business and a 30 percent drop in profit. The allocation system drove sales in the wrong direction.

One warehouse of a firm was about equally divided between heavy raw materials and lightweight finished stock. Warehouse costs were allocated by weight. Although an industrial engineer knew from his time studies that he could save $20,000 on a new method of handling finished stock, he could not prove it because he had to use the standard costs as a starting point. The cost system was militating against sound management decision. An executive must resist the normal accounting inclination to emphasize the cost of sound allocation as against the benefits of allocation to get the correct decisions. Allocation is not necessarily management reporting.

An example of management difficulties with a financial approach occurs in multiplant operations where accountants want to simplify the intracompany charge system. A plant of a container company was only given credit on a cost basis for everything it made for another plant. However, each plant was evaluated by the profit on its product. Of course, no plant was anxious to produce for another plant even though it was to the best interest of the company. The accountants argued that "it was all in the company, anyway, so why worry?" Besides, it might take an extra clerk to do the work.

When a company enters the international market, the domestic divisions are usually asked to do work for the international division, but they get inadequate credit for the time they spend for international and very often do not even charge the international division for this time. The argument here, too, is "It is all in the company," but the reasoning is false. The accounting system must reflect adequate credit to the domestic division for helping the international if it is to stimulate cooperation between them. Charges have a tactical effect, and can help get best concentration on management problems.

CHARGE THE SAME DOLLAR TWICE

To be effective, items may have to be charged to two people who must cooperate. In other words, the records should make cooperation rewarding to both. There is nothing wrong with charging both the training costs and the achievement of trainees to the training department as well as to the line. A maintenance department in a plant can bear an expense for maintenance cost as well as shutdown cost along with the supervision and the plant engineer. Many sales departments get a much better operation when promotion costs are charged against both the product managers and the district managers. Accountants resist charging in two places. It can easily be done with washout accounts, while still keeping the financial records pure. The decision, though, must be made by management. It is tactical; it is not an accounting decision. Its purpose is to encourage cooperation.

One of the invidious effects of accounting is the way current charges are made for long-range action, usually for tax purposes. A major overhaul is usually charged off currently; with a tight budget there is a strong inclination to postpone it. An overall management study aimed at long-range improvement is also charged off currently. As a result, the manager is disinclined to engage in it. Executives might make such charges current for financial purposes but spread them out when charging them to an individual manager's account. Managers should be encouraged to take action that will make the long-run improvement of the business possible.

Information people often feel that all that is necessary is to inform. Many computer and controller groups, therefore, feel that it is their job only to provide the information, nothing more. After all, they cannot make line decisions. If an executive accepts this reasoning, his information system will be both costly and inadequate. He should insist that they be accountable for the fact that some worthwhile action is taken because of the reports. If an information manager prepares a set of reports, ask him how much they cost to prepare. If he says $100,000, ask him where the firm gets $600,000 from them.

MAKE INFORMATION MANAGERS PART OF THE TEAM

How do you get information people in tune with the managers? The best way we know is the action principle which says that any person responsible for information should be accountable for the value of that information, not simply for presenting it. He should interpret the data but not decide the action. To show how this works, consider the case of a plant controller who developed a great deal of data for the plant manager and his key subordinates. He was, of course, the finger-pointer against everyone else and a pariah in the plant. He felt very uncomfortable under these circumstances and also felt that the data he developed could be used much better.

This controller was made accountable so that 50 percent

of his measurement was the percent achievement by the first-line foremen of their objectives. That seems like a poor measurement of a controller, doesn't it? After all, he did not supervise the foremen. His first comment was, "Well, now I'll have to talk to every one of those foremen." When he did, he found out that half of his data was not useful and could be eliminated. He then found that different methods of sub-totaling could be helpful. I talked with him six months later. He told me he was in trouble, but he was smiling when he said it. He had had so many requests for help from foremen and superintendents that he could not keep up with them. This is the same man who was avoided before. He was help-ing them now. Information people have been short-changed because they have not been put in a position where they must tie in to the general management stream. They, there-fore, do not develop management know-how and do not broaden the uses of the very information systems that they develop.

In fairness to information managers, the people on whom reports are kept must first be made accountable for action so that they take reports seriously. Managers often do little with reports they receive unless they are accountable to take action. They must first be accountable for objectives so that the information that is reported on deviations is utilized. Many executives make the mistake of assuming that if good people are informed about a problem, they will take action.

There has been a great deal of misinformation regarding the computer. It has two major benefits. First, it is a very fast calculator, and, second, it has a marvelous memory.

Ordinarily, two requirements must be satisfied, however, to capitalize on the computer. First, the data that is put into it must be timely, accurate, and complete. You cannot get out what you do not put in. The system must, therefore, allow for changing data with changing conditions. Studies such as many sale studies do not lend themselves to computer analysis because you cannot satisfy the data requirement. The changing competitive data are not available.

The second requirement is that the problems to which you direct the computer must lend themselves to programming to fit all possible solutions. A computer cannot pick from alternatives that are not programmed into it. This requirement is difficult to meet if the problems change often and fast, as they do, for example, in a job shop business. You must change programming very quickly; otherwise the computer will be a detriment rather than a help. This requirement has special relevancy to sales departments when you have changed objectives for different territories. The computer must lend itself to reporting data in light of those changing objectives. The same, however, could be true of any department. It is this requirement that suggests that programmers or systems people be in the line, or right from the line, so that they are aware of the line problems. It is hard for a programmer or systems man who has not had line experience to fully understand the need for changes.

The final problem with computers is that action records require fast data. In many cases computers are fast in computation but slow in giving action information to fit variable line needs. The delay must be overcome if the information is to be useful.

chapter thirteen

Capitalize on Each Individual

The basic job of any manager should be to make all his people successful. Without this attitude, a management system tends toward tighter and tighter control. People do not develop as well and they accomplish less. Good management must be based on a belief that all can achieve more. We have never been disappointed in this belief.

DEFINE RESULTS EXPECTED

The first step in making people successful is to define the results expected of them. If you want someone to accomplish something, tell him what it is that you want accomplished. The chief executive of a medium-sized company was sold on group dynamics. All problems were thoroughly discussed by his executive committee, and action was taken only after unanimous agreement. The company faltered. It took a real surge forward, however, when the chief executive more clearly defined the results expected from each member of that committee in his function, and problems came to the committee only when they had a broad interfunctional effect. Each executive was now firmly accountable for specific results that were necessary for the company profit. Executive bonus plans that are based entirely on profit fail to point up clearly to each executive what part of his results he is supposed to focus on. It is too easy to be covered by the overall blanket of corporate profit.

Results should be clarified for staff jobs, too. In a food company where there were constant competitive changes, the results of the product managers were not carefully defined in terms of actual results in the field. They felt that it was their job to provide promotion programs rather than to increase sales by meeting the timing, competition, and peculiar problems of every territory and district. Their programs were only partially successful.

TRAIN PEOPLE TO DO THEIR JOBS

The second step in making your people successful is to make sure that they are well trained. This emphasis is such an old refrain that it hardly seems worth mentioning. However, training is neglected in most companies. Why? First of all, because it is not emphasized in the place where it is primary, the first supervisory level. Lack of achievement and poor costs in most companies can usually be traced to this mistake. An executive can take a big step toward efficient operation if he insists that the major job of first-level supervision in all functions is training.

Most of us act through habit. If you teach a new employee the right habits, you gain from it for a long time afterward. Check in your operation. Has every first-level supervisor been thoroughly trained in how to train? It is a must.

Most people learn best by practice on the job and by being accountable for results. Many firms have done a poor job training in young college graduates by having them spend a week to two months in each of several departments watching a manager do a job. They do not learn the problems of the jobs, because they do not have to cope with them. It is a disservice to these young people and a waste of time and money so far as the company is concerned. Companies should put them on accountable work with coaching as soon as possible.

If training is so important on the first supervisory job, it is especially important that the second management level train the new first-level supervisors on the differences between their old jobs and their new supervisory positions. The primary training is in how to train. Secondarily, they should learn to inspire and direct people. Supervisory training is almost always done poorly in companies, especially in engineering departments. It is rare that a section head will take a young engineer who has just been made a supervising engineer and train him how to direct projects and supervise, inspire, and train engineers under him. Time spent on this training is always worthwhile.

In sales departments it is common for a new district manager to start his new job with only general instructions from the regional manager regarding payroll and the reports that he has to fill in. Since he has not been taught how to supervise or how to train, he tends to do the thing he can do best, sell, so he becomes a senior sales representative handling hot problems for his men. As a result, his salesmen do not grow and develop, and the total sales results are disappointing. It should be the job of that regional sales manager to spend a considerable amount of time with that new district manager training him on the differences between his old job and his new one.

Why are so many people poorly trained if everyone seems to agree that training is important? The main reason is the lack of follow-up. It is absolutely critical that whoever trains follows up with the employee afterward to help him over the tough spots in application, to correct any misinterpretations or misunderstandings that he may have had. And they almost always occur. The best general training program I know of is Job Instructor Training (training someone how to train someone else to do a job) fostered by the government in World War II, and yet this program has failed in 95 percent of the cases where it was used. Because of the lack of follow-up, people became discouraged in trying to apply the principles in their actual work. However, in one company a test was run by installing Job Instructor Training in an old department of about 100 employees where methods were fairly standard and understood. All supervisors were trained in Job Instructor Training, and a staff trainer worked with them for two months afterward coaching them in applying the principles in their work. By the end of two months productivity went up 10 percent. I do not know of any other training program that produces this kind of result, but it is successful only if there is a follow-up.

It is far better to have mediocre training and good follow-up than superb training with poor follow-up. The latter, unfortunately, is typical. The follow-up is done best on the job; it should, therefore, be done by the man's immediate supervisor. One reason many sales training courses are disappointing is that sales representatives are put through a three- to five-week course and then turned over to the district manager. He assumes they are trained and does not follow up on every angle of their training.

An executive should insist that all training programs be

devised, if at all possible, so that managers learn the programs and train their own people. First of all, it is the best way you can assure yourself of a follow-up. Second, there is hardly a manager who will want to put on a program for his people without boning up ahead of time. He does not want to look stupid, so he learns in the process. Third, if he puts on a program, it is for real. It is not a program put on by a staff trainer which can later be ignored. Fourth, he can immediately get to a practical discussion of the trainees' problems, and all training is much more effective if it can be discussed in terms of the problems of the people who are being trained.

Ordinarily, training departments should not conduct the training programs for the people down the line. They should devise programs that the managers can use to train their people. Managers can run even management training sessions for their own people with the aid of films and discussion guides. These programs are much more effective than those that are run by a skilled seminar leader trained in management philosophy. Programs conducted by managers start to develop a skill and are not just giving information. The essence of all training programs is to give people a skill that they can and will apply to their work. Every training program must have the requirement that something positive should happen in the work as a result of it.

People need encouragement if they are to be successful. Current follow-up on accomplishment of results is the third step in managing for success. The purpose of this follow-up is to make sure that sound progress is being made toward the accomplishment that the manager wants. He must provide for sound feedback to his people and to himself. His people must know when a deviation should be corrected. He, in turn, must know when an exception occurs that requires action on his part. He must, therefore, set up an effective information system that does this, as discussed in Chapter 12.

WE NEED LEADERS

The fourth step in managing for success is providing leadership and motivation for a group. People lag and need encouragement. I recall one plant manager who was reluctant to effect a major change in organization even though it appeared sound to him. He was not sure what the vice president of manufacturing really thought about it. At a cocktail party the vice president of manufacturing got him aside, put his arm over his shoulder, and said, "Jim, I'm depending on you to make this work." The man went ahead like a house afire. There is a place for charisma in every operation.

I know of a small company that was getting 90 to 100 percent efficiency without any time study incentive rate, a pace almost unheard of. This was due in a large part to the kind of man the president was. For example, he had bought a new car and asked one of the men to go over and get it for him. The man had an accident and reluctantly called the president to tell him about it. The first question the president asked was "Were you hurt?" When the man said, "No," the president replied, "That's all right. We can always get another car." Everyone in that plant would do or die for the "old man." When we are dealing with people, we are dealing with emotional beings.

IMPROVEMENT—A WAY OF LIFE

As a fifth step in making people more successful you need a constant influx of new and better methods. It is important to encourage men to apply new ideas and, therefore, to have a constant philosophy of improvement.

Improvement should be made easy. With people down the line who are somewhat unsophisticated with financial concepts, return-on-investment forms often seem to be too much work and trouble to complete. A foreman rose from the ranks and had a flair for methods improvement. He had great difficulty preanalyzing anything he was going to do, however, and putting it on a projected cost savings report. He was constantly working out improvements in methods, however. He was then made an industrial engineer and subsequently a chief industrial engineer and was one of the best I have seen in medium-sized plants. A requirement for projected cost savings reports would have stymied him.

Large corporations constantly miss improvement by taking a financial approach to budgets. Their executives feel that any new methods work should be charged like any other cost to the departments concerned. These firms should be constantly experimenting with new ideas in operation, management, marketing, merchandising, etc., in order to capitalize on their size. In a firm known for improvement, if a manager tried any idea new to the company, it was included in the corporate budget, not in his own budget. In other words, he had a free ride. It is a mistake to expect every manager to assume all improvement costs as part of his budget, especially when they are for a completely new idea in the firm. It discourages new methods.

A common executive mistake is to assume that the credit should go to the manager who originates an idea. This is wrong. The same credit should go to a manager who has an idea as to the manager who steals it. That is what responsibility for a result means. Is there any more value from the idea if the person thought of it himself versus getting it from someone else? In addition, the manager may not be inclined to give his people credit for results if recognition only goes to the idea man. Improvements from application of ideas will then dry up in the future.

As a sixth step, if a manager wants to make his men successful, he must plan ahead for the best accomplishment, provided he does not overdo the planning. To make planning practical, let each manager plan for his own results and certainly be in on the master plans affecting his work. Ask each foreman or superintendent whether he could not plan his own schedules. If he can, let him do it. Let sales managers plan their own approach to their problems. They will be better sold on them and apply more insight to their jobs.

The seventh step in developing successful people for future promotions is critical if the firm is to maintain virility. An executive should make sure that every manager gets recognition for the development of his people, since most of the development comes from the experiences and challenges that a man has on the job. Special courses in management may be helpful, but they are secondary to the development of a person on the job. Every manager, at every level, must be trained on delegation, and there must be rewards for developing people. Do you keep a record of the people who are promoted from a manager's group? Does he get credit for this? There should be recognition for the development of people for higher jobs as well as credit for accomplishment of results on the job. By contrast, if you require the same objectives of a manager after two or three of his key men are promoted, you are telling him that it is not to his advantage to develop people.

GIVE RECOGNITION

The last step to encourage men to be successful is a final recognition of their accomplishments. Such a recognition is necessary to make sure the direction is sound and to discourage misdirection. The man's superior should make the review, not the personnel department and not people two or three steps above.

A plant engineer actually followed through with the production people to make sure that his machines worked when the recognition system weighed in the downtime of new installations that he had designed. In a sales department, service had been the key item. They were so busy servicing existing accounts they did not seem to have time to contact new prospects. When the sales representatives were rated down because of a lack of new accounts, they changed their whole approach, spent a portion of their time on new accounts, and got some. They were then much more valuable to the company, because service to existing accounts did not suffer.

TIME—THE ESSENCE OF SPAN OF CONTROL

In order to carry through on these steps necessary to make men successful, a manager must have time to manage. Span of control is essentially a problem of time. It is a problem that grows insidiously with the growth of a company and is frequently unrecognized. A typical example occurred with district managers in an electrical products company. Initially, a district manager managed six sales representatives selling a simple line of shelf items. Gradually, new products and product lines were added, many of which were quite complex. Many required contacts with entirely different kinds of customers. In addition, the crew of each district manager increased until many of them had nine to twelve men. New products lagged; customer contacts were not quite what they should have been. The district managers simply did not have time to supervise.

How should you analyze span of control? If the work is simple, routine, and repetitive—and I mean very simple, like the basic kind of assembly work—a supervisor might handle twenty-five to thirty people and do all the necessary supervisory work. And it pays to insist that he do all the necessary supervisory work.

If, however, the work managed is variable, the supervisor cannot handle as many people. It takes more time to set objectives, to train, and to put in new methods. The management of conglomerates is especially difficult because the individual divisions have entirely different kinds of problems. The effect of variability on managing is the reason it is sound to organize by similarity of work, wherever possible. If a company grows with two different kinds of product lines requiring different kinds of contacts and products, it is usually better to have two separate sales forces. In a plant, the foremen can generally supervise men more easily if they are all on the same kinds of machines versus handling a variety of machines. The limit of this principle is the extent to which a result is fragmented. If a particular piece has to go through five different departments, there may be more loss than gain by combining similar work.

It is easy to be beyond your span of control if the work you are supervising is very complex. In product development and research departments, the work of the research men is quite complex; therefore an individual supervisor can supervise only a limited number of people. Supervisors are frequently beyond their span of control.

Much of the literature on span of control revolves around the interrelationships between subordinates. Relationships are a factor, and it is the job of any manager or executive to smooth them over. An executive has to be very careful about adding staff people reporting directly to him because of the added relationships. He often assumes that because these staff people are working with the same line functions that report to him, he can, therefore, easily handle the staff. This reasoning does not hold. By the very nature of the work, a staff man has to work through various line people, a ticklish proposition, particularly if it is a manipulative type of staff that digs into the everyday work of the line. A chief executive, a vice president, a branch manager, or a regional manager should directly supervise only a small number of staff people.

Outside relationships affect span of control. Sales departments, especially, are affected by outside relationships. The essence of the sales job is the customer contact. A district manger has to be sure that each is handled well, and it takes time to keep on top of the various customer contacts of his men.

Geography is often a related factor. Managing is about as effective as the face-to-face contact. Again, sales departments are strongly affected. A general sales manager, a regional sales manager, and a district manager are severely limited in the number of people each can supervise when his people are at different locations. The problem also occurs in any multilocation operation. A manager of location managers finds it hard to manage more than five or six if he is to do a good job of upgrading and developing these men to maximum performance.

Geography can be a problem even at one location. Most hospitals suffer from it in their maintenance. The housekeeping crews work on several floors of the building. It is difficult for a supervisor to control what they are doing.

NEW FUNCTIONS TAKE MORE TIME TO MANAGE

New functions usually take more time to manage than old functions. Many of the procedures and operations are unknown and people are untrained. The manager himself may be somewhat unfamiliar with the new function. He and his people, therefore, need more time to get acquainted with the function. The installation of almost any function requires more supervision than the maintenance of the function. If you are installing a job evaluation plan, a supervisor may be able to handle three or four analysts. After the plan is installed, however, it is questionable whether this supervisor does not now have a part-time job. If it is not recognized, the supervisor begins to make work by digging into the work of his analysts.

Even if the function is well established, it requires much more supervision if the people are new. As a rule of thumb, it takes at least double the supervisory talent when the people are new than it takes when they are well trained. People do not know policies, procedures, or methods. A startling example of this rule occurred in a supermarket chain. It usually took about six weeks to get a new store operating smoothly. The typical approach was to put in seven home-office staff men along with seven line supervisors—for example, a home-office staff meat man came in to help in the meat department. The staff men were generally helping the department manager, so there was a great deal of duplication. The setup was changed so that each department was divided and a staff man was given half the people to train and supervise in the break-in period. The department manager worked with the other half. The break-in time dropped to two weeks. What was needed was not more general staff help but simply personal training.

It is harder to supervise and therefore takes more time when people are in doubt about policy. They do not want to be criticized for incorrect action, so they tend to wait and see. It is important, first of all, that an executive establish sound policy and that it is communicated to everyone. Otherwise, his managers may get beyond their span of control. In a plant, for example, well-explained disciplinary policy makes it much easier for each of the foremen and superintendents to operate.

Executives often fail to recognize that detailed procedures cut the span of control of the managers under them. It is harder for a manager to inspire initiative, because everyone is afraid of violating the book. It takes more time to police procedures, resulting in less time available to work on true accomplishment. Whenever an executive shows me a shelf of procedure books, my first question is, "When are you going to start cutting them down?" While some procedures are necessary, detailed procedures are antagonistic to good management.

PAPER WORK REDUCES MANAGERIAL TIME

Administrative detail or paper work is similar to procedure and cuts down the span of control of a manager at any level. The more paper work required of a manager at any level the less time he has to supervise. Even at the first level, a foreman who must spend 50 percent of his time on paper work can only handle half as many people. Loss of management time is one of the great hidden costs of paper work. Sales departments constantly have this problem. District managers cannot get out and work with their men because they are too busy in their offices handling all the paper coming in from the home office. Even though the paper is ostensibly aimed at providing analyses that may later help him, all of this help will do him very little good if he does not have time to spend with his men.

Many executives have felt that they or their subordinates are not supervising too many functions or people. They arrive at this span-of-control conclusion by looking at the organization chart. They forget that people may be in a constant stream of meetings. A chief executive who is in meetings 50 percent of the time cannot supervise as many people. A laboratory head who is spending 60 percent of his time conferring with executives on projects cannot directly supervise as many section managers. Saving management time is a basic reason to cut meetings to a minimum. Executives should review all the meetings they call with their subordinates and ask the question, "Is the meeting time detracting from the effective dispatching of the responsibilities of each of the men under me?"

If an executive has too many outside responsibilities, he cannot handle as many subordinates. A president who has to do quite a bit of outside public relations work is especially hit. He may have to have an executive vice president to handle all inside operations. Perhaps he should consider getting someone else to do the public relations and devote more of his time to the actual operation of the company. Which is the more critical?

On the other side, the better the system of balanced objectives and the better the information system that reports to people, the broader the span that a manager can handle. In one plant the plant manager had to do relatively little day-to-day work with his foremen or superintendents. The group bonus system included the hourly people, the foremen, and the superintendents. Supervision knew exactly what they had to accomplish; they were accountable for it and were paid for it. The information on reports that went to them each day told them where they were off. They were very quick to take the necessary action before the reports went up the line.

SPAN OF CONTROL MOST IMPORTANT AT THE BOTTOM

Discussions on span of control have generally centered on the span of a chief executive, very often focusing on the number of interrelationships between his people. Of course, span of control affects an executive. In our experience, though, the most important area is not at the top but at the bottom of the organization. There is a tendency to feel that you have so many supervisors at this first level that you could easily cut out one or two, have each remaining one handle a little more, and still get by. It is an illusion. One large paper plant did this. Within three years, costs increased 15 percent, but higher cost was not traced to span of control. Since costs were increasing, more industrial engineers were added. Apparently, foremen were not what they used to be. Quality was slipping; therefore, the quality control department was increased. Supervision seemed to be weak, so more intermediate levels of supervision were established. The span of each foreman was then decreased so that he could handle his work. Because more problems were solved by foremen, the firm could cut the intermediate levels of higher supervision and staff by 30 percent. Both cost and quality improved substantially. Previously foremen had had difficulty communicating their problems up the line. There were too many intermediate levels of management and staff to go through.

An impossible situation developed with a district sales manager who had twelve sales representatives reporting to him on relatively complex lines. He just could not manage them. He got nowhere requesting an assistant sales manager from the home office. He then had a bright idea. He made out a complete statement on the need for establishing a senior sales representative classification for those sales representatives who would not be managers but were true professional sales representatives. The classification would give them a higher level of income and a better status. The idea looked good to the home office, and they approved it. The first thing the district manager did after approval was to assign three of his younger sales representatives to the new senior sales representative to keep an eye on them. It was a way around his impossible span of control.

Executives often fail to grasp that much of their communication problem comes from too long a management chain. If the first supervisory level is not beyond its span of control, the second and third levels can handle many more managers. In one plant a superintendent supervised four foremen. When the foremen were set up with more manageable spans and trained to supervise, a superintendent could supervise eight or nine foremen. Communications problems up and down the line were greatly decreased. The need for staff was also reduced because problems were solved in most cases by the foremen.

Executives should study their organization charts. A manager with only two or three subordinates probably has a part-time job. The natural inclination of a live-wire manager under these circumstances is to stick his nose into the work of his people. He tends to debilitate the managers below and leads toward a strongly centralized approach. The broader the span of intermediate managers, the less the tendency toward centralization. It is important for an executive to scrutinize not only the immediate organization under him but also the organizational plans of each of his subordinates. They will affect decentralization, communications, and, finally, the development of management people all the way down the chain.

LEAD MEN ARE TOO EXPENSIVE

It is tempting to some executives to refuse to add salaried personnel because it apparently saves money. The tendency, however, is to be lenient about adding lead men as the need arises throughout the company. (They are not salaried.) Lead-man supervision, however, is second-class supervision. A lead man is rarely solidly accountable for the full achievement of the people he supervises, especially if he is in a union. You ordinarily pay as much for supervision as if you had salaried supervisors, but you get much less for your money. It is an illusion of supervision and an illusion of economy. A senior sales representative, for example, very rarely does a good job training junior sales representatives. He is primarily accountable for his own territory. He may very well give the man a "snow job" and show him all the easy accounts or else show him all the difficult ones to pound home how tough this job is. Neither approach is very good training. He always has his own territory to keep up, so he cannot spend time training the man. He will not do the most important part of any training, the follow-up. Training becomes merely showing, a very inferior form of training.

Should you ever use lead-man supervision? You may, but only when you have no alternative. When four maintenance workers are sent to a job, someone should be in charge, although obviously supervision is not a full-time job. He would have to be a lead man. In the petroleum business, a drilling crew of five men may be out on a job. Although the crew may be small, someone should be in charge. A supervisor may go around to check various locations, but obviously it is not economical to have one man in the crew simply supervise. These are the exceptions rather than the rule. It is still poor supervision, but it is the best you can do under the circumstances.

If creativity is a very great factor in the work, it may suggest having a lead man. A top research man of proven ingenuity may operate this way. The project may move along faster if he has three or four engineers working on part of the project while he himself works on the major parts. But the situation is touchy, and it must be limited or he will do all the work. His engineers may not develop because they become merely leg men. Such a situation is justified only if the research man is very unusual and has that special knack, as they say, to see the obvious.

chapter fourteen

How to Capitalize on Central Staff

One of the great advantages of a larger organization is its ability to afford skilled central staff. Properly used, this is a way to capitalize on the advanced state of the art in almost any discipline. But it must be used sensitively or it detracts from the operation. Positively used, it can raise the level of the entire organization.

Some services, such as computers, are combined into a central service merely for economy. The kinds of staff discussed in this chapter are those that are advisory or control. These offer the greatest return.

CENTRAL STAFF SHOULD EDUCATE

What is the main job of central staff people? It is primarily to pass on their expertise to the rest of the organization, essentially to upgrade. Executives often make the mistake of looking at central staff primarily as experts to solve problems in their field. While the solving of difficult problems is one of their functions, it is a secondary, not a primary one. To be most valuable, central staff should develop advanced practical ideas in their fields and also ways to pass them on. They should keep abreast of the new ideas and experiment with them so that everyone in the firm does not have to "reinvent the wheel." Central functions in personnel, marketing, organization, and control should be given funds to try out new ideas for improvement in their fields. After they have proved a new idea, central staff should develop ways to train local line and staff to be effective in the new methods. In a supermarket chain the meat merchandiser, for example, was far more effective when he developed methods for the meat department and both trained the meat department head in these methods and acquainted the local store managers with them. If the store manager had not been trained, there would be no local supervision to make sure the ideas were utilized.

By all means, central staff should pick up good ideas from various parts of the company and spread them to other parts. In a steel company one plant developed a completely new and integrated materials control program. Central staff studied it and helped all the other plants install it. In an airline one district developed a ticket-office layout that was very appealing to its customers. The central staff picked this up and spread the idea throughout the system. Central staff should not have to be just a developer. It is unfortunate if the NIH factor creeps into central staff.

Central staff should help the rest of the organization install a workable and working function. They should be accountable for the fact that it works and helps the line. Then they should train local line or staff people to carry it out. Even in such a function as job evaluation, local personnel men can usually do all the local salary and job evaluation work once the system has been installed.

Central staff should not administer the plan once it is in. Once they install a plan, they quite naturally do not ever want to give it up. In a crushing plant an industrial engineer developed a fine approach to waste control. He wanted to control the system afterward, and in doing so interfered with supervision. When he was forced to train local supervision in the system, they did quite well on it and integrated it into their general supervisory system.

A central inventory staff developed a central inventory control to affect all plants. It did not fit sales problems as they occurred with the various products produced in the different plants. The plan should have been administered by the various local operations. Even though a central computer was used, it could have been attuned to the needs of the local groups. The system was good but the administration was poor because it was centralized. Central inventory control people were not close enough to the plant problems. If the local people are to administer a plan, there must be considerable leeway so that it can be adjusted to fit the local situation.

Central staff should make long-range studies in their fields for planning and policy purposes. An executive must make each of his central staff people accountable for anticipating and solving problems that occur in their fields. If they do not, they have failed. If personnel problems occur in the plants that the personnel director did not anticipate, he should be accountable. Purchasing should be criticized if material shortages occur that cause severe problems. It is their job as experts to look ahead and to make sure that executives are not caught short. Executives often make the mistake of freeing central staff from accountability for looking ahead. One reason you want experts is to make sure that you can look ahead in their fields.

CENTRAL STAFF SHOULD KEEP POLICY VITAL

Central staff should propose policy so that the executive is not surprised in that function. The financial vice president should propose financial policy. The director of sales and marketing should propose marketing policy that will keep the sales and marketing arm of the company strong under changing conditions. Ordinarily, central staff should not decide the policy but should propose it. Line executives should still determine the policy.

It should also be central staff's job to develop procedures that would help the line effect a policy. But note: the purpose of the procedure is merely to help people effect the policy; it should not be to control them. Central staff should, therefore, be accountable for the negative effect of policy and procedure on the bottom level. Before they propose any procedure, they should check its impact on the various bottom-level positions of the operation. They must be in touch with reality. As one chief executive put it, he must demand a travel schedule from each of his central staff people for the year. Without getting out in the field, they could not possibly be in touch with the problems.

If you are measuring results, long-range plans should be measured in the future. That is where the results should be. Most accountability systems are geared to six months or a year. Central staff often works on plans for results several years away. Whether the executive likes it or not, the measurements must be made at that time. It is the only true measurement of a result. An overall marketing plan, an overall employee relations plan, an overall inventory control plan, or a new computer system probably would not be effective for several years. A measurement system should be devised that will reflect the results later on, or the executive will have no way to evaluate his central staff for future decisions.

It is hard to keep a record on the long-term work of central staff. One of the stumbling blocks is accounting's normal penchant for short-term charges. Accounting will have to change, over the years, so that it keeps track of long-range impacts (longer than a year) wherever they apply. A management study would certainly be expected to affect the operation for several years to come, and the records should show this effect. For example, in a large equipment company, the central economics group studied the potential of entering the African market. The value of this particular study could be measured only five to ten years later.

The cost of installation of a new procedure should ordinarily be part of the cost of the initial study and charged to central staff. If a company is experimenting with a whole new approach to costing in a plant, the expense for it should be central corporate cost, not, as accounting normally dictates, local plant cost. The entire cost of installation should be charged against central staff.

It is usually inappropriate for central staff to engage in short-run studies. That work should be given to local staff or line. Central industrial engineering should probably not work on specific plant methods. This work should be done by industrial engineers in the plant itself. Central industrial relations should normally not handle grievances in particular plants. They should be handled by the local plant people. If there is to be a division cost study, it probably should be carried on by the controller of the division involved.

Central staff should also look at its job as that of helping the first level be more effective. The organization will then capitalize on their high expertise. In a smelting and refining company, machinery often had high maintenance and frequent breakdowns. The central engineers felt their job was done when they had developed designs for machines. Maintenance and breakdown problems improved when the engineers were made accountable for continuous operation without undue maintenance. They checked first-level operating problems more closely and designed to minimize them.

It is sometimes difficult to trace some staff operations down to their impact on the first management level so that an evaluation of the impact can be made. It is another reason why it is better to delegate the function as far down as possible. At least, the line results expected should be specified first before central staff works on a problem. The building department of a department store chain found it was much more effective when the expected merchandising results of a particular installation were defined before any design work was begun.

If the impact of central staff on the first-level line is hard to find, it is a signal for the executive to question the function. One company had a staff of eight procedure writers in the central office. When the critical question was asked as to what the company was getting from them, it was hard to pin it down. The department was eliminated, and those procedures necessary for individual functions were then written by the individual departments. The procedure book was cut to about one-eighth its original size, with no apparent loss in results.

In a technical company, the purchasing department reviewed all requisitions and then passed them through the various experts in the engineering department to check. As a consequence, almost every requisition went through twelve different hands, resulting in over-review. When the requisitions up to a certain level were approved only by local engineering and operating people, there was no observable loss. However, twenty central engineers could be eliminated.

WHEN CENTRAL STAFF PAYS OFF

The more a staff is removed from its impact the more difficult it is for it to contribute to results. Central staff has to go through more people than local staff does to have its final impact on the first level. If central staff is to work on a project, there must, therefore, be much more at stake. If a local staff could justify its cost working on a project with a $60,000 potential, for central staff to work on that same project there probably should be double that, or $120,000, at stake. It has to go through at least one more level. Should the central staff be corporate and go through both the division staff and the local staff, there should probably be $240,000 at stake. It is another level removed. While this is only a rule-of-thumb approach, it is helpful for a chief executive in evaluating where to use skilled central staff efficiently.

The major weakness of central staff is that it is not accountable for line contribution. Usually, authority is not a problem when central staff is accountable for the same results as line. For example, a controller who is measured by whether or not some action was taken in the line is not inclined to over-control the line.

One way to gear central staff to the solving of line problems is to try to hold each one accountable each year for solving a specific problem in a particular area in his field. One company with a major safety problem had assigned that responsibility to the vice president of personnel. One year the chief executive set a specific objective for him to improve the safety record in one plant where it was especially bad. This objective forced him to get down to the practicalities of operation in that plant. A market research function was made accountable for improving the sales record in New England when a particular plan was applied in New England as a test. A corporate controller was made accountable for the percent improvement in cost in a particular plant where he was to install a record and control system. He was encouraged to find out what was actually needed to best meet problems on the firing line.

A major cost of central staff is not the direct cost but the added cost resulting from its negative impact. As far as possible, record systems should be developed to charge in as much of the cost of the negative impact of central staff as possible. If a credit man develops a tight system on accounts receivable, some way should be developed to charge in the loss of business that results from being this tight. Many central staffs require the time of the line people in meetings. No record is ever kept of the losses involved. One way to approach this expense is to charge central staff with all the time people spend with them at a certain charge per hour. They soon find ways to get information and discuss problems without unduly wasting the time of the line. As a consequence, less time is spent on meetings.

Because the available figures are difficult to interpret, chief executives sometimes misuse their central staffs by having them investigate and explain variances. The local line then spends more time telling central staff the reasons things happen than they do correcting the problems. Central staff should be there primarily to help the line, not to keep tabs on them and explain variances.

A chief executive should not demand explanations from his central staff why something went wrong: the prime purpose of central staff is not control. He should demand that the staff help correct the problems. Financial people often spend their time pointing up deficiencies to executives, but it is a grave misuse of financial talent. It should be their job, too, to help point up problems to the people involved, if possible, not to the executive. A financial man who points up all the problems to the chief executive should be criticized rather than complimented. He should be encouraged to get down and help the line and staff at different levels solve their financial problems.

Most central staff work should be voluntary rather than compulsory. Occasionally, there are procedures that require compulsory adherence, but these should be only on items where uniformity is absolutely necessary on an overall corporate or division basis. Compliance or control should not be a major function of central staff. If it is, the function should be questioned. In salary administration you do need to have an overall salary approach that is equally fair throughout the organization. Specific increases and methods of handling people, however, could be entirely different in different divisions. The salary system should be a motivating tool to be used by each manager to encourage work toward the required results. With the advent of the computer, there is a strong tendency, however, for central salary staff to go much farther on compliance activities. They get computer runoffs and are inclined to question any deviations from "normal" distributions, particularly if chief executives ask them to explain the reasons for them. The procedure detracts from a sound concept of authority for the line.

In fairness to central staff people, presidents often err by asking them detailed questions about what is going on.

Obviously, then, they have to check up. They are being used as an extension of the chief executive to keep him informed. If he asks staff a question on a cost deviation, he is likely to get an explanation but not the correction. He may even get action that does not work or adversely affects someone else. If the explanation sounds good, it is likely to get by. Down the line, however, people drop everything to work on the items questioned by the chief executive. This reaction is natural but usually leads to poorer results because it tends toward imbalance.

MAKE CENTRAL STAFF HELP VOLUNTARY

A good way to keep central staff in perspective is to list all of its functions, even down to minor ones, and classify them as compulsory or voluntary. The classification of the functions should then be publicized throughout the organization so that everyone knows which items he can ignore and those on which central staff has a control responsibility.

When the central staff is made voluntary, it is forced to apply its high expertise to help the line, or it has apparently not accomplished anything. Paradoxically, local staff then has the authority to turn down or change a suggestion by central staff. In a chain store operation the home-office buyers made some excellent buys of certain merchandise. It did not sell very well in some localities, however. The buyers still felt that they had done a good buying job. When the local people had the right to pick the inventory that applied to their particular merchandising area, the buyers had to fit the variations in customer needs.

In a company with many plants, a home-office analyst developed a fine production control system. When local plant inventory people were allowed to use the information but change it to fit their needs, almost every plant changed it to some extent. Each plant's problems were different from the theoretical perfect envisaged by the central production control analyst, even though his broad ideas were very good.

Should the chief executive, then, let a local, less expert man second-guess the central staff expert? It is actually a better way to capitalize on the expertise of central staff, because the local man is closer to the problems as they occur in real life. Central staff skill is then better applied to the existing problems.

Chief executives must fight the tendency to be unduly influenced by their central staff people. Organizationally, there is a tendency for a chief executive to assign all line functions to an executive vice president who reports to him along with the various central staff heads. He feels the setup keeps him closer to the experts and, therefore, better informed. It is far better organization to have a vice president of administration supervise all or most of the staff functions and have as many of the line operating units as possible report right to the chief executive. The line functions, where the action is, are then close to the chief. Strangely enough, he can utilize his central staff better by keeping in touch with line problems in this way. Otherwise, he will overweigh staff activities too much and not direct them as well to the line problems they are supposed to solve. Their skills will actually be underutilized.

CENTRAL STAFF SHOULD BE EXPERTS

Since the key value of central staff comes in using their high expertise to help the line, above all things, they should be experts, not, as so often occurs, castoffs. It is inappropriate, too, to place inexperienced, though bright, young men in these functions. Central staff should be the best men available in their fields.

Central staff should be used only in the part of the function where an expert is required. Central staff is at a great disadvantage because they do not know local problems and become somewhat inflexible. In an industrial engineering function, a high-grade expert may work out a complete system for approaching industrial engineering problems that could be helpful to all operations. Local industrial engineers are better at applying the specific methods to a particular department, however. Central personnel functions can work out overall plans that may be effective in all areas. Local personnel people can solve local personnel problems far better, however. They are closer to the variability of personnel problems as they occur in real life as against someone sitting 1,000 miles away.

There is a popular misconception, too, that if you have a central staff in a function, you need a counterpart at every level below. You may not. You may need a corporate public relations man but no division public relations man, even though you may have regional public relations people. Staff should be set up only when needed, not just to have uniformity of organization. Any extra levels simply add extra problems in administering the function. One company found that they needed a central labor relations negotiator but did not need other experts in any of the divisions except for the personnel people in the individual plants.

chapter fifteen

Faith in People—
The Key to Optimum Results

Many management plans fail because their prime purpose is to put a hedge around possible deficiencies of people down the line or to try to control any deviation. To the contrary, the purpose of the art of management is to get the most effectiveness from all subordinates. Great managers create a climate that taps the unused 50 percent of the abilities of all their people.

Management plans can accomplish more through faith in the individual. The management climate should be based on accountability for results to permit this faith, rather than on a detailed system of checks and balances.

PEOPLE CAN THINK

Executives must believe that people can do more than carry out specific orders and, right down to the first level, can solve many of their own problems. In a typical plant, inspection departments are set up to check on the foremen. With sound commitment, many foremen can be trusted to do their own inspection and do it well. With a commitment to profit from the district and careful training, district managers in a petroleum company took on the responsibility for station maintenance and credit.

In most firms first-level supervisors are beyond their span of control. They do not have time to handle all their problems, so costs, methods, waste, quality, etc., are not attacked well. The situation seems to prove to executives up the line that they cannot depend on these supervisors, and seems to justify a lack of faith in them. If problems are occurring at the first level, it is more likely that the supervisor does not have the time or the authority to handle them. The top executive should approve budgets for smaller crews for the first-level supervisors and an authority setup that permits more leeway at the first level. The supervisors can then be relied on to solve many of their own problems.

If the first level is set up properly, an executive can trust middle management to assume more responsibility. Regional managers who formerly supervised three district managers could direct seven when these district managers were within their span, trained to supervise, and given authority; in other

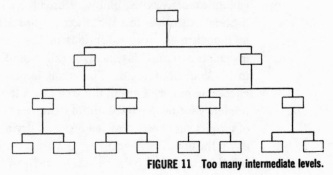

FIGURE 11 Too many intermediate levels.

words, when they trusted the first-level district managers.

In one large plant where the foremen were beyond their span of control, it appeared as though they could not be trusted to manage. Managers were, therefore, added at intermediate levels to compensate for this, resulting in an organizational setup of one over two, one over two (see Figure 11). The managers at each higher level did not have enough to do, so they would go below to dig into problems that were occurring because the foreman was not taking care of them. When the first level was set up properly, two intermediate levels were eliminated. Problems were handled by the foremen at their source. Pay problems were also reduced. Usually you need differentials at every management level. With extra levels, the pay of individual managers gets too close to that of the plant manager because there is a limit to what you would pay a plant manager.

Decentralization is based on faith. To make it effective, an executive needs a management mode of operation that he can set up through all the intermediate levels. Many managers have failed in decentralization because they have not guided such a management mode down through the operation. They feel that each manager should develop his own. On the contrary, he should make his own decisions but within an overall corporate management system. Only then can an executive trust him with broad delegation.

Some executives feel that their major staff should operate as though they were extensions of the executive—general assistants to him. This type of operation implies a lack of trust in his line subordinates. The result is that each staff man checks on minor items all the way down the line. There is a tendency for people to be afraid to move and for a great deal of nit-picking to occur, all leading to a drying up of initiative down the line. The executive gets a great deal of information, but this check and balance system reduces initiative.

A similar problem occurs in many audit groups. Executives rely on these groups to get all kinds of information. They become a sort of control group to check up on the line because the line is not trusted. Instead, these audit groups should be trying to help the line correct its problems. Personnel departments put all appraisals into a forced distribution because they do not trust the line evaluation. They should have confidence in the line and help them use the appraisal system to better motivate people.

Specialization is a sound organization principle, but it is often overdone because of a lack of faith in people to carry through on a total result. Specialization is especially evident in technical groups where many separate disciplines are required. Ostensibly, you cannot trust any of the specialists to get enough knowledge of other specialties to carry through on projects. At times, of course, certain of these highly specialized groups are justified, but in many cases the work does not require the high level of specialization that is implied by the groups. An experienced engineer could be relied on to do much of the work.

If nonspecialized but trained and experienced technical people could do an average job on the work at hand as against a specialist who could do a top job on only one phase, your gamble is usually with the nonspecialist. You cut out all of the wasted time in cross-discussions and sometimes poor technical work because the specialist does not want to compromise his specialty for the total.

Even at the work level, good management suggests combining rather than breaking down into specialties. In an insurance company the paper work was combined so that instead of fifteen people handling a particular piece of paper, only three did; each one was relied on to do five parts of the work. A 35 percent decrease in personnel resulted. The arrangement cut down a great deal of extra handling.

There is a tendency for a manager to give all the difficult assignments to the unusually good person in his department. In other words, the manager does not trust the other people to handle them. This approach tends to further reduce the development of those who are not quite as good, thereby justifying the manager's lack of faith. Instead, he should train and upgrade these people and still delegate a total responsibility to each. Much greater accomplishment results, plus the increasing development of each of these people.

One management error is to assume that delegations below are different from those above. In one large company, for example, an executive made the comment that only as a division manager did one learn to take into account the whole business. There was a fault in this management setup. People below division managers were not trusted to make sound business decisions. Every level in the organization should be developed so that it is a small replica of the jobs above. People should be encouraged to make decisions at their level like those occurring in higher jobs but of smaller scope. The delegation and accountability of an area sales manager should be, in a smaller way, the kind he would have to handle as a district manager; and those, in turn, should be similar to those of a regional manager, and so on up the line. This approach is the best way to get maximum development and accomplishment into the job. Most people come through.

An executive often fails to build lower jobs because he does not trust the people down below to operate as he would. He forgets that he was at that level at one time, too, and could make reasonable decisions. Unfortunately, many pay plans encourage this elitist thinking. A manager is paid more if he reports to a higher level in the organization. The pay plans, therefore, encourage poor organization. Every decision should be made at as low a level in the organization as possible.

A purchasing department of fifteen people was reluctant

to permit purchasing to be done by people in the various divisions. They said that purchasing was too complex for division people to do. In spite of this feeling of the purchasing department, the executive cut their staff to five and pushed the buying down into the divisions. The local people not only handled it well, but the divisions got much faster service because local purchasing was attuned to the current needs of the divisions.

In an airline, the central advertising department contracted for all advertising. They felt that advertising was a specialized art. It was found, however, that some of the local advertising was more effective when the district manager placed it, so it was given to him. There is nothing wrong with breaking up a function in this way and relying on the nonspecialist.

Many long-range plans have gone by the board. Usually it is because the line people who are to carry out the plans do not have the basic responsibility for the planning; executives do not have confidence in their ability to do it. Long-range plans of staff people are usually very detailed. (If the detail is great, you can be sure that the plans were not prepared by the line.) The line, however, knows very well that the future cannot be planned in detail. Since the executive still would like to have everything all laid out in detail, he relies on staff instead of line. The line is then expected to operate in a preplanned, impractical straitjacket.

When an executive tends toward a high degree of centralization, he usually does not trust people down below. He feels that he must have better control over them. In a department store, buyers and merchandisers control the materials and inventory for the various branches because the branches are not trusted to do it themselves. In government and in many large companies, centralization is carried to an extreme in that everything must go by the book. A central office determines every procedure and the way to handle every kind of work. This approach is antagonistic to creative stimulation. The first step should always be to decentralize as much as you can and put faith in people.

There is a powerful reservoir of untapped ability in the management team of every organization. Through sound management tactics this ability can be tapped and intelligently directed toward the organization's overall strategic plan. While the management sciences and modern computer techniques can help to improve the performance of management people, these techniques can never eliminate the need for good executive tactics—instead, they demand a more sophisticated application of them. Results must still be achieved by people, but they can be achieved to the optimum degree only if people are provided with an organizational climate that demonstrates management's faith in them.

Index

Rule of influence, 61-63

Cuttin'
Up

Craig Marberry

Doubleday

New York   Toronto
London   Sydney   Auckland

Cuttin' Up

Wit and Wisdom from Black Barber Shops

PUBLISHED BY DOUBLEDAY
a division of Random House, Inc.

DOUBLEDAY and the portrayal of an anchor with a dolphin are registered trademarks of Random House, Inc.

Book design by Terry Karydes

Library of Congress Cataloging-in-Publication Data

Marberry, Craig.
Cuttin' up : wit and wisdom from Black barber shops / Craig Marberry.—1st ed.
p.   cm.
ISBN 0-385-51164-7
1. African American wit and humor.   2. African American barbers—Interviews.
3. African Americans—Social life and customs.
I. Title: Cuttin' up. II. Title.

PN6231.N5M37 2005
818'.6020803553—dc22
2004058213

PRINTED IN THE UNITED STATES OF AMERICA

June 2005

First Edition

10   9   8   7   6   5   4   3   2   1

To my father,

Fred Nolan Marberry,

who took me to get my first haircut

And in memory of my grandfather,

Louis Henry Ford,

who never thought my hair was short enough

Contents

We wear the mask that grins and lies,

It hides our cheeks and shades our eyes,

This debt we pay to human guile;

With torn and bleeding hearts we smile,

And mouth with myriad subtleties.

—From "We Wear the Mask"
by Paul Laurence Dunbar (1872–1906)

Cuttin' Up

Author's Note

A man never forgets his boyhood barber shop. L&M was mine. It stood right across the street from our apartment on the south side of Chicago, near 87th Street and South Park (later named Martin Luther King Drive). It was a dangerous intersection. Tires squealed. Horns honked. Fenders crunched. In fact, our cocker spaniel Alison was killed by a car one summer when she slipped out of the backyard to follow my four brothers and me to the barber shop.

But once inside L&M, the distinct sounds of the barber shop—sounds so vivid you could almost touch them—drowned out the perils of heavy traffic. The trumpet of Dizzy Gillespie or the drums of Art Blakey or the voice of Sarah Vaughan poured in buckets from a radio perpetually tuned to WBEE-AM. On hot days, a rotating fan, whose blades looked large enough to propel an airplane, crooned in competition with the radio, swirling with great gusts the talcum powder and menthol-cigarette smoke that dusted the air, the smoke puffed by old men who roared at jokes I didn't understand.

Ray and Ray, the shop's barbers, would greet my brothers and me, their voices the very sound of smiles. "Our mother said to put our haircuts on her account," my big brother, Marc, would announce with aplomb, never failing to convince me he was a man among us boys. We'd come with just enough pocket change to split a bottle or two of Coke and a big bag of O-Ke-Doke cheese popcorn. Then, waiting our turn, we'd sit near the front window and play checkers on a sun-bleached board, a few bottle caps standing in for pieces lost long ago. And so, for my brothers and me, the barber shop was a different world: a world of kinetic jazz and air you could see and grown-ups who actually knew how to laugh and a cold Coke drunk straight from the bottle. The barber shop was back then, as it is today, a place to kick back and have a good time.

Over the last seven years or so, I've become an accidental chronicler of good times in the barber shop. While waiting for a haircut, feeling like the lowly caboose on an endless train of customers, I bide my time by taking notes on the colorful conversations whirling around me. I immediately jot down the best quips in my laptop.

Now, in any other setting you might call that eavesdropping. But in the barber shop, there's no presumption of privacy. In fact, most speakers would feel honored to be quoted since, in truth, that's what they're aiming for: to utter statements so singular, so funny, that everyone says, "Did you hear what so-and-so said the other day?" Besides, as my barber, Tony Parker (page 75), once proclaimed concerning the privacy issue, "Folks can't tell your business if you don't tell it first."

Here's a sampling of the one-liners I've collected.

One barber to another on the sober realities of life in the hood: "Careful with that razor. 9-1-1 don't rush to this neighborhood. They give our blood time to clot up on its own."

An elderly customer on the demise of corporal punishment: "I'm tired of parents yellin', 'Time out! Time out!' Raisin' up a child ain't no game. Bad kids don't need a time out. They need a *knock* out."

A customer on a distinction between presidents Bill Clinton and George W. Bush: "I trust Bush with my daughter, but Clinton with my job."

A married barber on why his flirting with other women is harmless: "A dog will chase a car, but if he catches it he won't drive."

I had no immediate plans for the clandestine collection of quips. I recorded them simply because they made me laugh whenever I read them. So when Doubleday executive editor Janet Hill, who edited my two previous books, mentioned that she always wanted to publish a book about barber shops, I leapt at the opportunity. Based on my collection of quips, not to mention the experience of a lifetime of haircuts, I knew I'd find plenty of material to work with, plenty of subjects to explore. To be sure, barber shops are peopled by some of the nation's funniest comedians and sharpest pundits: real characters with fascinating stories to tell. And they come to the barber shop eager to take the stage. The title came to me immediately: *Cuttin' Up.*

African-American men commune at the barber shop. It's where we go to be among ourselves, to *be* ourselves, to unmask. More than even the church, where reverence for God's house curbs one's enthusiasm, the barber shop is where we gather for true fellowship, for a respite from a society where black men are often scorned and excluded. Barber Reginald Attucks (page 121) calls the barber shop the final black frontier. "It's the last public place," he says, "(where) black men can go to be separate." We come for a haircut, of course, but we also come to connect, to converse among brethren—sometimes in spirited debate, sometimes in jovial accord. We spice our dialogues with braggadocio, poured so generously that the air hangs heavy with witch hazel and testosterone.

Governing most exchanges in black barber shops is an unwritten rule: comments shared with the group must both entertain *and* enlighten. Proverbs must merge with punch lines, comedy with profundity. Those unskilled in the art of being one part humorist and one part sage bite their tongues and play the role of audience. I count myself in that number: an appreciative spectator.

And so, over the course of eighteen months, this spectator crisscrossed the country, visiting cities from Detroit to Orlando and from Brooklyn to Houston. I wrapped my ears around topics ranging from the sometimes comical rite of passage of the first haircut to the raids by state inspectors to catch unlicensed barbers before they scoot out the back door. And when I plunged beneath the mirthful surface of black barber shops, I found much more than humor.

Some of the oral histories I accumulated convey how the barber shop, one of the nation's earliest black businesses, is as much a think tank as it is a comedy showcase. As Reverend John McClurkin (page 101) observes,

"I would venture to say that every time I preach I talk about something I heard in the barber shop." Other stories impart the spirit of community that thrives in barber shops. Albert Ghee (page 39) describes how his two uncles organized strategy sessions in their Virginia barber shop to decide how to educate black children when, in 1959, Prince Edward County closed public schools rather than submit to court-ordered desegregation. And then there are the stories that inspire me most, the ones that talk up the notion of barber shop as classroom.

As I visited barber shops across the country, I observed, among barbers and customers alike, an informal yet earnest proclivity to teach, to enlighten, to "school." Knowledge is passed on, not salted away. It's a custom that runs canyon-deep. As George Evans (page 14), a fifty-year-old customer, insists, "More black history is taught in barber shops than in schools." Sometimes, the schooling takes the form of advice, relationship advice in particular, since women tend to be the topic of choice. "My wife has a Master's in psychology and she's working on her PhD," says barber Fabian Shorey (page 148). "But I do more counseling than she does." And sometimes the schooling is as fundamental as how to prevent a crop of tomatoes from getting brown spots or even the right cop to see about fixing a ticket.

Barber shops can be celebrated without having to idealize them. Some black men, sad to say, can be quite small minded about female barbers. So, in an effort to tell the whole truth, I've let that chauvinism rear its ungroomed head within these pages.

In closing, a note on the spelling of "barber shop." Dictionaries spell it as one word. However, on their signs, business cards, and calendars, barbers themselves spell it as two words. With all due respect to Mr. Webster, I've sided with the barbers.

This collection of oral histories, in the end, takes you where only exclusive brethren are privileged to tread: inside the captivating world of the black barber shop. That sound you hear, rising above the throaty buzz of clippers and the metallic chirp of scissors, is the easy hum of men among men.

– Craig Marberry

Hairitage:
Passing It Down

Robin Pickard 32, Customer

When I was little, my mom always said, "If you cut a boy's hair before his first birthday— or if you let it grow uncut longer than a year—the texture of his hair will change."

**— Robin
Pickard**

When I was little, my mom always said, "If you cut a boy's hair before his first birthday—or if you let it grow uncut longer than a year—the texture of his hair will change." I don't know about that, but that's what the old folks believed. Every mother I know cut her son's hair when he was one. But Isaiah was almost two and a half and I still hadn't taken him to the barber shop.

All my sisters were like, "That doesn't make sense. You need to cut that boy's hair." My five brothers said, "The older he gets, he's not gonna like the buzz of those clippers. He's gonna fall out and act his color."

Isaiah hadn't got a haircut because his father liked it long. Me, I was ready long time ago. I have an eleven-year-old daughter, so I was doing three heads every day: hers, mine, and Isaiah's.

I had to fight Isaiah every night to braid his hair. Then he would take them down in his sleep. So I had to do them again in the morning. And when I picked him up from day care, he would have taken them down again. This was *every* day. I could just scream. I think he did it to mess with me. He'd come up to me and say, "I pull hair loose." I'd say, "You sure did. And you're a wonderful little boy." But, oh, he was a monster!

I gave his father an ultimatum: find someone else to braid his hair or it's coming off. He promised to find someone, but after a month it was still my job. So I took Isaiah to the barber shop. I know a boy's first haircut is a daddy thing. It's a rite of passage, like back when a father would take his son out in the woods to shoot his first buck. But his daddy wouldn't do it.

There's a whole ritual around a boy's first haircut. Isaiah's grandmother schooled me. She said, "I know you been thinkin' about cuttin' Isaiah's hair." I said, "I can't take it anymore." She said, "Well, before you take him to the barber, make sure you plant one braid right at the top of his head." I said, "Why?" She said, "That's the center of his soul." I said, "Okay, I didn't know that." Then she said, "Have the barber cut the braid before he cuts anything else. Then you take the braid and tuck it in your Bible." I said, "My Bible?" She said, "That will preserve Isaiah's strength." I said, "Really?" She said, "Don't you remember the story of Samson and Delilah, how Samson's strength was in his hair?" I said, "Yeah." She said, "Well, if you save the braid you'll preserve Isaiah's strength."

When the barber saw Isaiah he said, "Oh, that's the prettiest little girl." I said, "He's a boy." The barber said, "Lord, let me cut that child's hair." I didn't know how Isaiah would react. I imagined all these angry men looking at me and shouting, "Woman, take that crybaby outta here." But he didn't make a sound.

When I got home, I placed the braid in the first page of the book of Isaiah. Then I turned to the family-tree page in the front of the Bible. I wrote: "On May 30, 2003, Isaiah became a little man."

But, actually, he looks like a bald-headed girl.

*The sweet sorrow
of the first haircut*

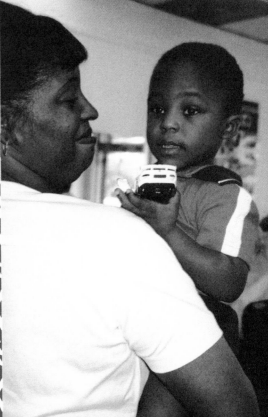

*Robin and her
"little man"*

Alexander Parker 70, Barber Shop Owner

I tell the young guys that the secret to repeat business is good manners, a clean appearance, and a professional attitude. Don't nobody raise hell up in here but me.

✂ **Alexander Parker**

You know, I could teach these young boys a thing or two about cuttin' heads, about making money cuttin' heads. I've had my barber's license for fifty years. Still, can't teach them nothin'. They know it all. Well, there's such a thing as being "over learned." Some things they don't teach in school. I got a PhD, in "street" and a Master's in "white folks." White man up the way asked me once, he said, "Why don't colored folks do business with the colored man?" I said, "They're afraid they'll get screwed." He said, "They're not afraid the white man will screw them?" I said, "Yeah, but the white man got a smaller dick. Black man screw you, you *know* you been screwed."

My first barber job was in Davidson, North Carolina, a small college town in a rural county. The shop was owned by Ralph Johnson. He was black, but he looked white. Said he was the wrong kind of nigga on both sides of the tracks. All his customers were white: farmers, professors, students. Back in those days, you couldn't cut white heads *and* black heads. Whites wouldn't have it. You had to choose. Ralph and I couldn't even give each other a cut during business hours. Ralph said a man made a better livin' with "CW" on his barber's permit, so that's what I chose. "CW" meant colored cuttin'

Alexander stands tall at barber college in 1952.

white folks' hair. "CC" meant colored cuttin' colored folks' hair. There wasn't no "Whites Only" sign in Ralph's window. Black folks knew where they could go and where they couldn't.

Ralph had a good mind for business. Made a whole lot of money. And I don't mean "nigga rich," all flash and no cash. He had money like the white folks. Some of them didn't like that. Tried to run him out of business, tried to burn his place down. I learned a lot from Ralph and I try to pass it down, but these boys won't listen. Some barbers want to make money and some barbers want to make noise. The young guys get too friendly with the customer, talkin' all the time. You should have a new head in your chair every fifteen minutes. Four and thirty-two. That's the formula. Four heads an hour, thirty-two heads a day—forty on Saturday. In my day, I was a workhorse. But these young guys don't want to work that hard. Got "butt-itis." Always want to go sit on what their mamas should've kicked.

And they always want to run have their "social experience" with the girls. I tell them that Sally will spend more time with John, who can help her out, than with Dick, who ain't got nothin' to give but romance. Keep it zipped up and you'll keep somethin' in your pocket.

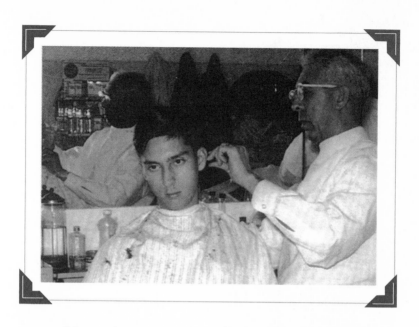

*Alexander's first boss, Ralph Johnson (right),
aka "the Wrong Kind of Nigga"*

I tell the young guys that the secret to repeat business is good manners, a clean appearance, and a professional attitude. Don't nobody raise hell up in here but *me*. I'm old, but I ain't too old to run you the hell out of here. Gotta be humble, too. Can't talk cash from a man's pocket unless you're smaller than him: "Thank you, sir. Come back, sir." And you have to keep your mouth shut. I say, "Customers will tell their business, but if you tell all you hear, you won't get to hear much."

Look here, where can a man go today and get a good laugh? Think about it. The barber shop is about it. Men need that. So I tell the young barbers that they can joke, but don't let joking slow you down. The customer ain't payin' for laughs. Barberin' has been good to me. But I've had my turn at the plow. Now I'm tryin' to teach the young ones.

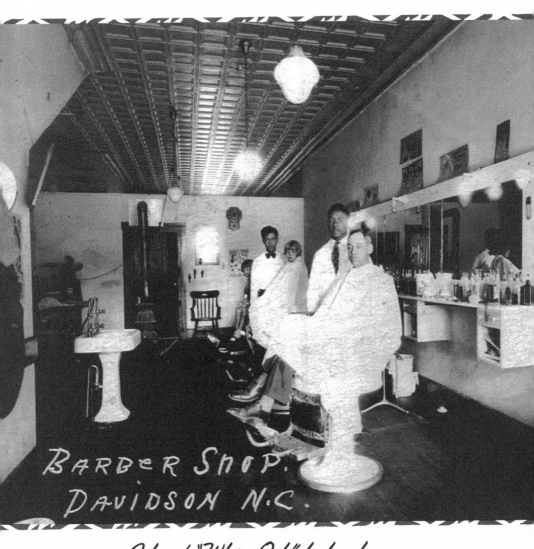

BARBER SHOP. DAVIDSON N.C.

Johnson's "Whites Only" barber shop

George Evans 50, Customer

Mr. Woods, who was every bit of seventy years old, was my first barber. He was a member of our church, Hanes CME, and he had a barber shop set up in his garage. Customers sat in fold-up chairs along the walls. One exposed lightbulb hung from a black cord in the center of the ceiling. He had a real barber chair and it sat right under that light. He had those posters on the walls that showed different styles of haircuts, but they were just for show. Mr. Woods could do only one style: the Broach, which was very short, one step from bald. In fact, some parts of your head *were* bald 'cause Mr. Woods couldn't cut. Not a lick.

Mr. Woods's barber shop was four blocks from our house. My father would walk me and my brother over. Always had plenty of customers. Some men would sit up there and drink likker. Back then, a lot of men didn't leave home without their tin can, their flask of white lightnin'. Some of them poured it in a little mayonnaise jar. Just enough to hold 'em till they got back home. Kids would listen while the men talked and swigged. Nowadays, these young boys have the answer. But kids back then, you didn't open your mouth while grown folks were talkin'. Might get popped.

The men talked about things that all of them had an opinion on. If they were talkin' politics, now that ran out quick. But if it was sports, that

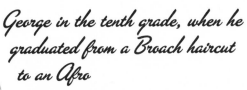

George in the tenth grade, when he graduated from a Broach haircut to an Afro

might go on forever. They'd talk on one topic till everybody got their say. They even got to double dip. That's when you get your say *twice*. If somebody out-talked you, you'd want to double dip.

The old folks, they loved to talk about the olden days. Dad would talk about pickin' cotton in the country all week long and walkin' ten miles along the train tracks on Saturday nights to get to the poolroom in the black section of Winston-Salem. When he was too young to go inside the poolroom, he would sit out front and his cousins would come out every now and then to give him a Nehi and a honey bun or a RC Cola and a Moon Pie. He'd say, "Family looked out for family."

More black history gets passed on in barber shops than in schools. When I talk to young guys, I like to say things like, "I bet you don't know that Charles Drew, a black doctor, made blood banks possible." Even when we talk sports, there's some history in it. One young guy, a Cowboys fan, he said to me, "You a Redskins fan, right?" I said, "That's right. Why? You wanna lose some money on the game?" He said, "Well, as a loyal fan, you know that the *great* Redskins were the last team in the NFL to integrate. And soon as Doug Williams won the Super Bowl for them, they let him go the next year. Kicked the brother to the curb." I said, "That's true. But why didn't your Cowboys pick him up?"

Even when a man's got a point, you gotta have a comeback. Gotta keep your gun loaded in the barber shop or they'll shoot you down. I *always* got ammunition. Old folks are always tryin' to school young folks in the barber shop. Guess I'm one of the old folks now.

Y'all in
the Family

Ronald Couthen 37, Customer

When Ron, Jr., was old enough to sit up, I'd put Teniqua in his lap before I got in the barber chair. It taught him to look out for his little sister.

 Ronald Couthen

Kids shouldn't run all around the barber shop. It ain't an amusement park. They're *supposed* to be bored. When my children were younger, I would take them to the barber shop with me every Saturday. I always held them in my arms till the barber was ready for me.

One thing 'bout me, I believe in discipline and reward. The book of Proverbs says, "Train up a child in the way he should go and when he is old, he will not depart from it." That's why I have such wonderful kids to this day. They were trained up. Ron, Jr., is fourteen now and Teniqua is twelve. Both of them are honor roll students. When Ron, Jr., was old enough to sit up, I'd put Teniqua in his lap before I got in the barber chair. It taught him to look out for his little sister. He's almost my height now and, believe you me, ain't a boyfriend Teniqua gets that Ron ain't aware of. First boyfriend she had, Teniqua didn't tell me. But Ron did. He said, "Dad, I know how he looks, where he lives, and who his people are." I said, "Guess I don't have to worry 'bout nothin'." He said, "I'm on it."

My kids liked comin' to the barber shop, but I hated for them to have to wait so long. Some barbers take appointments nowadays, but it's still "first come, first served" in most shops. You never know if you're gonna be next in the chair or if you'll have to sleep in there overnight. And nothin' you do to speed things along really works. Sometimes I'll call ahead and ask the barber how many customers he got. They always say, "Oh, one or two." But when you rush over there, there are always three or four ahead of you. That's how they do you. They know you're thinkin', *Well, I'm already here so I might as well wait.*

A lot of barbers watch who comes in, and in what order. They'll say, "You next." Or, "I got two, then you." But customers also have to keep up with their spot. That's why we greet other customers as they come in. It lets the next guy know that you're there. It's sort of like when customers come into Fairway I Stop, the convenience store where I work. I greet them and that lets them know that I know. You know? I say "Hello" or "Mornin' " or "How you doin' today?" Part of it is being friendly. But part of it is business. Same thing in the barber shop.

Once, my barber tried a number system to cut down the wait. But guys would come in and take a number and then they would leave to get lunch or somethin'. When they came back they expected to be next, even if their number had passed. It messed up the flow. Number 21 would be in the chair and you were holdin' number 22, but then number 12 would walk in and want to go next. It happened to me several times. I talked to my barber 'bout it. I said, "Hey, I been sittin' here all day and some guy gets to go mow his lawn, eat lunch, hug on his woman, and stroll back in when he's ready? That ain't right." My barber agreed. He dropped the number system.

On average, I wait 'bout an hour for a haircut. The Bible says that the tryin' of your faith worketh patience. Your patience gets worked big time in the barber shop.

Ronald plays the waiting game in 1992.

Bruce Simms 39, **Barber**

I looked up and Jim hadn't moved. He froze in the chair. I had to reach up and pull him down to the floor before he got shot.

 Bruce
Simms

Jim Gallmon was in my chair when two guys bust in the shop one night, pointing guns. I've known Jim since he was bald—his head *and* his face. Now he's all dreads and beard. Yeah, we were staring down the barrel of a gun that night. But this is (Washington), D.C., Congress Heights. Gets kinda rough.

It was two young guys, a little dude and the leader. They had on black ski masks. They didn't need masks 'cause I didn't want to identify *nothin'.* The leader, he was shouting: "Y'all know what the *'f'* this is. Everybody on the floor!"

Our shop is small, so it gets loud in here. But it got quiet in a heartbeat, like someone pulled the plug. The leader said, "Drop your money and get on the *damn* floor." I ain't gonna lie. I was scared. But I was mad, too. Just so happens I had fifteen hundred dollars in cash on me. I had three hundred in my right pocket to make change for customers. And I had twelve hundred in a wad in my left pocket. To tell the truth, it was a couple of weeks before Christmas and I was hoping to buy a hot big-screen TV, if someone walked in to sell one. And they always do.

I saw one barber drop his money on the floor and lay on top of it. I didn't want to give up all mine, either. As I was laying down, I dropped 300 on the floor, in plain view, with my right hand and threw the wad behind some boxes with my left hand. I looked up and Jim hadn't moved. He froze in the chair. I had to reach up and pull him down to the floor before he got shot.

Bruce to Jim: "Chin up."

The leader told the little dude to search our pockets. Little dude said, "If I find somethin' in your pockets, you gonna get popped." Guys started saying, "Hold up, hold up, hold up," and they gave it all up.

They took my watch, my rings, my wallet. *And* my three-hundred dollars. Found out later that when they left, they went up the street and shot a man in the chest. Killed him. As soon as I stood up and started brushing my pants off, the phone rang. I answered it. It was my daughter, Jamiya. She's four. She said, "Hi, daddy. I love you." I ain't gonna lie, it moved me. I was dealing with all these emotions. Fear. Anger. Revenge. And then to hear my daughter's voice. It was like God was telling me I should be thankful to be alive. "Hi, daddy. I love you. . . ." I cried.

There are no accidents. You know, I had almost left the shop ten minutes before those guys robbed us. If I had, I'd still have my stuff. But I would have missed out on a lesson: *things* can blind you, hold you back. This life is more than money or a watch or a few rings. I have a daughter . . . and she loves me. How much is that worth?

My new business card is a little different. It shows me kneeling at the altar of my church, Campbell A.M.E. You only see my back, not my face. People ask me what that's about.

It's about gratitude.

Altar call

Robin Simmons-Blount 47, Customer

My children can hear stories about their ancestors from a barber who knew them when, and from other men who knew them when. That's <u>living</u> black history.

✂ **Robin Simmons-Blount**

About nine years ago, my father sat for a picture with my kids. There are two things about that picture. First thing is I forgot to put shoes on my daughter, so I asked my father to hide her feet with his hands. But she kept kicking herself free. The other thing about that picture is that I can tell that my father had just been to the barber shop. I can tell because of his nose. There's no hair on it. Long white hairs grow on the tip of his nose. He laughs when Roman and Rycal pull on them. But his barber cuts the hairs off, which is how I can tell he had just been to the barber shop.

My father is eighty years old and has diabetes and congestive heart failure. Doctors gave him six weeks to six months to live. That was four years ago. His legs are weak and he doesn't get around like he used to, so I bring him to his barber shop once a week. Sometimes I bring my children along. I tell them, "You're here to absorb some wisdom."

I make them listen to the conversations amongst the men. I say, "If you listen, you get fed." Our kids are being taught they can learn something out of chaos. They can't. They need the lessons being taught in the barber shop.

Kids need a framework of reference. Otherwise, they can't appreciate who they are. That's what the barber shop gives them, a frame of reference.

Daddy Will sits for his last family portrait.

The owner of my father's barber shop is a virtual griot. He knows all the black history of the town. He knows that my children's great grandfather negotiated for the property our church is located on, and that their grandfather was honored for rescuing two children from a runaway car, and that their Uncle Gene was a botanist. My children can hear stories about their ancestors from a barber who knew them when, and from other men who knew them when. That's *living* black history.

If someone in the barber shop asks my kids their names, I tell them to speak up. I say, "Announce your name clearly. That's a sign of confidence." One time, a man came in and seemed like all he could do was grunt. It was a good time to show them the pitfalls of a monosyllabic vocabulary. If you don't have sense enough to articulate what you want or what you think, you're going to be in trouble in life. You have to learn to express yourself.

You also have to learn how to carry yourself. Some of the kids come in the barber shop with do-rags, chewing gum in public like a cow, their pants falling—crotch down to their knees—showing their underpants like a diaper, walking like a baby because they're tugging at their britches so much they can't keep their balance. What do they think belts are for? Ain't got sense enough to open a door for an older person. And if they had sense enough, their hands would be too busy holding up their draws. These are not practices that undergird success. Who's going to take the time to de-program that? *Who?*

The barber shop also teaches my kids the value of hard work. These men aren't digging ditches for somebody else. They're working for themselves. And one of them *owns* the place. I tell my children, "Use your business sense. Make your head work for you. And be diligent. A lazy man can't get his crop in."

You've got a lot of lessons at your fingertips in the barber shop, if you have sense enough to use them.

(AUTHOR'S NOTE: Robin's father, William Otto Simmons, Jr., died four weeks after this interview.)

Vernon Winfrey 71, Barber Shop Owner

and Father of Oprah Winfrey

I'm seventy-one.

Old but not spent.

Somebody asked

me if Oprah is my

only child. I said,

"The only one

so far."

 Vernon Winfrey

I'm from West, Mississippi. You heard of a one-red-light town? Well, West had one caution light. Real small town. So I left Mississippi and moved here to Nashville. Opened my barber shop in 1965. Don't have a big-name business, but I have an important business. My main objective is not to make money. It's to make men look good. Then I want my money.

When she was young, my daughter wasn't happy with some of the men who hung out in my shop. Oprah frowned on the drunkards, the off-course men. What some people consider undesirable folk. But they were harmless. And some of them were really comical. A preacher was talking to one man. Preacher said, "You *know* you shouldn't be drinkin'?" The man said, "Preacher, you right." He said, "I'm not gonna drink no more . . . or no less."

Not that I've catered to those men, but I don't turn them away. Might give them a little change or buy them a pack of cigarettes. On holidays, I invited them home for dinner. When she was a girl, Oprah didn't like that. Thought family dinners should be for family. She talked about that in her speech when she got that humanitarian award at the Emmys. She talked about Slim and Bootsy and Willie Fox, all the off-course men from the barber shop. Oprah wanted to know why we had to have these kind of people in our house. I told her, "Christ comes in different forms. You never know who you turning away."

28

That Willie Fox was a drinker. He went out the house one night and his landlord locked him out. Tired of his drinking. I saw Fox on the street, shivering. It was *cold* out. Fox had mucus hanging down to his knee. Picked him up and carried him home. Know what Oprah did? The girl who didn't want men like Fox in our home. She pulled the quilt off her bed and made a pallet on the kitchen floor. Gave Fox a warm place to sleep that night. She forgot to mention that in her speech. You see, the world knows her heart now. But I knew it then.

The men who come to my shop, I tell them, "Don't love your children too much to tell them no. Don't let them lead you. You lead *them*. When

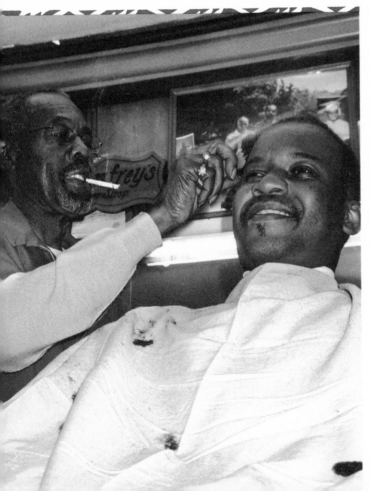

Smoke gets in your eyes.

you teach a child discipline, you never know what they can be . . . or *will* be." Oprah told me if I hadn't been such a strict disciplinarian, she would have been somewhere in public housing with a bunch of babies.

When Oprah spoke at the Emmys she said she couldn't get me to retire from the barber shop. Well, that was about two years ago and I'm still working. I'm so old, when you look at me you're looking at black history. I'm seventy-one. Old but not spent. Somebody asked me if Oprah is my only child. I said, "The only one so far."

Marcus Iverson 32, Barber

I couldn't believe it. Michael Jackson sat in my chair. He twisted and twirled in it like a little kid. He said, "You're a barber! I've always wanted to be a barber."

✂ Marcus Iverson

When I was fifteen, my mother bought me some clippers. She said, "Cut my hair." I said, "What?" She said, "Yeah, taper it just a little." She wore a Bob cut: short on the sides and back, like Anita Baker, the singer. I said, "Ma, I don't know." She said, "You can do this. I *know* you can." We had several barbers in the family: a cousin in Washington, D.C., one in Atlanta, and my grandfather was a barber. I guess my mother thought it was in my blood.

So I cut it. And know what? I *tore* her head up. It was full of patches. Terrible, terrible, *terrible*. I felt so bad. My mother looked in the mirror and said, "It's okay. You'll get better. You did a good job."

The next day, she went to work looking like that. She could have gone to a real barber to fix it, but she wore that haircut for a couple of weeks. She wanted it to grow out so I could try again. The next time . . . I *fixed* it. It was like that feeling when you learn to ride a bike, or the first time you slam dunk. My mother said, "A mistake can always be corrected."

I don't make many mistakes anymore. I work in downtown Detroit, near the Marriott in the Renaissance Center. A lot of celebrities stay there. I've cut Biggie Small's hair, the mayor, Mick Jagger—who gave me a hundred dollar tip and tickets to his concert. Two years ago, Michael Jackson walked by with these two big bodyguards. A parade of fans were following him. He glanced through the window, turned around, and came

Marcus cuts it close.

in. I couldn't believe it. Michael Jackson sat in *my* chair. He twisted and twirled in it like a little kid. He said, "You're a barber! I've always wanted to be a barber."

Years ago, Michael Jackson's hair caught fire when he was shooting a Pepsi commercial. I wanted to see if his scalp was damaged and how he covered it up if it was. But he hopped up before I could peek. He didn't want a haircut. He just wanted to play in the chair and talk. As he left, cameras were flashing outside the window. Oh, man! I would *not* want to be in his shoes. Can't go anywhere without a crowd, but what a lonely guy.

Jam Master Jay, the hip-hop DJ from the group Run-DMC, he came in whenever he was in town. He always wore Adidas shoes. One day he had on a real nice pair. I said, "I've never seen those in stores." He said they were called Clima Cool, the lightest pair Adidas made. A few days later, a box arrived. Jam Master Jay had sent me a pair of Clima Cools.

He called to check on me one time and said he was working on a movie. I told him he should include a barber-shop scene and let me star in it. He said he'd see if he could work it in. Next thing I know I'm driving to work, listening to the radio, and I hear that Jam Master Jay got murdered. Someone shot him in his studio. I turned around. Didn't go to work that day.

Some mistakes can't be corrected.

Everyone has a calling. This is mine. Celebrity or not, I love to give customers a great cut. After I got good, my mother reminded me about the first time I cut her hair. She said, "You know what? You *jacked* my hair up!" We can laugh about it now. I love that woman. She gave me everything I have.

Bernard Mathis 47, Barber

I tried talking

Don King into

a haircut.

Seriously. . . .

He looked just like

he looks on TV,

like he stuck his

finger in a socket.

✂ Bernard
Mathis

I tried talking Don King into a haircut. Seriously. He was in town promoting the Tyson-Holyfield fight. He'd just left Freeman's shoe store on Mitchell Street, right near my shop. He had a small entourage with him. He looked just like he looks on TV, like he stuck his finger in a socket. I walked up and said, "Brother King, who you think's gonna win the fight?" He said, "Mike Tyson." I said, "Well, you in Atlanta, Evander Holyfield's hometown." He said, "I'm sorry. Did I say 'Tyson?' I meant Holyfield." Everybody laughed.

I said, "Mr. King, I'm a barber. Do me one favor. Come into my shop." He said, "Oh, no, no, no!" I said, "Just sit in the chair for a second and let me stand there with the scissors." He said, "Can't do it." *Man*, I wanted that picture. I was gonna sell it and make millions. Guess he knew that. That or he's allergic to scissors.

I used to cut Holyfield's hair. And I gave Lennox Lewis a haircut when he fought here on an undercard back in '94 or '95. He wore a Box style back then. He gave me a picture of himself holding the British heavyweight belt. He wrote on there: "Thanks for the cut. Lennox Lewis, future heavyweight champion." That was five or six years before he actually won the title.

But the client I remember most wasn't famous or glamorous. She was a single parent, had five kids. Three of them were boys—ages six, eight, and

To
Bernard
Thank for
The
Cut
↓

Best
wishes
Lennox Lew
"future
Heavyweight
Champion!

ten. They lived a hard life in the projects, the Eagan Homes, where there was a lot of drugs and gang bangin'. One day she said, "I've noticed the way you run your business, the way you always wear a suit and tie." So she asked me, "Would you mind if I bring my boys to watch you one afternoon? I want to expose them to a black man doing something positive."

The way she asked, I knew she thought I'd be doing *her* a favor. But she was entrusting me with her children, the possessions she loved most. I told her, I said, "I'd take that as an honor. By all means... bring them here. I'll do my best to inspire them." She was happy and in tears. I was happy and in tears.

The day she dropped her boys off, I took them next door for soda pops. I wanted them to relax, to get to know me. I told them, I said, "If you work hard in life, you can make it. You *will* make it!" When we got back to the shop, I said, "Make yourselves at home." Which meant they had to do chores.

I told one boy to grab the broom and start sweepin'. I told the next one to check the tissue in the bathroom. I told the other one to straighten up the magazines in the reception area. I told all three of them, I said, "When a customer gets out the chair, you can make tip money if you whisk them off." They spent the whole day with me. I don't know if I touched those boys. It was only one day. But for that day, they were surrounded by black men dressed clean as the Board of Health. For that day, they met black men who were lawyers and college professors. For that day, they got a good dose of a better life. That meant more to me than chewin' the fat with Shaq or Don King or Lennox Lewis. Much more.

Civil
Wrongs

Albert Ghee, Jr. 47, Customer

Playin' the numbers was done so quietly in the shop because it was illegal. It's <u>still</u> illegal— unless you're the government and call it Lotto or something.

✂ **Albert Ghee, Jr.**

Shorty, a midget, worked in back of my uncles' barber shop in Farmville, Virginia. Shorty was the shoe shine guy. If you gave Shorty an extra dollar, he'd play tunes with his rag as he shined your shoes. He might play "The Star Spangled Banner" or "Michael, Row the Boat Ashore" or "Amazing Grace."

I was thirteen before I heard one of Shorty's songs. That's 'cause you had to be a teenager before Uncle James and Uncle William let you in their barber shop, called Carter's. No kids allowed. But on Sunday morning, all the young boys they didn't allow in, my uncles would come to their houses and cut their hair before church. The barber shop was where grown men did business and exchanged information. You had local politicians and candidates comin' through to toot their horn before an election, even some white guys. They'd say, "I don't believe in bad talkin' nobody, but that other guy's no good . . . and let me tell you why." You had your church news—like who had a revival comin' up—and your religious debates. They'd put young, nervous preachers to the test: "Okay, preacher, what does John 3:16 say? And how do you interpret it?" You had farmers arguing about who raised the best cantaloupes or cucumbers. If your tomatoes were gettin' brown spots, somebody would say, "Oh, you gave them too much water." Or, "Cut back on the nitrogen in the fertilizer." And if somebody had a problem with their taxes or something, one of my uncles would say, "There's a customer who comes in Friday mornings who can help you. Come back then."

There was one man ... I couldn't figure out who he was. He'd never get a haircut. He'd just come in and speak to everybody. Then he'd sit in the furthest chair. Every so often a different man would come in and walk to the bathroom. Then the mystery man would go into the bathroom with the guy. A few minutes later, the same thing over again. Somebody would go in the bathroom and that man would follow. After a while, I found out. He was the numbers man. If you had a nickel, that nickel could pay off five dollars, *if* you played the right three numbers. A dime paid ten dollars. A quarter paid twenty-five.

Playin' the numbers was done so quietly in the shop because it was illegal. It's *still* illegal—unless you're the government and call it Lotto or something. But the foot traffic was easy to conceal because white stores wouldn't let blacks use their facilities. If a black man had to go, he had to go to the barber shop. For some reason, *lot* of brothers in Farmville had to go.

Farmville is in Prince Edward County, which has a shameful past. Back in 1959, the county closed all public schools rather than desegregate, as the Supreme Court had ruled. It was one of the only counties in the whole United States to do that. Whites started private "academies" for their kids but, for five long years, black kids were shut out. It was a hateful thing. I was nine years old before I went to public school for the first time. Well, what happened is the men started having small meetings in barber shops. One idea they came up with was that black teachers start holding school in churches. The teachers got paid by the farmers—sometimes with cash money, sometimes with food. But a lot of kids slipped through the cracks and never went back to school.

Yeah, my uncles' barber shop wasn't just a barber shop. It was a gathering place. A gathering of men.

Albert reflects.

James Butler 66, Barber Shop Owner

One day, Jesse Jackson came in the shop and told us, "If I don't see you down there protestin', I'm gonna tell students to boycott the barber shop." Jesse was president of the student government. He was a big jokester. He'd always come down to the shop and get somethin' goin'.

— James Butler

We used to cut the heads of the students who started the sit-in movement: McCain, Richmond, and the rest. That was back in 1960, at North Carolina A&T State University. They'd come down to College Barber Shop, which was in the basement of Cooper Hall. I think it's a laundry room now.

Lookin' back, I can't believe the price of those haircuts. Haircuts in the rest of Greensboro were about a dollar and a quarter. So we raised our price from a dollar to a dollar and ten cents. The students complained and the university made us drop the price to ninety cents a head. Ninety cents! A dime less than we were gettin' in the first place. Those students were good at protestin'.

But they weren't so good at tippin'. Sometimes they'd give us a dollar and let us keep the change. But then we had to give the shop owner thirty cents on the dollar. So you had to cut a few heads before you could pay for lunch.

We'd go to Moms for lunch, me and the three other barbers. Moms was a black woman named Helen George. She had a boardin' house over on Lyndon Street near Sycamore, a big two-story house. She made home-cooked food every day: meat loaf, fried catfish, pinto beans, all that stuff. Her food was so good that the place would fill up. She had tables in the dinin' room, tables in the livin' room, tables in the kitchen. She even had a card table back in the bathroom.

I had to eat in the bathroom once. Moms had a big ol' rusty bathtub in there. I looked in it and it was filled with turnip greens, a good little batch. I looked at the greens on my plate. I was hopin' that Moms had more than one bathtub. Everybody ate there because we couldn't eat at the white restaurants: Mayfair, S&K, and the lunch counter over at Woolworth's on South Elm. And that's what got the sit-ins started.

One day, Jesse Jackson came in the shop and told us, "If I don't see you down there protestin', I'm gonna tell students to boycott the barber shop." Jesse was president of the student government. He was a big jokester.

James (left) with student customers in basement of Cooper Hall in 1960

He'd always come down to the shop and get somethin' goin'. So we didn't know whether he was jokin' or not. But we didn't chance it. That afternoon, the four of us joined the picket line. There were two or three hundred people out there at the square, a big crowd of folks, lined up singin' and chantin' and carryin' on. All of a sudden, here come the police. They brought a city bus with them. They were goin' to load us up and take us down to the box. One of the leaders told us to sit down. Some people, mostly students, sat on the sidewalk and some sat along the curb. But I tried to find me a hole back against the wall. I wasn't tryin' to go to jail. I supported the cause, but I supported a wife and two children, too. Can't pay your bills sittin' in the box.

The police hauled a lot of students off. The rest of us went on home. We barbers protested for two or three afternoons. And we made sure Jesse saw us each time. There was a student named Wilbur Mapp. He played football with Jesse. Mapp had a bad stutter. He came to the shop and told us he asked Jesse, "Wh-wh-wh-wh-why you make *us* go to jail? Wh-wh-wh-wh-why don't *you* go?" Mapp said Jesse said, " 'Well, somebody's got to get y'all out.' "

Kenneth Norton 75, **Barber**

My father would take white folks' money, but he wouldn't take no lip.

✂ **Kenneth Norton**

My father would take white folks' money, but he wouldn't take no lip. In 1910, he opened a barber shop in Davidson, North Carolina. All of his customers were white. Blacks weren't allowed. That was the only way he could keep the whites' business. They'd come in for a shoe shine, a haircut, and a shave. Most of them worked at the college . . . or they were students. But some poor white men would come in, too. They didn't have running water in their homes and they would come to the barber shop to have a shower. Cost a quarter.

I was sixteen when I got licensed as a barber. That was in 1945. I went right to work for my father. I remember the time when the white man who ran the five-cent popcorn stand came in, fussin' up a storm. He was upset because the college passed over his wife for a promotion. Well, like I said, most of my father's customers were associated with the college. So my father asked the popcorn man to hush or leave. But he wouldn't do either. Just kept bad mouthin' the college. Think he'd had a nip too many. My father said, "Get on outta here, now. Go on take that up the street." The street was a different matter. Out there, my father was a black man in a white man's town. But he didn't put up with no mess in his barber shop.

Well, the popcorn man kept on and my father had more than his fill. He went over and grabbed the popcorn man by the collar and shoved him toward the door. He said, "Didn't I tell you take that outta here?" He opened the door and kicked the man where he sits. None of the white customers said a word. And my father wouldn't care if they did. Nobody was gonna run his business but him.

The popcorn man didn't hold a grudge. He kept coming to the shop for a haircut. He kept running his mouth, too. But he didn't talk about the college. He knew if he started up, my father might punt him out the door again.

We integrated the shop's services in 1964. It was time. But our main competition, a black man named Ralph Johnson, he stuck to the old ways: all black barbers cutting for whites only. Students marched on his shop in 1966. And when Ralph Johnson was finally forced to serve black men, many wouldn't go to his shop. Hurt his business.

I learned a lot from my father. He wasn't perfect but he was a good man, a strong man. He cut his last head on a Saturday, got sick on Sunday, and died on Monday. He was seventy-four. I'm gonna do the same thing: work till they run me out. I want to die on my feet. Can't think of a better place to leave this world than working in the barber shop, among friends, doing what you love.

*Kenneth (far right)
in his father's shop, which served "Whites Only"*

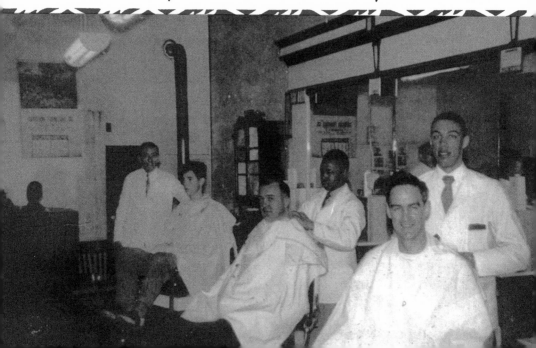

Wheeler Parker 65, Barber Shop Owner

In my barber shop

I tell boys to

remember my

cousin. How he

suffered. The

opportunities he

never had. I tell

them to remember

his name:

Emmett Till.

✂ **Wheeler**
Parker

Daddy used to cut our hair on the porch, me and my two little brothers. He used manual clippers. Had to squeeze the handles to make the blades work. When his hand got tired, he'd end up pulling your hair out instead of cutting it. One day, Daddy gave me those clippers. They were Osters, the Rolls Royce of clippers. I was proud. He said, "Son, it's time you learned. I'm tired."

I grew up in Money, Mississippi. In 1947, when I was eight, my father settled up the crops and we took the I.C. to Chicago. Know why so many blacks in Chicago are from Mississippi? Because it was a straight shot on the I.C., the Illinois Central train. You see, blacks migrated in straight lines. That's why folks from Carolina went straight up to New York. Now if you were from Carolina and ended up in Chicago, people wondered what was wrong with you.

One summer, back in '55, I went back to Mississippi to visit my grandparents. My cousin Bo came, too. But they didn't want him to go. See, Bo grew up in the North. He didn't know the rules.

I liked Bo. If there was something going on, he was right up in the thick of it. After supper one day, eight of us kids borrowed my grandfather's car to go buy some candy and things. We drove to Bryant's grocery store. Roy Bryant's wife, Carolyn, was there alone. She had on a pretty dress and Bo whistled at her. That whistle froze time. Bo was just making a

joke—he *loved* pranks—but we were shocked. A Southern rule had been broken.

Three days passed, so we thought it was over. But then they came. White men in the middle of the night: Roy Bryant and his half brother, J. W. Milam. It was about 2:30 Sunday morning. It was so dark you couldn't tell if your eyes were open. But they had flashlights. And a Colt .45 automatic. They were beating on the front door and yelling. Felt like the whole bed was shaking. Man, you talk about terror.

My grandfather let them in. I heard them ask for the boys from Chicago. My grandmother offered them money. Roy Bryant started to take it, but his half brother said no. They came in my room. Lights flashed in my eyes. I was praying: *Please, God. Deliver me from this place.* Then, the lights were gone. They had moved on to the next bedroom. They wanted Bo.

When they found his room, Bo broke another rule. He didn't call them "sir." They cussed words never spoken in that house. But Bo wasn't afraid. He stopped to put on his socks. They told him he didn't need socks. Bo was so calm. He said, "I don't wear shoes without socks."

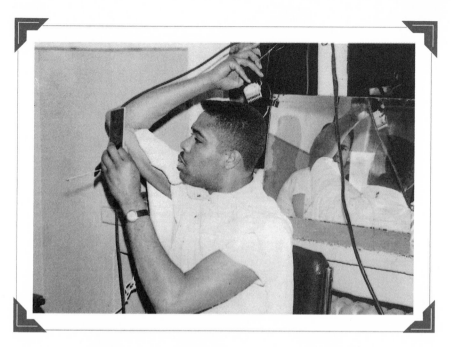

Self-service: Wheeler cuts hair in 1964.

His body was found in the Tallahatchie river three days later. To hold him down, they tied a big gin fan around his neck—tied it with barbed wire. He'd been beaten—tortured—and shot in the head. The bullet went clear through. His face was like mush, his body all bloated. He looked like a monster. There was a trial. But the jury let his killers walk.

I wanted to be a barber. Bo wanted to be a fireman. Whatever he did, he pushed to the top. So I'm sure he would have been chief.

When I think about black folks today, what we've survived only to turn around and destroy ourselves, I feel a pain I can't describe. In my barber shop I tell boys to remember my cousin. How he suffered. The opportunities he never had. I tell them to remember his name: Emmett Till. He had a short life. Fourteen years. But if we remember, then it wasn't a wasted life.

Sense of
a Woman

Karen Regina Graham-Oliver 47, Barber

One time a guy said, "I ain't never sat in a woman's chair." I said, "Well, don't start today."

✄ Karen Regina Graham-Oliver

The worst day of my life was when I cut my first head. It was a Saturday, the busiest day. The customer was a tall, brown-skinned guy with a big Afro. It took me forever. Couldn't get him even. I work with eight guys, eight barbers. They kept looking at me through the mirrors. Customers think those mirrors are for them, but they're for the barbers to spy on each other.

When I finished, the guy started acting out: "Oh, my God! You messed up my head." All the clippers shut off and the whole shop went quiet. One of the barbers came over and helped me get the guy straight. The guy hid his Afro under a hat and left. I went outside and took a *long* walk.

But I came back.

The next guy I worked on had real curly hair and wanted a V cut in the back. I'm like, "Come on. This is my first day and you want me to cut letters of the alphabet?" He said, "I know you can do it." I asked him why he didn't leave after I messed up the first guy's Afro. He said, "When you came back for more I knew you had confidence." I said, "I don't know why that guy was so upset. It's just hair. It grows back in seven days." He said, "I guess it's those first six days that matter."

I couldn't get that V thing going on. He looked at it and said, "Well, this isn't exactly what I asked for. But it'll be okay. I'm gonna keep coming

In the
lion's den

back. Eventually, you'll get it." That guy's name is Carl. He's one of my best customers to this day. He gave me the confidence to go on.

But later that first day, I cut off half of a guy's mustache.

One time a guy said, "I ain't *never* sat in a woman's chair." I said, "Well, don't start today." Give a sistah a break. It's tough for a woman in a barber shop. They say it's the black man's country club. He comes here to socialize and relax. But if a woman's around, he feels like he has to sit up straight and watch his language. Cars don't speed around cops.

A young fella came in one day. I'd say he was in his thirties. He sat in the chair next to me. Then this woman came in. Looked like she was about seven months pregnant. She was holding an envelope of photos that the young guy had left in the glove compartment. She said, "Ray! What the *hell* were you doing at Brenda's house?" She threw the pictures at him and started yelling that he was a no good so-and-so. Then she hauled off and slapped him. She slapped him so hard that the chair spun. He followed her to the car like a spanked puppy.

One customer said, "Naw, naw, *naw.* Y'all shouldn't allow *that.* A man can't come to his barber shop and get beat down by his woman. This is our sanctuary. Can't shame a man in his sanctuary." A woman who had brought her son in disagreed. She said, "If you commit a crime you can't tell the law where it's okay to bust you."

Men just aren't accustomed to having a woman in this environment. They don't like change. That goes for their haircuts, too. A man will get so many bald spots that his head looks like a crop of Afro puffs. Don't matter. He ain't changin'. But like it or not, women are everywhere now: the army, corporate America, firefighters. One Saturday, a guy said, "This is a man's world." I said, "Yep, and a woman makes it turn."

Betty Reece 69, Former Barber

I'm sure I had a bad reputation in the shop. Sometimes I'd sit there all day and not get a single customer. I did a lot of waiting. Felt like I was watching hair grow.

✂ **Betty Reece**

I've always been bashful. In school, I was tall and real skinny. My legs were so thin a boy told me, "Let me get you some paper 'cause you walkin' on pencils." I took off runnin'. If a boy even looked my way, I'd fly. That was just me. Being such a shy person, especially around men, I don't know why I chose to be a barber.

There were forty men in my barber school. Clara Poke was the only other woman. She was from Connecticut. If it hadn't been for Clara, I probably wouldn't have finished. I'm good at starting things I don't complete. We went to barber school five days a week for eight months. They made us study the *whole* body, anatomy and all that. I don't know why. I didn't want to cut on nothing but hair.

We had a teacher at barber school named Mr. Mercherson. He was a young man, but he had a bad case of asthma. Sometimes he had to sit down and catch his breath. Mr. Mercherson was so comical. He would say, "Miss Reece, I bet you whisper when you think to yourself." He thought my shyness was holding me back. He would say, "Miss Reece, you so slow you miss the boat *and* the bus."

I got my first job in April of 1967. I was so nervous that I broke out in hives. My face got so big that I scared myself. I messed up a man's hair so bad that first day. Took a whole chunk out the back. I was afraid he was

Betty waits for a customer in 1967.

gonna hurt me, but he was real nice. I messed up a whole lot of heads. I had the right training. I was just scared to death. Never could relax. To build a customer base, a barber has to be friendly and outgoing. Most customers don't talk unless you talk to them, and I wasn't the talking kind. So that hurt me. I just don't meet people easily. I hate that about myself. Now, my mother, she didn't meet strangers. She could shake your hand and make you feel like family.

I'm sure I had a bad reputation in the shop. Sometimes I'd sit there all day and not get a single customer. I did a lot of waiting. Felt like I was watching hair grow. After six months, I gave it up. I told the owner I found a job over at Lorillard Tobacco. He told me that was a good opportunity. I think he did me a favor by letting me go. He knew I wasn't a good barber. He knew it wasn't for me. But, you know, if I hadn't been so nervous and shy, I could have succeeded.

I put in thirty-three years at Lorillard. I retired three years ago. But I'm ready to work again. And I might go back to barbering.

I'm still a shy person. But if I went back now, I think I could handle it. I don't have my tools anymore, but I've kept my license up. I send in my thirty dollars the first of every year. I've done that for thirty-five years. Just in case.

I feel good about myself now. I've come a long way. I think I can do it. But no barber shops have offered me a job yet. So I guess that tells me something.

Carolyn Braboy 53, Barber Shop Owner

The sign in the front yard says, "Cuts by Carolyn." If they can't deal with a woman, they can keep on walkin'.

 Carolyn Braboy

When clients walked in where I used to work, I'd say, "May I help you?" Some would act like they didn't hear me. One client said, right to my face, "No woman is gonna cut my hair. You'd take my strength away." He pinned his ignorance on Samson and Delilah. One client even laughed in my face. And sometimes customers who tipped the men, they wouldn't tip me. I didn't count.

It was like they were tryin' to run me out of there. But I had two little boys to feed. I wasn't goin' *nowhere*.

There was one boy, I cut his hair since he was a little bitty guy. One day, when he was about twelve, he came in with a couple of his friends. He told them, "I'm waitin' on Miss Carolyn." His friends laughed at him, so he switched over and went to one of the male barbers.

After he got his haircut, I pulled him to the side. I said, "Tim, it didn't hurt me to lose your business." I said, "What hurt me is that I've watched your mama raise you up to be a nice guy." I said, "You should never let anybody pull you down." I said, "You pull *them* up so they can go further."

Sometimes I would cut the water on at my sink so nobody could hear me cry. Late one night, when it was about time to go home, this client walked in. All the other barbers were busy except me. The client asked the receptionist if a barber was available. She said, "Yes, Carolyn is open." I heard him whisper, "Can she cut?" The receptionist said I was good, but the man came over and asked me, "Are you sure you can cut my hair?" I said, "Well, we close in ten minutes. You've been thinkin' about it so long

Can she cut? Carolyn works at her old shop in 1993.

that I'm not sure I have time." I said, "What do you do for a living?"
He said, "I work in a bank." I said, "How many blacks work there?" He
said, "Right now I'm the only one." I said, "Can I ask you a question?
How would you feel if a white customer came in the bank and questioned
your qualifications because you're black?"

I saw a soft side in him open up. He said, "I'm sorry . . . never thought
of it like that." This time he said it nicely, *"Will* you cut my hair?" I
said, "Yes, I will. What would you like?" He said, "A Bald Fade with a
low blend." I said, "Fine." Then I said a little prayer: *God,* please *let me
throw down on this haircut.* And when the man got up out that chair,
God sho 'nough had helped me 'cause that haircut was *somethin'.*

After three years of that mess I said, "No more!" One day, this client
kept fussin' about the way I was cuttin' his son's hair. He had a little juice

in him. I said, "Look, I didn't sleep in your bed last night. I didn't make you bring your paycheck home. And I don't even cut your hair. You're *not* gonna talk junk to me." All the barbers sort of gasped. One of them said, "Don't mess with those quiet ones. They'll cut ya."

From the very beginning, my goal was to have my own shop. And I finally got it. It's an extension in back of my house. I work alone. And I love it. The sign in the front yard says, "Cuts by Carolyn." If they can't deal with a woman, they can keep on walkin'.

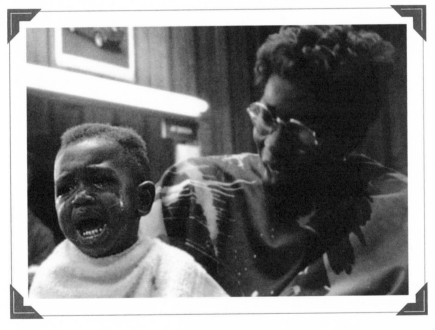

Bawl-headed

Evelyn Burgard 56, Customer

Breaking in a new barber is hard work.

✂ Evelyn Burgard

I'm not shy. I don't mind telling a man what I like, when I like it, and *how* I like it—or whether I like it at all. There's no shame in my game. Same thing goes with barbers. I don't get up from the chair until I'm satisfied. What can I say? I'm hard to please.

Barbers hate to see me coming. One time, I went to the shop and my barber was out. One of the barbers said, "Now who's gonna cut Evelyn's hair?" Another barber said, "I'd rather take a beatin'." (Laughs.) Then another one said, "Don't believe your lyin' eyes, Evelyn. I'm off today."

I think I must be a challenge.

I've been getting haircuts since 1994. Back then I owned a fire restoration business in Richmond, Virginia. When you enter a building that's been damaged by fire, the stink of smoke permeates your clothes, your skin, your hair. I had to wash my hair every day. That just became too much of a hassle so I decided to go for a shorter, more manageable style. I went to a shop on East Broad Street. I sat in Frankie's chair. Frankie is in his fifties. Definitely old school.

The man in the chair next to me had a very short cut, almost to the scalp. I asked Frankie, "Can you cut my hair like that?" He said, "Yeah, I can. But I won't." I said, "Wait a minute. Why not?" He said, "A woman shouldn't look like a man. I'll cut your hair similar to that, but it will be a feminine look." So Frankie cut it short and left bangs in front. I loved it. It's wash-and-go. No curling irons, no do-rags, no nothing.

Frankie was always overbooked so I had to find another barber.

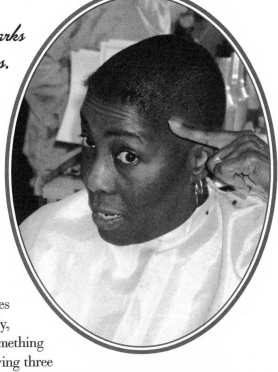

Evelyn barks instructions.

I found a young guy named Danny. He's short, about five feet tall, but he's the best barber I've ever had. I almost cried when I had to move to Greensboro four months ago. At first, I couldn't find a decent barber so I drove back to Richmond two or three times to see Danny. I said, "Danny, you're gonna have to do something about this. I can't keep driving three hours to see you every other Wednesday." Danny wrote some instructions on the back of his business card and told me to give them to my next barber. He wrote:

One eighth against the grain, all the way back.
Fade in the sides.
Taper in back.
Long sideburns.

I gave those instructions to a barber in Greensboro named A.J. I told him, "You don't have to cut my hair if you don't want to, but I'm warning you up front that I'm *very* particular." When he reached

for the instructions, his hand was shaking like a leaf. I went to AJ three times, but he was so nervous that he never got it right. I found another barber, a guy called Bug.

Bug can't cut as well as Danny, but he's getting there. I'll have him trained pretty soon. I've been getting on Bug about buying a new hand mirror. The handle is broken on the one he has. He said, "I'm gonna buy a new one for you." I said, "And get a new comb, too. That thing's been in everybody else's head."

Breaking in a new barber is hard work.

Suffer the
Little Children

Randy McKendall and Maliek Ray Barber, 32, and Customer, 7

MALIEK: Ouch! That hurts. Are you almost done?

RANDY: I just started.

✂ Randy McKendall and Maliek Ray

RANDY: Hop on up here and I'll take care of you.

MALIEK: I never seen you before.

RANDY: I just started a few weeks ago.

MALIEK: Oh.

RANDY: Your granma will be right back from the Dollar General. She said to give you a regular cut.

MALIEK: What's a regular cut?

RANDY: Let's call it a Even Steven.

MALIEK: That's the name of a show on the Disney Channel. . . . I want it bald.

RANDY: Your granma might punch me. Ready? Hold still.

MALIEK: What kind of clippers you usin'?

RANDY: Master Andis.

MALIEK: Will it cut me?

RANDY: (Laughs.) Not your skin. Just your hair.

MALIEK: Ouch! That hurts. Are you almost done?

RANDY: I just started. Hold your head down.

MALIEK: What's your name?

RANDY: They call me Pie.

MALIEK: Pie? Why they call you that?

RANDY: My granma gave me that name when I was little. 'Cause I like pie.

MALIEK: I was gonna say that. Ouch! Softer, please.

RANDY: Okay.

MALIEK: Are you done?

RANDY: Almost. But you have to stop movin'. (Maliek flinches again.) Tell you what. I'll use a softer pair of clippers. (Randy pretends to change clippers.)

MALIEK: Will those hurt me?

RANDY: These here aren't gonna hurt at all.

MALIEK: Ouch! After this, are you done? (Phone rings.)

RANDY: Bet that's your grandma right there, checkin' to see if you sittin' still.

MALIEK: How you know?

RANDY: I'm just messin'. I don't think it's her.

MALIEK: (Smiles.) I don't, either. Are you going to give me something special when you're done?

RANDY: Yeah, I'm gonna pick you up and give you a body slam.

"Softer, please." Randy gives Maliek an Even Steven.

MALIEK: (Laughs.) I'd rather have some candy. Ouch! Softer, please.

RANDY: Just let me get around the ears.

MALIEK: (Laughs.) That tickles.

RANDY: Okay, done. Come on here and get some candy. (Randy cleans Maliek up, then removes the lid from a can.)

MALIEK: What kind is it?

RANDY: The free kind. Take two. (Maliek takes a fistful.) I said two. (Maliek takes three.) I said *two*. (Maliek takes two. Randy smiles.) Here come your granma.

MALIEK: *Where?* (Maliek sprints to the door to greet his grandmother.)

RANDY: (To no one in particular.) I used to be like that. I *loved* my granma.

MALIEK: (Turns to Randy.) Will you be here next time?

RANDY: God willin'.

"That tickles."

Arlandor Davidson 35, Barber

It's a long day when you're cutting kids. That's why most barbers don't want to bother with them. Plus, kids can't tip.

✄ Arlandor Davidson

When a kid sees a barber in a white smock, he thinks of the doctor's office. He thinks he's gonna be poked and prodded with cold instruments and pricked with needles. So it ain't easy getting him in the chair. And when you do, he kicks and screams and fusses up a storm. Even when we changed the color of our smocks to burgundy, the kids felt it was the same scenario: this big man is gonna do something to me that's gonna hurt. One little boy, Matthew, Jr., when he was about eighteen months old he was so afraid of a haircut that he did a somersault out of the booster seat. He launched like a rocket. I froze. I just stood there holding my clippers and a comb. His father, who was standing next to the chair trying to calm Junior down, he froze, too. Fortunately, another barber was walking by and actually caught Junior in midair. If he hadn't, Junior might have cracked his head. I was working with some barbers who had decades of experience, but none of them had ever seen a kid spring from the chair like that. They all said it would never happen again, but I thought about installing a seat belt.

It's a long day when you're cutting kids. That's why most barbers don't want to bother with them. Plus, kids can't tip. The price of the haircut is cheaper, too, so you make less from the jump. That's why your rookie barber gets stuck with kids. I'm not a rookie anymore, but I still cut kids because I enjoy it. You get a special feeling from them. They can't

*Steal away: Mr. Jay tries to coax
a young client into a haircut.*

pronounce my first name, so I have them call me "Mr. Jay." Over the years, I've learned some tricks that make it better for the kids . . . and for Mr. Jay.

I have one three-year-old customer named Micah. The only way to cut Micah's hair is to constantly feed him. I used to give him candy, but now his mother brings in a bag of snacks. He wants some Goldfish crackers, then he wants some drink, then he wants some candy, then he wants more drink, then he wants some fruit snacks, then he wants more drink. When he's full, he thinks it's time to go. But with all the stopping to un-wrap stuff and the digging in bags and the eating and the swal-lowing drink, I'm only halfway done.

You'd think he'd be chunky, but Micah's a little bitty guy. His mom says he doesn't eat until he comes to the barber shop. I tried to cut his hair without the snacks one time. It took me about an hour and a half. We went back to feeding him.

I cut more kids' hair than anybody in the shop. I do about twenty or thirty a week. They call me the kiddie barber. That's been my calling card since I started. One Saturday, a man was waiting for a haircut and my chair was open. The man looked at me funny. He said, "Can you cut adults' hair?"

I have one customer, I started cutting his hair when he was eight. He's twenty-one now. I cut him *and* his son. I have quite a few customers like that. That's what most barbers don't realize about cutting kids. When they get older, they keep coming back. You make a customer for life.

Kwame Bandele 39, Customer

I was accustomed to silence during a haircut, but Mr. Wallace's barber ran his mouth like a marathon.

 Kwame Bandele

When I was a kid, a haircut was a pain. I grew up in Morgan Park, a black, working-class neighborhood on the south side of Chicago. On Saturdays, my father would give my three brothers and me haircuts, always in age order. I was the youngest so I was last. Dad had served in the army, so when it was your turn for a haircut he would call your name. Loud and hard. And *once.*

Dad would take an old shirt or a sheet and drape it around your neck like an apron. He never said much while he cut. He let his scissors do the talking. I always thought Dad cut our hair too short, but he didn't take requests. I wanted to wear my hair long as Jimi Hendrix's, the rock star who my brother David idolized. But Dad hated Afros more than he hated rock.

I've got a school picture from the second grade, when Dad let me wear my hair a little longer. When I got to school that day, I picked my hair out to make it look even longer. But it only looked messy and I was sad. You can see it in my face.

I was five or six when I saw the inside of a barber shop for the first time. I think the shop was called Midget's. Mr. Wallace, our neighbor, was babysitting me and his son, Nukey, who was my age. Mr. Wallace took us to the barber shop with him, although only he got a haircut. Mr. Wallace owned a motorcycle. He drove us in his car, of course, but his motorcycle made him my hero. He and his wife were younger than my parents. Mrs. Wallace wore lipstick and I remember watching her paint her toenails red one time. I just thought that was *amazing.* My parents were members of the

Church of God in Christ, and COGIC women weren't allowed to wear "the Devil's paint."

When we got to the barber shop, I was surprised at how small it was. My mother used to drive past it on the way to the savings and loan, but I had never been inside. There were four or five chairs for waiting customers, but Nukey and I stood near the front window.

I was accustomed to silence during a haircut, but Mr. Wallace's barber ran his mouth like a marathon. He was upset about a local protest over the Vietnam war or something. Maybe it was about the riot at the Democratic National Convention, which was held in Chicago in '68. I don't remember. All I know is that the barber got very agitated and, as he spoke, he was stabbing the air with his clippers. Mr. Wallace would just nod his head as the barber fumed on and on and on.

The barber said things like: "What's got into these young kids? Runnin' round, lookin' like fools. Can't get no respect that way. Know what they need? They need a haircut and a shave. Now *that's* how you get respect. Get yourself a haircut and a shave. *Then* somebody might listen. A hot bath wouldn't hurt, either. Nobody cares what they're sayin' with all that hippy hair. You can't change nothin' out there marchin' no way. Ain't no *big* mystery. You want somebody to pay you some mind, get a haircut and a shave."

I was so scared because the barber seemed so angry. I turned to Nukey and asked, "Does he want us to get a haircut and a shave?"

That experience put me off barber shops. But I didn't like my father cutting my hair, either. For a long time, I associated a haircut with harsh discipline. I couldn't figure out why barbers made hair such a big issue.

Kwame pouts over his "do" in 1972.

Tony Parker 48, **Barber**

There was a white man from the state who'd come through every now and then. He made sure no one was cutting without a license. Daddy would take him on down to the wood-pile and give him some white likker and he'd go on 'bout his business.

✂ Tony Parker

I was eight years old when I started cuttin'. My first customer was a man named Irving. I stood on a wooden soda crate to reach his head. Actually, I was so short I had to stand on two crates. Irving would let you practice on him so he could get a free haircut. Hair-cuts weren't but fifty cents, but Irving didn't have no money. Never knew him to work. Could lay a job at his feet, he wouldn't pick it up. He was one *lazy* man. When half his roof collapsed, he didn't fix it. He just moved to the other side of the house. Now *that's* lazy.

But Irving sat still while I cut him bald. That's how Daddy started me out, with bald heads. Then I moved up to a Julius Caesar, which is even all over. Then I did an En-glish, which ain't nothin' but a Fade today. Then I moved up to a Hustler, which is short on the sides with a little more on top.

Daddy was a barber. He owned a shop since 1939, but he stopped cuttin' in 1945—soon as my big brothers were old enough to work. All nine of my brothers ahead of me were barbers. We lived on a dirt road off highway 109, north of little Mount Gilead. The road didn't even have a name. Our postal address was Route 3, Box 329. The shop was in a little building right next to our house. We had some good

Tony outside the shop

times in that place. In the country, you opened the barber shop on weekends only. When we got out of school on Fridays, we opened from about four to nine. We opened again Saturday morning, from eight in the morning till nine at night. Sometimes Daddy made us open at seven on Sunday morning to cut Buck Collins, the local police, and Hubert Ellerbee, a hustler. They were big shots who didn't want to wait with everybody else on Friday and Saturday. But we started charging them five bucks and that broke that up.

We had three barber chairs. People came from all the nearby towns: Troy, Exway, Peedee. They'd talk or play checkers till their turn came. Some wanted to play cards, but Daddy didn't allow that.

Some of Tony's big brothers in 1954, taken the month Tony was born (the building on the right was the family's barber shop)

If customers got hungry they could go in back and get chicken dinners, fish dinners, hot dogs, chitlin sandwiches, pies, cakes, all that kind of stuff. Lord have *mercy* it was good! We had a little woodstove back there and some tables and chairs where people could sit down and eat. But we didn't have no toilet. If you had some business to do, you went out in the woods.

I ran the shop when I was in the tenth grade, but I wanted to play football. Daddy said, "The barber shop opens at four o'clock on Fridays. If you can play football *and* open the shop at the same time, you go ahead." Now, what you think I did? I didn't have a barber's license back then. None of us did. We weren't nothing but kids. There was a white man from the state who'd come through every now and then. He made sure no one was cutting without a license. Daddy would take him on down to the woodpile and give him some white likker and he'd go on 'bout his business.

When I was eighteen, I went to barber school to get a license. But the day I enrolled I was *already* a barber. Had been since I was eight.

Hair
Cutups

Omar Rasul 25, Barber

Majority of the time, clients don't come to the barber shop for a haircut. Not really. They come 'cause it's therapy. It's therapy for us barbers, too. You can make fun of your reality. . . . It's relaxing to laugh.

✂ **Omar Rasul**

The barber in the chair next to me calls me a hairy-back animal. Says I have hair for skin. If a client asks for me when I'm out, he says, "He's out chasin' rabbits." Or "He ran up the tree to get a nut."

That barber has a big nose. I'll tell him, "You worse off than Pinocchio. At least he had to tell a lie for his nose to grow."

We go at it in the shop. We have "cut down" sessions. You target a person's flaw and roll with it. It's all about making people bust out laughing.

Since my name is Omar, they call me Osama's brother. One time a client asked one of the barbers, "How does it feel to work next to a terrorist?" The barber said, "It's cool. Omar know where all the oil products at."

There's a girl in the shop, she has two babies. People be like, "Careful when you walk past her. If you bump into her she'll get pregnant." Or like, "Man, she's like a flower. She get pregnant out of the air."

Majority of the time, clients don't come to the barber shop for a haircut. Not really. They come 'cause it's therapy. It's therapy for us barbers, too. You can make fun of your reality. It's good to get away from being so serious all the time. It's relaxing to laugh.

Like, some mothers bring their kids in looking any kind of way.

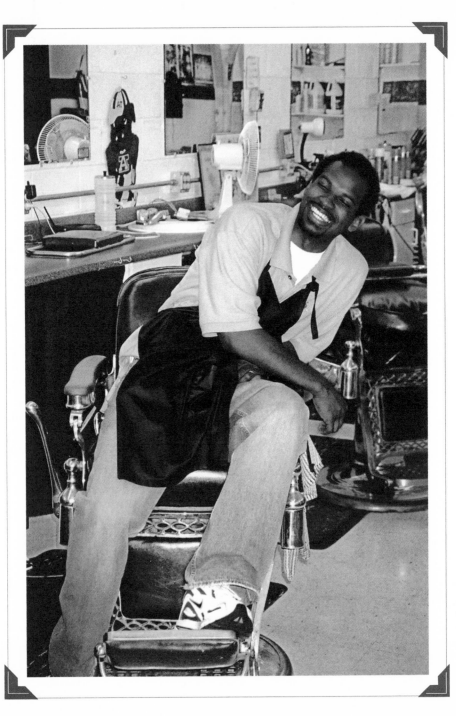

We talk about the mothers bad. One time, a woman had her little girl in a funny-looking terry cloth dress. The girl was about two or three and the outfit looked like it was made for fourteen months. It was way too small. We unloaded on her.

"Why you dress that child like that? She look like a stripper in trainin'."

"Somebody need to call Child Welfare on you. That ain't enough cloth to blow your nose."

"We gonna take up a collection for you. Pass the plate, y'all."

Actually, we did take up a collection. It's good to give a little blessing away, even if you do give somebody a hard time.

That little girl caught on. She spoke out for herself. She said, "Shut up, watermelon heads." Children are just little adults. Sometimes they're the funniest ones in the shop.

In a cut down session, it ain't a whole lot of lines drawn. But we chill out if someone starts to get offended. If they get offended, we don't talk about them till they leave. Like the dude who wears a Shag still. The Shag went out in the '80s, but older guys hold on. They'd rather go down with the *Titanic* than jump on a new boat. When Mr. Shag leaves, people tell his barber, "Man, you ought to charge him more. A Shag is like three cuts in one: an Afro, a Fade, and a Taper all mixed up." But don't nobody talk about the older dudes to their face. They'll go out to their El Dorado and get a gun. They're not into fighting, but they *will* shoot you.

It's always something going on. Naw, sometimes *nothing's* going on. Sometimes we just *look* at each other and bust out laughing.

Omar busts up.

Clarence Richmond III 32, Barber

In our shop, everybody feels like family. But families don't always get along.

✂ **Clarence Richmond III**

I can tell when America is at war by reading the day's receipts. If they're off more than half, something's goin' on. Our shop is near Fort Bragg Army Base and Pope Air Force Base. We do a lot of what we call military cuts: your High and Tight, which is fairly close to the skin coming up to the crown of the head; your Medium Taper, which is almost like a Fade but not as well defined; your Brush Cut, which is even all over. But sometimes what we do the most is repair work. There are two or three barber shops on post, and those military barbers can't cut to save their lives.

Happens all the time: a soldier walks in and says, "Man, I just got my hair cut on post. Can you fix it?" His Fade will be all lopsided. His edges will be crooked. I'll say, "He *sho* messed you up." One guy was supposed to have a Medium Taper, but it was clean on the sides with a patch of hair sittin' on top like one of those Chia Pets. He said, "I can't go off base this weekend looking like this." I tried not to laugh. Yeah, we do a lot of fixin'.

I can't believe barbers let those guys out of their chairs looking like that. But on post it's all about speed. One soldier told me what it's like: "You sit down, the barber turns the chair a couple of times and, *bam*, you're through." He said, "I ain't used to gettin' kicked out the chair like that. That's premature ejection."

What a military barber doesn't understand is that a man wants more than a haircut. He wants some . . . some back-home atmosphere. But on post, it's strictly business. They don't talk, they don't debate, they don't

A slow day during the War in Iraq in 2003

laugh, they don't *nothin'!* You just sit in the barber chair and you're out in three to five minutes. But in our shop, something's always going on.

One time a soldier came to pick up his boots. We cut hair and spit-shine boots. The guy had lost his ticket so I asked him what type of boots they were. The guy in line behind him was with the 82nd Airborne. He was impatient so he butted in. He said, "They're F-in' *leg* boots." The first guy said, "Yeah, that's right. I'm a leg. And I'm proud of it." A "leg" is any-one who isn't a paratrooper. Then the leg said, "But they ain't *leg* boots, they're basic-issue boots." The paratrooper kind of laughed and said, "Legs are cowards. You're just afraid of heights." The leg said, "I ain't afraid. I'm smart. Why would anyone jump out of a perfectly good airplane?" The paratrooper said, "Because he gets paid to do it." The leg said, "Paid? Shoot, ain't enough gold in your teeth to make me jump." The paratrooper said, "Like I said, legs are cowards." The leg said, "I just don't see the point. Floatin' like a leaf, landin' in trees and stuff. I heard about that guy who got caught in the wind and landed in Sanford, twenty miles up Highway 87. Missed the target zone by several towns. I can hear him on the pay phone now, 'Hey, can y'all send a leg to pick me up?' "

It didn't lead to anything. They were just having fun. But that conversation would never have happened in a barber shop on post. That's why soldiers like to come here. They want that happy atmosphere. It reminds them of their barber shops at home. In our shop, everybody feels like family. But families don't always get along.

John Moning and Pat Spencer
Customer, 70, and Barber (who insists she's 39)

The difference between scissors and clippers is like the difference between a knife and a blender. You wouldn't stick your head in a blender, would you?

✄ — John Moning

JOHN: I moved to Dallas back in '61. I'm from Oakwood, a little Texas town. When I met Pat, she was dirt poor. Didn't have nothin' but a boot and a shoe.

PAT: Quit tellin' that lie.

JOHN: A boot and shoe. When the heels got run down, she switched up and wore them on the wrong feet.

PAT: You a mess.

JOHN: She was a skinny thing. Had a skinny little French poodle, too. What was that dog's name?

PAT: Cocoa.

JOHN: Cocoa. That dog wasn't big enough to make a sandwich.

PAT: Just quit.

JOHN: What people want with a dog? I don't need nothin' that's gonna sit down and watch me leave for work. Everything in my house that eats, works. But Pat don't think that way 'cause she don't work much herself.

PAT: Say what?

JOHN: Don't do nothin' but sleep.

PAT: I work *every* day.

JOHN: That's true. But how *long* you work? She'll come in at eleven, take lunch at twelve, go home to nap, and don't come back. Tell you what, Pat

Pat and John go way back.

may leave work hungry, but she won't leave tired. And I don't know how she'll leave this world, but I know hard work won't kill her.

PAT: I ain't studyin' you.

JOHN: How long you been cuttin' my hair? Since '77 ... '78?

PAT: No, I didn't even have my license in '78 ...

JOHN: Oh, oh, oh! Now you shavin' years off ...

PAT: ... so how could I be cuttin' hair since '78? ...

JOHN: ... shavin' 'em off like nappy hair.

PAT: 'Sides, I ain't but thirty-nine.

JOHN: Thirty *what?*

PAT: Thirty-*nine.*

JOHN: ... Okay, Pat. Maybe you right. I was drinkin' a lot of Crown Royal back then. Anyhow, I been gettin' the same haircut most my life. Ain't nothin' changed but the price. Used to cost thirty-five cents. But back then a loaf of bread cost a nickel.

PAT: That's right.

JOHN: How you know? You weren't born yet.... You know, I used to didn't believe in letting a woman cut my hair. Pat was the first. She gonna do it right, but she gonna do it her way ... which is slow. *Real* slow.

PAT: That's 'cause I use scissors, not clippers.

JOHN: The difference between scissors and clippers is like the difference between a knife and a blender. You wouldn't stick your head in a blender, would you? Pat's old school. These here young barbers ain't used scissors since kindergarten. But, look here, it's gonna take her a while. If she charged by the hour, I'd be broke.... Pat, what ever happened to that dog?

PAT: Cocoa? Got old. Died.

JOHN: Oh.... But *you* ain't aged a day. Thirty-nine and holdin'.

Lance Dalton 23, Barber

**Don't nobody
want to lose a
crack session.
So if somebody
throw a crack at
you in the barber
shop, you gotta
crack back. If you
can't crack, you
gonna get chumped
on _all_ the time.**

✂ **Lance
Dalton**

Don't nobody want to lose a crack session. So if somebody throw a crack at you in the barber shop, you gotta crack back. If you can't crack, you gonna get chumped on *all* the time. Know what I'm sayin'? But if you learn how to crack, everything's gonna be all right. That's what I've learned.

Best thing to do is have a nickname for all the barbers. That's a instant crack. The guy in the first chair at my old shop, we called him Motor Booty. He was always movin'. That dude, he could walk from the barber shop to the post office to the laundromat before he finished sayin' he'd be right back. He had some long legs and when he walked it was like he was runnin'. But, hey, if you can't be fast about removin' yourself, you gonna get run over. Know what I'm sayin'?

Me and my home boy, Ramón, we came up with a song about Motor Booty. It go:

> *Get down on it,*
> *Motor Booty.*

That's it. We kept it simple. When you crack, you got to get your laugh and keep on movin'.

There was one barber I called Pig Pen. He was always dingy and wrinkled. He wore Nikes that he found in a trash can. He was like, "Yo, man, these some good shoes." I was lookin' at him and I was like, "But you got them out the trash can. And plus they *thirty-eights.*"

That's what we call regular Nikes. When I was growin' up, we went *bang! bang!* when we saw a guy in thirty-eights. Thirty-eights ain't like three fifty-sevens. Those are your Air models: you got your Air Jordans,

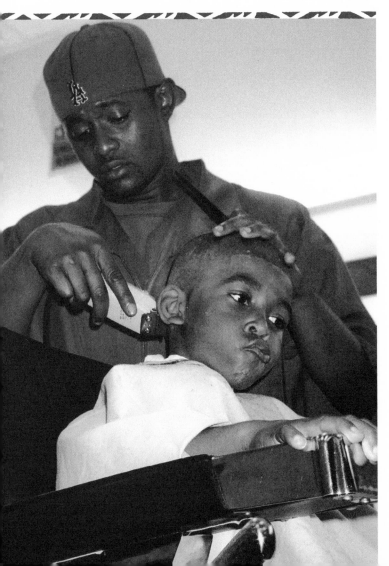

A buzzing in the ears

you got your Air Hardaways, you got your Air Max. They can cost you a couple hundred dollars, which is why I ain't got none. Know what I'm sayin'? Thirty-eights ain't the max but they ain't like twenty-twos, either. That's like your Puma. Below that, you got your Derringers. That's shoes so low you better off barefoot: like thirty-eights you pull out the trash can.

There was another barber I called End Zone. You seen those wreckin' balls that be knockin' down buildings? End Zone's head was big as a wreckin' ball. But there wasn't much in it. He was in his own world. Everybody else was runnin' plays on the field, but he was lost out in the end zone. Know what I'm sayin'? We could be talkin' 'bout a Camero and he'd start talkin' 'bout a Corvette. Yeah, a Corvette is a car, but it ain't the car we were talkin' 'bout. That was End Zone. We'd set the subject, and he'd change it.

If a pretty female walked by the window, one of the barbers would go, *Whoop, whoop!* All of us knew to look up. Except End Zone. Actually, I think he knew. I think he knew a lot, but he pretended like he didn't. You can get away with a lot when people don't expect much from you.

There was another barber I called Hot Head. We didn't mess with him too much. He got mad. But he wasn't supposed to get mad. Crackin' help the day go by. It's all good. Anyway, anger is a sign of weakness. Know what I'm sayin'?

They cracked on me, too. They called me Baby Boy. I was the youngest in the shop. The energizer. Into everything. Sometimes I could go too far, say too much. But a barber supposed to be real, straight up.

The owner of the shop didn't have a nickname. We didn't chump on him like that. He controled the money. I'm Baby Boy, but I ain't no fool. Know what I'm sayin'?

D'Clarence Reynolds 50, Barber Shop Owner

Hustlers come up with some <u>good</u> stories. There's one guy who always finds some suits or watches that just fell off a truck or something. I tell him, "You must be the luckiest joker in the world. Doors always just fly open on trucks right in front of you."

✄ **D'Clarence Reynolds**

My barber shop is in the heart of downtown Detroit, near the intersection of Randolph and Monroe. We see some of *everything* around here. One day, a man decided to relieve his bladder in our doorway. I tossed a bucket of water on him so he'd know how the doorway feels. Some people walk by looking shell-shocked, like they've just lost their house gambling around the corner at the casino in Greektown. And one day a drunk white guy stumbled in and said, "Do you remember where I parked my car?" I said, "No, sir, I don't. And I hope you don't, either."

Looking out the front window of my shop is like watching a big-screen TV. Only difference is there's no remote. Can't change the channel. Some real characters roll in here. They try to run all kinds of hustles, so sometimes I bait them. One time a guy said, "My car broke down on the freeway. All I need is a couple of dollars to get some gas."

"Which is it? Did you break down or did you run out of gas?"

"Both. All I need is a couple of dollars for gas so I can drive to a mechanic."

"Okay, have a seat."

"Well, I'm in a hurry. My wife's in the car."

"Why didn't you bring her with you?"

"She's pregnant."

"You left a pregnant woman on the freeway?"

"Somebody had to watch the camcorders and VCRs."

"The what?"

"I got a bunch of camcorders and VCRs in the U-Haul. Anybody need one?"

"U-Haul? I thought you were driving a car?"

"Yeah, the U-Haul's hitched to the car."

"Do you want to use the phone to call U-Haul?"

"No, man, if they see all those high-end electronics, they might ask questions. All I need is five or ten dollars to get me off the freeway. If you help me, I'll give you somethin' off the truck."

"Oh, so now it's a truck?"

"You know what I'm sayin'."

"Yeah, I know. I know you must think this is my first night out."

We don't allow the sale of stolen goods on the property, so hustlers come up with some *good* stories. There's one guy who always finds some suits or watches that just fell off a truck or something. I tell him, "You must be the luckiest joker in the world. Doors always just fly open on trucks right in front of you." Now we just stop that guy at the door. Before he can open his mouth I say, "Is that something you can sell over at 1300 Beaubein?" That's the address of the police station.

Hustlers come to the barber shop for the captive audience. They like the odds. It's better than trying to scam people one at a time on the street. We get 'em all. It's like they have a franchise, like Toys 'R Us. But theirs is We Be Slick.

No hustlers allowed

James RaeFord 68, Barber Shop Owner

I used to make up things in the barber shop, just to keep the day movin'. If things went dead, I'd bring 'em back to life with a whopper.

✂ **James RaeFord**

Growin' up in eastern Carolina, we saw a lot of hurricanes. One time this guy was sittin' on his bed, talkin' to his girl on the telephone. Storm roared through and blew his house off the foundation. Next thing he knew, he was sittin' on his bed out in the woods. And, look here, the bed was on top of a tree. And the phone was *still* in his hand. He told his girl he had to call her back.

That's the kind of tall tales I used to tell when I was a young barber. Mr. Potts, the owner, would say, "RaeFord, come on, man." I'd say, "Hey, that's a true story." His son Mickey would say, "Man, you need to quit."

I used to make up things in the barber shop, just to keep the day movin'. If things went dead, I'd bring 'em back to life with a whopper. Mickey told his father, "Daddy, one day lightnin' is gonna strike RaeFord up in here and kill us all." One time, I went to dry this guy's hair and when I turned the drier on it shot fire. There was a loud explosion and flames were blowin' instead of hot air. I dropped the drier and Mickey said, "See, Daddy, I told you lightnin' was gonna strike RaeFord one day."

Wasn't lightnin'. That drier shorted out because the cord got twisted. That happened to a lot of my clippers and driers. I had the tendency to tangle my cords up bad. I had my Oster, a heavier clipper for thicker hair. I had a Wahl, a intermediate-size clipper. And I had two Andis trimmers.

Course, I had a hair drier, too. Cords everywhere. And all of them were about eight feet long. They'd tangle up if I looked at 'em wrong.

Course, all of us had problems with our cords. But mine were the worst. Mickey always teased me. Said I was gonna break my neck or get electrocuted. He teased me so bad that I came home and put my mind to it. There had to be a way make it neater, safer.

Some barbers keep their clippers in a drawer. But cords tangle up in the drawer, too. So I was thinkin' of a way to store the cords, a way to roll 'em up. Those old-timey window shades came to mind, how they rolled up and down. You don't see those kind anymore. Venetian blinds took over. But we used to have those draw shades all over the house. I kinda went

from there. I talked to an engineer about a roller in a box that would retract the cords, just like those old-timey blinds. He did a drawing and made a prototype. I got a patent on it. The prototype is being tweaked in China right now. Wanna get all the bugs out.

When you tell tall tales like I used to tell, your mind is always spinnin'. Deep down, you're thinkin', *How can I make this story work?* Well, it's the same thing with an invention. That takes imagination, too. I guess makin' stuff up is just my nature.

James reels 'em in.

What a Fellowship!

Reverend John C. McClurkin 53, Customer

You know, the barber shop is tantamount to the dinner table. . . . Except nobody's trying to hide their vegetables.

✂ Rev. John C. McClurkin

I've often wondered if men go to the barber shop on the same day and time out of habit. Or do we go because we want to run into the same crowd each week? If you go to the barber shop on, say, Thursday between ten and eleven, pretty much that same core group will be there week after week. So then you develop these bonds, sometimes with men you only know by face, not by name. I've had long, rolling conversations with the same men in my barber shop—over a span of fifteen or twenty years. And I would venture to say that every time I preach I talk about something I heard in the barber shop. The barber shop is my link to the community.

I'm the kind of preacher who wants my sermon to be applicable to life today. You know, we can spend forever talking about how Delilah revealed Samson's secret: that his strength lay in his uncut hair. But if I can't break that story down to a level where it applies to daily life, then I've failed. I like to deal with issues that people are struggling with.

One day we were talking about entrepreneurship in the barber shop, about having the willingness to sacrifice, about the fortitude to struggle, about the faith to make something happen. So when I was invited to Evangel Fellowship Church of God in Christ, I preached. I preached about tools. I preached about the tools we can use to unlock doors, the doors to our blessings.

*Rev. McClurkin, with dyed hair,
preaches the "starter's pistol" sermon.*

I brought some props with me: a padlock, a crowbar, a hammer, and a starter's pistol, which shoots blanks, not bullets. I wanted to get across that I believe in the American dream. I believe we all can have a piece of the pie. But I also believe you have to put faith in action, you have to go out and make things happen, you have to work hard to unlock the doors to your blessings.

When the pastor of Evangel, my good friend Otis Lockett, saw the starter's pistol he said, "Now, Elder, you're not going to fire that gun are you?" I said, "Yeah, I want to drive home a point." He said, "Man, don't shoot that gun in my church. Somebody's heart might stop." I said, "I've got to fire it." He said, "No, you don't." I said, "Lockett, I'm shooting this thing so leave me alone." But when I pulled the trigger in the middle of my message, the pistol wouldn't fire. I pulled the trigger again. It still wouldn't fire. I pulled it *again*. Still wouldn't fire. After the service, Lockett explained what happened. He said, "I prayed, '*Lord*, don't let that gun fire in my church.'"

And as soon as I got outside, I pulled the trigger again, and it fired.

I preached that sermon about seven years ago. That was back when I used to have my hair dyed to hide the gray. My barber would cut my hair, dye it, wash it—all in one sitting. Some customers looked upset because I'd tie up the chair for about an hour. I always felt bad about it, but my barber would say, "The man in the chair has my *undivided* attention. He ain't done till he's done."

You know, the barber shop is tantamount to the dinner table. The dinner table is the forum for family members to share their lives with one another, to enjoy fellowship. Well, in the barber shop you have that same dynamic at work. Except nobody's trying to hide their vegetables.

Damian Johnson 30, Barber Shop Owner

The name of our shop is "No Grease!" Our logo is a character in black face. . . . Some people say we shouldn't dig up those buried symbols of racism. But we're making a statement: no more shufflin', no more tap dancin', no more grease or gel or chemicals.

✄ **Damian Johnson**

There's one customer I'll never forget. He looked like he was in his early forties, but the man was in rough shape. His left eye was missing, and he didn't wear a patch. Just an empty socket staring at you. There was a big scar on the left side of his neck. The edges of the scar looked like fat staples. His front teeth were chipped and rotting away. I knew he was abusing drugs because that's what happens to your teeth. He was dressed like a house painter. He had on old work shoes and overalls that were splattered with all colors of paint.

I met him on Thanksgiving about four years ago. When I walked in the shop, my brother was finishing him up. When the man reached for his pocket, my brother said, "Don't worry about it. Happy Thanksgiving." The man got excited. "Praise God! Thank you, brother. Thank you." We exchanged names and he was about to leave. But something about him moved me. I dug in my pocket and gave him all the cash I had. My brother did the same thing. We didn't count it. We just gave it to him.

Two weeks later, a man in a suit came in. He had a tie on and the whole nine. It was a brown suit, but the jacket and pants were different

Damian (right) and his twin, Jermaine, sport t-shirts bearing their barber shop's controversial logo.

shades. And he had a Bible in his hands. I said, "Good to see you again, Gary." He looked pleased that I remembered his name. He said he just wanted to come by and share how God had used me and my brother to be a blessing to him on Thanksgiving.

The thing that's unique about Gary is his voice. It's like thunder. It commands attention. So everyone in the shop listened.

Gary said he grew up in Grier Town, the bad section of Charlotte. They called him Boss. He said he had been strung out on drugs for over twenty-three years. He said how he confronted two drug dealers on his block one night. They beat him down with a broomstick. One of the blows poked his eye out. Another time, a drug dealer shot him in the back with a sawed-off shotgun. Some of the buckshot hit Gary in the neck. Surgeons had to slice him up to remove the pellets. He said, "I been through everything but death. Ain't afraid of nobody but the Lord."

By that time, Shonda had come in. She's a stylist in the beauty shop next door. She had heard Gary's voice booming and she sat down to listen. Gary started talking about Thanksgiving. He said when he counted up the money we gave him, it was a couple of hundred dollars. Then he started preaching from the book of Job. He talked about Job's trials and tribulations, and how his friends had turned their backs on him, but how God blessed him double for his troubles—like we had blessed him. Shonda was weeping. And so was a customer who came in for a haircut. Gary took their hands and began to pray with them. They found salvation that day.

The name of our shop is "No Grease!" Our logo is a character in black face. Not everybody thinks it's on point. Some people say we shouldn't dig up those buried symbols of racism. But we're making a statement: no more shufflin', no more tap dancin', no more grease or gel or chemicals. We need to love who we are and move forward. That's what we're about.

Before he left that day, Gary said, "This is no ordinary barber shop." We liked it so much we started using it in our marketing: "No Grease! This is no ordinary barber shop."

Alexander "Bug" Parker, Jr. 41, Barber and Mortician

Since way back, black people have gathered in two locations to share news: the church and the barber shop. And you'd be surprised how fast news travels <u>all</u> through town that way.

✂ **Alexander "Bug" Parker, Jr.**

Most people don't know that hair keeps growing days after you die. It feeds on the protein in the body's cells. That's why a man's corpse usually needs a shave and a touch-up. Most people don't know that, either. *I* know because I'm a barber *and* a mortician. I cut hair for twenty years before it occurred to me: *What am I going to do when I get old and have migraines in my feet?* That's when I decided to go to mortician school. When I prepare a body, I always ask the deceased's regular barber to do the final haircut. He knows what look to go after. But it *ain't* easy getting barbers to come into the funeral home. They come up with all kinds of excuses. First it's, "Give me an hour." Then it's, "I'm on the other side of town, but I'm on my way." Or, "I'll be through there first thing tomorrow." Tomorrow never comes.

The ones who do show up are a little jittery. One said, "I hear that dead people take their last breath. Has he done that yet?" Or they might say, "His eyes are closed, right?" Or, "Well, what if he sits up? He won't sit up, will he?" One barber said, "What if the body falls off the table?" I said, "*Man*, he ain't gonna fall off that table. But you gonna help me pick him up if he do." You just have to laugh sometimes.

One time, I was in the preparation room while a barber was cutting his old client. I said, "I have to go to the bathroom but I'll be right back." I was halfway down the hall when I turned around and the barber was right there with me. They're something else. A barber can know a client most of his life, but not want to be in the same room with him after he dies.

I try to give the barbers a few tips. I say, "The right side of the face is called the "show" side. When people approach an open casket, it's the right side they see. So you want the right side to be on point." I try to make them relax, too. I say, "Live customers can sneeze, cough, nod off, turn to see who's coming in the door. But you don't have to worry about that. He ain't moving."

Alexander
on the clock
at the funeral home

"Bug" cuts up at the barber shop.

The odd thing for most barbers is having to wear the surgical gloves before working on a corpse. It's like putting gloves on a pianist. Barbering is an art and an artist has got to feel his tools. He's got to touch his work. Your eyes are one thing, but you want to feel the hum of the clippers in your fingers.

I'm in the funeral home most days, but I still have a few good clients who prefer for me to take care of them. So every opportunity I get, I go over to the barber shop. In there, everybody calls me Bug.

I love the barber shop. It's like my stage. People know I'm gonna get something going. And I look forward to the fellowship. Since *way* back, black people have gathered in two locations to share news: the church and the barber shop. And you'd be surprised how fast news travels *all* through town that way.

When I'm in the funeral home, I always have to wear a face of concern, of compassion. But in the barber shop I can be myself.

Marcques Tatum 23, Barber

Some boys from the projects came in one day. . . . They said, "Did you hear that our boy got robbed?" They said, "There's gonna be trouble. If you hear who did it, let us know." I was like, "I'm a barber. I don't know nuttin' but hair."

— Marcques Tatum

Some young cats from the projects just *love* the barber shop. They come and sit down like they in a lounge. I want to tell them, "If you don't want a haircut, y'all should come in and say, 'hey,' and be *out*." But I don't. Some of 'em got weapons . . . and no sense. You could have a killer sittin' in your chair and never know. But you can't think 'bout that. If you did, every head you cut would be whack.

The projects are right behind our shop, right across the tracks. Some boys from the projects came in one day. They said they had just jumped a dude, a kid who hustled drugs and liked to flash what he had—wanted people to know he got juice. When those boys left, another clique of boys came in. They said, "Did you hear that our boy got robbed?" So I was thinkin', *Oh, my goodness! Those guys just left.* But what came out of my mouth was, "For real? Is he okay? I hope he get right." They said, "There's gonna be trouble. If you hear who did it, let us know." I was like, "I'm a barber. I don't know nuttin' but hair."

Marcques rubs customer the right way.

I used to carry a gun, but I stopped. If I pulled a gun in here somebody could get hurt. I ain't tryin' to take nobody's life for tryin' to survive. They can take the cash. I can make more.

'Cause I'm so young, those boys look at me and want to be where I'm at. They see barberin' as a legitimate hustle. But they don't know how to get here. I tell them they got to stay in school. I'm like, "You got to try somethin' positive. Negative will always be waitin' on you."

Some people think I wear a do-rag to look all hard. But usually I wear it 'cause I need a haircut. A barber should always have a fresh cut. Or a do-rag to hide under. A reporter came and interviewed me about downtown development once. He put my picture in the paper. I had on my do-rag 'cause I didn't have time to get my hair right. I haven't sent the article to my grandma. Gram would be like, "Boy! What you down there doin'? Got that thing on yo head, lookin' *just* like a nigga."

I'm a barber, but I like to do music, too. Rap music. My rap name is Barber-Q. I'm workin' on a song:

It's in tha barber shop,
you can get that dough,
find wha ya need to know,
and get a cut fa sho.

It's in tha barber shop,
you can see new things,
find out people's dreams,
and you can flip that cream.

It's in tha barber shop,
they all know your name,
everybody is tha same,
it ain't about no game.
It's in tha barber shop.

Toni Mosley and Tracey Mosley
Customers, 46 and 43

TRACEY: People "download" a ton of information in the barber shop. If a doctor comes in, they'll ask for medical advice. If a real estate broker comes in, they'll ask about mortgage rates. . . .

TONI: . . . If a cop comes in, they'll ask if he can fix their tickets.

✂ **Toni Mosley and Tracey Mosley**

TONI: My husband and I were visiting Macon, Georgia, for a convention. . . . .

TRACEY: . . . And one night I said, "I need a haircut". . . .

TONI: . . . I said, "We live in Atlanta. How're you going to find a barber shop in Macon?"

TRACEY: And I said, "Same way I find one in any city. Just point me to Martin Luther King Drive . . . or Martin Luther King Boulevard . . . or Martin Luther King Avenue."

TONI: That's what he said.

TRACEY: When I was looking for a barber shop in Chicago, I asked for King Drive. In Philadelphia, I asked for King Drive. Augusta, King Drive.

TONI: And sure 'nough, we found our way to King Drive, turned left, and not two blocks later . . .

TRACEY: . . . There was a barber shop. That's how I found my barber here in Atlanta. I moved here from Knoxville, Tennessee, and when my hair got bushy, I looked for King Drive.

TONI: All the men in my family visit barbers here on Martin Luther King, too. My father, my brother—their barbers are all within three or four blocks.

TRACEY: And, wherever you go, barber shop conversation is always the same. Everything from world affairs to extramarital affairs.

TONI: In Macon, Tracey's barber was in his early thirties. He kept talking about all the kids he had by these different women...

TRACEY: ... His babies' mamas weren't actin' right....

TONI: ... It was like a soap opera.

TRACEY: The barber shop is also a forum for great debates.

TONI: Don't let there be a big trial in the news.

TRACEY: Guys in the shop know more about the Kobe Bryant rape case than the prosecutor and the defense team put together.

TRACEY: People "download" a ton of information in the barber shop. If a doctor comes in, they'll ask for medical advice. If a real estate broker comes in, they'll ask about mortgage rates...

TONI: ... If a cop comes in, they'll ask if he can fix their tickets.

TONI: And when local politics heat up, you'll hear everything. Insider information. Who's gonna run...

TRACEY: ... And who doesn't stand a chance.

TONI: The barber shop is a place where men can go and, across generations, hear each other talk about different issues. It's about relationships. People need places they can turn to, people they can count on.

TRACEY: ... That's the thing about black barber shops. They never change. They're anchors in the community. As long as a brother needs his "do" done, they're not going anywhere.

Waiting for Dad
(Tracey gets haircut in the background)

Willie Simmons, Jr. 59, Customer

There are three things I never want to change: my church, my wife, and my barber. A good relationship is a good relationship.

✂ **Willie Simmons, Jr.**

There are three things I never want to change: my church, my wife, and my barber. A good relationship is a good relationship.

I've been married going on thirty-five years. And I was a longtime member of El Bethel Baptist Church in Houston. I'd still be there if I hadn't relocated to Missouri City, Texas, about thirty minutes away. When you're attending night services and prayer meetings and Bible study, the drive gets to you. But I did it for thirteen years, driving back and forth to the Third Ward. My old barber has her shop there, too. Johnnie has been my barber for over thirty years.

Johnnie is a good barber and a good friend to me, like family. She's very encouraging. Always has positive things to say. She's just that kind of person. Every time I thought about finding a shop in my neighborhood, I felt... disloyal, unfaithful. One day, I was talking to Deacon Darby at my new church. I said, "Man, at my age, I need to stay close to home. Know a good barber?" He said, "There's a great shop right down the street from you. That's where I go." I said, "I'm not into all these young styles that look like carved wood. I'm looking for a barber who can cut an old man's hair." He said, "Ask for CB. He'll do you right."

Johnnie means so much to me that I felt guilty going to a new barber on that Saturday. When I walked in, CB greeted me kindly. He said he had six men waiting. I didn't mind. It gave me a chance to check out what kind of shop it was. I listened to the conversation.

Willie gets a trim.

The men were talking about the San Antonio Spurs and their chances in the playoffs. About Tiger Woods's slump. About the war with Iraq. It was a healthy conversation. Polite. Wholesome. I liked that. When I visit a barber shop, I don't like to hear a whole lot of garbage: girlfriend talk, nightclubbing, negative gossip. Yeah, men can gossip, now.

I didn't do any talking myself because I was a new customer. That's the way I was brought up. You don't jump in strangers' conversation. You could land on somebody's toes.

When I got in the chair, I told CB what I wanted. That felt odd because Johnnie always knew what I wanted. I wear the old Flat Top from years ago. Another thing I didn't have to tell Johnnie was to trim my mustache and eyebrows. Wild, gray hairs pop up there when you get old. They don't lay down flat with the others. I asked CB, "Do you mind taking the scissors to those wild hairs?" I wanted him to use the scissors because I wasn't sure how steady his hand was. If he messed up using clippers, I was still going to attend Sunday service, but I'd be praising the Lord with half an eyebrow. CB said, "I want you to trust me to use the clippers. I promise you I'll do a professional job." I said, "Go ahead on." And the man did a good job. I *am* going back. Think I've found a new home. But I feel uncomfortable about leaving my old one. I know it's a business, but I've been concerned about hurting Johnnie's feelings. I haven't told her yet. It's hard. There's a slash on my heart. Kinda like loving someone most of your life and then having to say good-bye. But I had to leave. Had to save time. Time is important to me now. You never know how much you have left.

All Shape Ups and Sizes

Reginald Attucks 54, Barber Shop Owner

The cop's gonna

come. The

preacher's gonna

come. The gansta's

gonna come. The

barber shop's the

one place where

you can put all the

wrong people at

the same time. It's

the final black

frontier.

✂ **Reginald
Attucks**

No matter your walk of life, you gonna come to the barber shop. The cop's gonna come. The preacher's gonna come. The gansta's gonna come. The barber shop's the one place where you can put all the wrong people at the same time. It's the final black frontier. It's the last public place black men can go to be separate.

I've been a barber for thirty-five years. Wanted to be one since I was in my teens, sporting a pompadour. And I ain't beating my chest when I say I am the consummate barber. My family has lived very large off barbering. But it's not about the money. It's about what I love to do. You *have* to love it to be good at it.

See, this job ain't just about skills. You got to know things. You got to know when a customer wants you to lift his spirits ... and when he wants you to shut your damn mouth. There's only one way to know that kind of thing. You have to be intimate with the customer.

A haircut is a personal thing, an intimate thing. That's because it involves touching. When you're in my chair, I'm on you. I don't mean touching the wrong way. Now, everybody's funny about a stranger touching them. But once a barber starts touching a customer, he breaks down a wall.

Reggie sports a pompadour in 1963.

You develop a comfort zone with me and I develop a comfort zone with you. It's almost like relations with a female. Once you're intimate with her, you gonna have some new conversations, some deeper conversations. That's if she liked it.

Now, on the other hand, some skilled barbers lose customers because they have no rapport. A man will think, *This guy gives me a good haircut, but it's somethin' about him I don't like. Know what? I don't want him touching me.* If you don't like me and I keep touching you, then you gonna feel like I'm forcing myself on you. I'm violating you now. I'm taking liberties.

But if we establish rapport, you start telling me things and I start telling you things. We share. Pretty soon, you don't think about no other barber but me. I might not even be that good no more, but you ain't gonna cheat on me. You ain't gonna leave me for another barber. I'm telling you, a haircut is an intimate thing.

Now, there are some customers you *don't* want to be intimate with. This guy walked in one day. When I went to comb out his hair, all kind of stuff fell out: dirt, lint, dandruff. Just looking at it made me itch. I asked him, "Hey, when's the last time you washed your hair?" He said, "Uh, my hand's messed up." I said, "Man, you can pay somebody three or four dollars to wash your hair." He said, "Well, you can go ahead and wash it." I said, "Wash it? I can't even *look* at it." Wouldn't cut his hair with another barber's clippers.

In my peak, I did as many as forty-five or fifty heads a day. But now I don't want to do no more than twenty-five or thirty. I'm comfortable with that. I've even gotten to the place where I don't really want to do walk-ins. I just want to do my regular customers, my steadies. See, if you don't know me, I got to prove myself. I don't feel the need to do that anymore. I'm done with courtin'.

John Sullivan 53, Customer

Coming up as a boy, my dad cut my hair. He'd give me a Bowl cut. When you're a child, it's no big deal looking like that. But when you start smellin' yourself, around fifteen or sixteen, that Bowl cut ain't gonna do it.

✄ John Sullivan

When it comes down to it, I'm a black man who needs a white man's haircut. Straight hair is all up in my bloodline. My great, great grandfather was white. My hair is too straight for electric clippers. Have to use scissors and thinning shears. All manual. And that's a dying art for black barbers.

What happens is my hair grows in so thick that a barber needs to thin some of it out so I can get it to lay down. Thinning out my hair takes time, twice as long as a normal haircut. The barber parts my hair, separates a small section, and pins down the rest with hair clips. Then he takes a special pair of shears that have staggered teeth, which take out only about a fourth of the hair between the blades. It's like pruning a tree. After he thins out my hair, he uses scissors to bring down the length.

I know only one black barber in my town who knows how to use thinning shears and scissors: Reggie Attucks. So I've stayed with him for more than thirty years, more than half my life. I don't know who else is out there. I'm afraid to look. White barbers, they know how to deal with my kind of hair. But I couldn't be who I am in a white shop. I'd have to sit there and shut up. Same thing with a beauty shop. I'm sure that black beauticians could cut my hair, but there again I'd

Black to the bone.
Reggie, without his pompadour,
thins out John's hair.

miss out on the barber shop atmosphere. In black barber shops you have the freedom to express yourself. We look at both sides of everything: religion, politics, race. Well, with race we leave the white man's side out of it.

Coming up as a boy, my dad cut my hair. He'd give me a Bowl cut. When you're a child, it's no big deal looking like that. But when you start smellin' yourself, around fifteen or sixteen, that Bowl cut ain't gonna do it.

So I started going to black barber shops. I'd sit down and explain what I wanted. I'd say, "Take it down some and thin some out. No clippers! You gotta use scissors. I know that's going to take longer. But look, man, take your time and do me a good job and I'll throw in an extra five dollars." They'd say, "Okay." But then they'd reach for the clippers and butcher me. I don't think they heard a word I said, except the part about the extra five dollars. And then, after they messed me up, they'd actually expect me to give it to them.

I didn't participate in the Afro era. My hair was long but it wouldn't stand up. I wore a big mustache and a chin beard. A sixties, sort of hippy look. I was all hair. Straight hair. And it didn't get me any more or any less women. Women like what they like. If they like a light-skinned man with straight hair, then they like a light-skinned man with straight hair. If they don't, they don't. Straight hair ain't gonna get you no more or no less. It's ladies' choice.

Some black people look at me a little different, like they're not sure what I am. But all my mannerisms and expressions are the same as theirs. I might look white to the eye, but I'm black to the bone. Guess I'm sort of a square peg in a round hole, but I force the fit.

I am who I am. And I'm not ashamed. I look like my father and, hey, I'm proud of him. I'm my father's son.

Jabreel Ali 29, Customer

Somebody asked me if I'd ever cut my dreads. Only for two reasons: for a really good corporate job . . . or if I start going bald. I won't be that guy who expects people to pretend like they don't notice.

✂ **— Jabreel Ali**

I got my first bit of facial hair when I was twenty-five. Four years later my barber says all I have is peach fuzz. My head, that's different. Hair grows on my head faster than weeds, which lets me experiment a lot.

I've had every hairstyle you can think of: Jheri curls, the Fade, the Flat Top—like Kid of Kid 'N Play used to wear—the Ramp, the Stair Step, the Bird, which is that slanted style like Bobby Brown used to wear. I've had a part down the left side, down the right side, but not down the middle. I've had so much graffiti cut into the back of my head that I could have been a billboard: my name, the Nike swoosh, the number ten—which was my number on the basketball team. You name it.

Actually, my hair grows so fast that I got tired of going to the barber shop. Eight months ago, I decided to grow dreadlocks. But if you want your dreads to look nice, it's a lot of work, too. When the new growth comes in, the scalp between your locks start to blacken, which looks pretty sloppy. Bob Marley wore the wilder looking dreads, but I like mine to look sharp. So at the salon they shampoo it and retwist it with a gel. Some people use beeswax. I go to a salon every two weeks to get my locks done.

And after all that, I *still* have to go the barber shop every week to get my edge up. The hair that grows around your ears and down your forehead, you want to get that sharpened out. But even if I wasn't getting my hair lined up, I would still hang out in the barber shop. See what's going on, who's doing what, who's doing who. It's like the news center.

There are a lot of myths about dreads. People think they are dirty and low maintenance. But the easiest thing to take care of is *no* hair. That's why they cut it off when you go into the army. That's the first thing they do.

Somebody asked me if I'd ever cut my dreads. Only for two reasons: for a really good corporate job . . . or if I start going bald. I won't be that guy who expects people to pretend like they don't notice. That's like Stevie Wonder. He's a legend, but somebody ought to tell him that his hair is missing in action. Those braids are barely hanging on. It's not his fault. The man can't see. It's his peeps fault. They need to make Stevie put those braids down . . . like an old dog.

As time goes by, people will start to see that it's not threatening to hire a person with dreadlocks. My mother said when she was growing up, black men in corporate America couldn't wear a goatee. White people looked at that as militant. Black Panther Party type of stuff. Now a goatee is okay. But my mother still wants me to get rid of my dreadlocks. I told her, "If my hair was meant to be short, it wouldn't grow back when I cut it." She couldn't come back on that one.

Mom says dread not.

Corey Morgan 25, Customer

Some people stick with a certain cut all their life. It becomes who they are. I'm glad I grew out of that Slant. I think my wife is, too.

✂ Corey
Morgan

When I was thirteen I wore a Slant, where the hair is real low on the sides and the back, and it slopes up to one side on the top. Sort of like a lopsided mountain. I wore a part that curved through the top. Like a hiking trail. That was how rappers wore their hair.

And ballplayers. And all my friends. I was cool.

Two years ago, my girlfriend came over to my mother's house. My girlfriend started looking through some photo albums. When she came across an old picture of me wearing a Slant, she laughed. Had a *good* laugh off me. Yeah, a haircut like that doesn't say much about your judgment. But she married me anyway.

What was I thinking? That's all I can say about that haircut. I blame it on my mother. When I was young, she had the barber cut my hair the same way all the time: low all over, pretty much skinned. One day, I told her I didn't like that style anymore. My eyebrows are too thick, and short hair made me look funny. So my mother told me I should try something new. So I started wearing haircuts like the Slant. One week I'd want it flat on top. The next week I'd want the part to zigzag. The next week I'd want to outdo the last week. My mother had created a monster. After a while, she had enough. She said, "We *can't* have this." She made me start telling her my new ideas *before* I went to the barber shop. She wanted to "yea" or "nay" them.

I've had the same barber all my life. For the longest, he had a picture of me sporting a Slant on his wall. He'd point it out to customers when I came in: "See that picture? That's him ten years ago." It was embarrassing. He took it down recently to do some renovations to the shop. I hope he forgets to put it back up.

I can't blame the Slant on him, though. I asked for it. And he's a great barber. Even when I lived in Pittsburgh, I always waited until I could get back home to get a haircut. I've gone more than two months without a cut just to wait for my barber. Only two people can cut my hair: him and me. And if I cut it, I'm just going to shave it off. Some people stick with a certain cut all their life. It becomes who they are. I'm glad I grew out of that Slant. I think my wife is, too.

I have two sons. They're one and three. Who knows what haircut they'll be wearing when they're teenagers. I'm just hoping the Slant doesn't come back. We can live without that one.

Corey's 1991 "Slant" on life

Kevin Session 46, Customer

A good barber is like a good lady: once you find the right one, hold on tight. The first time my current barber gave me a Razor Line I said, "Hey, what's your number?"

— Kevin Session

When I was a boy, Sunday meant church. And men wanted to look their best. That meant getting a Razor Line on Saturday. A good cut is like a Cadillac, but a Razor Line is a Rolls. Men who didn't get a Razor Line looked . . . unfinished.

I grew up on the west side of Detroit, near Eight Mile and the Monte Vista area. I would go to Mr. D's barber shop on Saturday mornings and watch men get a Razor Line. Young boys like me couldn't get one because you'd get sliced if you didn't sit real still. I couldn't wait till I was a man.

I forgot to blink when I watched men get a Razor Line. First, the barber would spread hot foam around a man's hairline: the forehead, the temples, around the ears. Some men even got a squared Razor Line, which includes the back of the neck. After applying the foam, the barber began to sharpen the straight razor. I was fascinated by that. A big leather belt hung from the barber's chair. He would take the belt in one hand and scrape the edge of the razor back and forth across the surface: away from him then toward him, away from him then toward him. It was a swift, rhythmic motion that made a distinct sound. Like a brush across a snare drum, followed by the beat of a high-hat cymbal. *Shh-tup. Shh-tup.* And then, the barber would stabilize the man's head with his free hand and sculpt a perfect frame around the guy's face. It was like music. It was like a dance. It was like art.

*Lookin'
sharp*

When I was a kid,
every barber knew how to do a
Razor Line. It was a required skill. Automatic. But these days it's your rare
barber who can pull one off without drawing blood.

A good barber is like a good lady: once you find the right one, hold on
tight. The first time my current barber gave me a Razor Line I said, "Hey,

what's your number?" You got to keep up with a guy with skills like that. But he moved on me.

When a barber leaves a shop, the other barbers act like they don't know where he went: "Who? What? Couldn't tell you." They *could*, but they won't. They want your business, you see. I ended up going to two or three different shops looking for a good barber. Oh, I got some bad cuts! One barber was giving me a Razor Line around my mustache and he cut me over my lip. That's the worst place in the world. Every time you talk or eat or smile, you feel it. I jumped and he said, "Oh, man! I'm sorry." I said, "That's okay." But I was thinking, *Sucka, you cut me!* I was *highly* upset. I was thinking, *Pull a razor on me? Don't you know I'm the police? I'll shoot your butt.* I've been on the force six years. I never went back to that barber. Why pay for torture? I know some neighborhoods where I can get cut up for free.

After a few weeks, I tracked my old barber down. I said, "Now, don't you do that again, brother. Where you go, I go."

Society will always look at a black man in a certain way. But what matters most is how we see ourselves, how we present ourselves. Your appearance says a lot about pride and self-respect. I like when people look at me and think, *That guy must be somebody.*

It's true what they say: clothes don't make the man. The *barber* makes the man.

Courtland Byrd 51, Barber Shop Owner

If you make a donkey of yourself in the barber shop, they'll ride you.

✂ **Courtland Byrd**

Thing 'bout this business, a barber never knows what kind of hair is gonna walk in the door. Got one guy in his late fifties who wears a wig. I guess he want to look young, but you can see his gray hair stickin' out from under the edges. If you're gonna sweep dirt under a rug, you gotta sweep it clean. There's more. This guy dyes his mustache and his eyebrows jet black. Old men don't have hair that black unless it comes from a bottle. When this guy come in, it takes all you got to keep from laughing 'cause he looks so false. Like a black Groucho Marx. But he's *cool* as he want to be. He don't get no haircut himself. He bring his little boy, who is five. So I guess he got it like that.

Now here's the thing. This guy's wig is a Jheri curl. I could see it if he wore fake hair that looked natural. But who would go shoppin' for Jheri curls to slap on top of his head? They're too high maintenance. You *know* he got to spray that lawn down all the time. I was in Mississippi a week ago Sunday, and I saw more Jheri curls growin' than cotton. I'm not lyin'. But you don't see that many here in Houston anymore. And that's fine by me.

I hate to see a Jheri curl walk in. You won't believe the number they do on a pair of clippers. All that gook clogs up the blade, dull it out real quick. I let guys with Jheri curls go once or twice, but then I break it down. I say, "You know, trying to cut your hair is like trying to run a lawn mower through wet grass."

Got it like that

"NOTHIN LIKE A BARBER'S TRIM"

Big Afros are a fad again. I hate to see a big Afro walk in the door. It takes a lot of work to get one even. But it's *more* work for the guy himself. He got to keep blow dryin' his hair and pickin' it out to make it look good. It's a big headache. Lot of guys last a month or two before they say, "Oh, no! I can't handle this. Cut it off." Some of 'em will start wearing their hair in braids 'cause it's less trouble. When they come in to get an edge up, I barely recognize 'em. Those braids are so tight that their eyes look Chinese. Tight braids are a poor man's facelift.

Got one longtime customer, Murphy. Good man, Murphy. Comes in with his brother-in-law. Always glad to see him. One time, while I was finishing up Murphy, I got caught up in the crosstalk. We were all laughin' and clownin' around, the barbers and the customers. Had a full house that day. When I was done with Murphy, I handed him the mirror. But he wouldn't take it. Just sat there. Thought maybe I had offended him, said something wrong. Everybody in the shop stopped talkin' and they stared at me and Murphy. I was like, *Is he gonna look at the haircut or what?* All of a sudden, the whole shop burst into laughter. You see, Murphy is blind. They get on me to this day about that: "Ol' CB showin' a blind man a mirror."

Murphy don't wear those dark glasses, so you forget. And when we get to jokin', he joins right in. Women, ball games, politics—don't matter. He don't miss much. But none of that matters at the end of the day. If you make a donkey of yourself in the barber shop, they'll ride you.

Women
on the Brain

Kola Olosunde 27, Customer

There's a natural rhythm to barber shop talk. It's like the call and response between a preacher and the congregation. And an ill-timed question throws the discussion off beat. You wouldn't ask for a point of clarification in the middle of a sermon, would you?

✂ Kola Olosunde

There are no out-of-bounds conversations in the barber shop. Guys will talk about their wife in one breath and their girlfriend in the next. It's not *what* we say that amuses me but *how* we say it.

Half of my barber shop is a beauty salon, so guys speak in code oftentimes, so as not to offend the sensibilities of the ladies. Your crude colloquialisms pop up anew every week, totally silly things designed to elicit a laugh. For instance, guys might refer to women as sandwiches:

"Did you try that grilled chicken you were talking about?"

"Naw, I went home and got a burger again."

"Hey, burgers are good. Especially if you get one with the works. Sometimes I can't pull myself from the table."

"I don't know. After a while, even a happy meal can bring you down."

"Well, you gotta shake things up. Try different condiments. All my life I thought I wouldn't like honey mustard. Wouldn't go near it. But I tried some once and, man, burgers have never tasted so good."

"Real men don't eat honey mustard."

"You ain't a real man till you do."

The references we use are constantly being invented and reinvented, mixed and remixed, but we all know what's really being said. And if you don't know, you don't ask. You just sit and follow the conversation. That's one of the unspoken rules in the barber shop. You never ask the group to fill you in. No, no, no! That'll make you look unschooled—unfamiliar with the vernacular. Also, you don't want to disturb the flow of the narrative. That's another rule. There's a natural rhythm to barber shop talk. It's like the call and response between a preacher and the congregation. And an ill-timed question throws the discussion off beat. You wouldn't ask for a point of clarification in the middle of a sermon, would you?

If you want to discuss a personal problem, you have to be honest or they'll see right through you. That's an important rule. You have to be careful about that one. Because the second you say something like, "A buddy of mine has a problem," they're all over you. "A buddy of yours.

Kola (second from left) hangs outside the shop.

④

Yeah, right. What's his problem, *buddy?*" It's so much better just to say, "Here's what happened to me," and move on from there. Because if you get caught being reticent, you look like a jerk. And in the barber shop, they'll have at you like a fat man on a slab of ribs.

I once got into a heated debate about African dictators with another customer. He said how wrong he thought it was for the dictators to exploit their starving people. I told him that I agreed. But I contended that things aren't always black and white. I pointed out that the dictators grow up in austere poverty, too. When they get into a position of power, I said, it's only logical that they'll consume to the point of gluttony and cling to power with brutality.

The customer said, "Look, college boy. Big words don't make you right. I went to the school of hard knocks. Know what I learned there? I learned that wrong is wrong. And it's wrong to take advantage of people."

The barber shop is the great homogenizer. I graduated from the University of Massachusetts and I investigate allegations of misconduct against the NYPD. But education and career mean nothing in the barber shop. You may be a drug dealer or you may be a doctor. Doesn't matter. When you enter the barber shop, you leave who you are at the door.

Dasia Thomas 29, Customer

I've been inside a barber shop only once in my life— when I took my little brother, Bernard, to get a haircut. It never occurred to me that I would be out of place . . . a swan amongst apes.

✂ Dasia
Thomas

Almost every block here in (Washington) D.C. has one of three things: a church, a liquor store, or a barber shop. I think it's a law. I've been inside a barber shop only once in my life—when I took my little brother, Bernard, to get a haircut. It never occurred to me that I would be out of place . . . a swan amongst apes.

There're a lot of years between me and Bernard. He's eight now but back then he was five or six. It was a Saturday and my mom wanted Bernard's hair cut for church. Everybody else was busy, so I took him.

When we got there, it was a long line. All the chairs were taken. Standing room only. Everyone looked at us. Then one guy smiled at me and said, "You can have my seat." He was about twenty-five or thirty. A real gentleman.

But it didn't take long for them to forget a lady was in the room. You should have heard their language. I was surprised how men talk to each other in a barber shop. They talked about women a lot, about their latest conquest in the neighborhood. It got very explicit very fast. It sounded like the plot for a porno flick.

I don't remember word for word, but one guy would start talking about how he had relations with some woman, and how well he performed, and how she'll remember him for a *lon-n-n-n-ng* time. Another guy would say,

Dasia's view

"Yeah, I had her already." Then another guy would say, "I haven't had her, but my boy has. They call her birthday cake. Everybody gets a piece."

It was disgusting. I kept thinking, *Why would they discuss this in a barber shop?* What's that all about? Competition? Male bonding? Whatever it was, you'd think they'd show a little courtesy. But they acted like I was one of the boys.

When women are with women, like in the beauty shop, we feel open to talk—about men we're dating, about their *attributes* or lack thereof. But if a man is around, we won't say much of anything. But those guys didn't care that a lady was in the house. If Bernard didn't really need a haircut, I would have left. So I just picked up a copy of *Ebony* and tried to ignore them.

I had no idea what men talked about when they were alone. Know what I came away with? Men gossip just like women.

Lora Butler and Timothy Butler Barbers, 34 and 32

One time a guy came in and said, "Where your wife at?" I was like, "Hold up. Why you need to check on my wife?" And then I remembered that she's his barber.

✂ Timothy Butler

TIMOTHY: The first time I saw Lora she was pulling up on a motorcycle.

LORA: I had a Kawasaki 750. I like street bikes.

TIMOTHY: She came to interview with my father about a job. I couldn't believe she wanted to cut hair. She was such a beautiful woman.

LORA: People at my barber school recommended that I go see Mr. Butler. They thought it was a safe shop for a female. They said Mr. Butler was an older gentleman who had respect for ladies....

TIMOTHY: ... What'd they say about me?

LORA: ... Mr. Butler told me, "If you can ride a motorcycle, you can cut hair." I started the next week.

TIMOTHY: In the beginning, she was just another barber. I'd tell her how to get started on certain haircuts. Shortcuts to take.

LORA: Both of us were in bad relationships. Sometimes we'd sit down and cry on each other's shoulder.

TIMOTHY: She worked in the chair beside me so it just snowballed. But I didn't want my father to know. He always said, "Don't date anyone you work with."

LORA: One day, one of Mr. Butler's customers came in. Mr. Abdoo, an older African man. He said, "Butler. Have you looked at Tim and your lady

145

barber lately?" Mr. Butler said, "I look at 'em every day." Mr. Abdoo said, "I telling you, Butler. They got someting going on. Mr. Butler said, "What are you talkin' about?" The whole time I'm thinking, *Why don't this man shut up.*

TIMOTHY: I'm thinking, *Why don't he get his haircut and leave.*

LORA: Mr. Abdoo said, "I see it in their eyes. I telling you. I telling you. They got someting going on, someting strong."

TIMOTHY: He had never seen us out or anything. Couldn't have, because we hadn't been out yet. We were just testing the water.

LORA: It was spooky because we thought we were hiding our feelings.

TIMOTHY: Oh, we thought we were good!

LORA: Mr. Butler didn't say anything for two or three days. Finally, he called us back to the office. He said, "Do y'all got somethin' goin' on?"

TIMOTHY: Both of us said "yeah" at the same time.

LORA: He said, "Well, what you do outside of work is your business. But in the barber shop, keep it strictly professional."

TIMOTHY: And we have. We work well together. In spite of all the non-sense. When some guys come in they tell Lora, "You cut it the way you want." What they're really saying is, "How would you want my hair to look if I was your man?"

LORA: Sometimes I'll cut a guy's hair and he'll leave the shop and call right back to talk to me.

TIMOTHY: Half the time, they don't realize it's *me* answering the phone. Or they don't care.

LORA: Same goes with the females. They'll come in and go right to Tim's chair. Some of them send him greeting cards.

TIMOTHY: The same customer who will sit in my chair and not tip me will sit in *her* chair and give *all* his money away. One time a guy came in and said, "Where your wife at?" I was like, "Hold up. Why you need to check on *my* wife?" And then I remembered that she's his barber.

Bride and grooming

Fabian Shorey 32, **Barber**

My wife has a Master's in psychology and she's working on her PhD. But I do more counseling than she does.

✂ **Fabian Shorey**

I work at a barber shop in Brooklyn named Skilzs. When you walk into Skilzs, it's like two different barber shops in one—hot and cold. The front of the shop is sort of quiet, all business. But when you go to the back, past the coatrack, that's where the brothers be kickin' it. We call it the dungeon. Doctors, bus drivers, businessmen. One guy's a federal agent. We're like family in the dungeon. Guys advise each other on real estate, legal problems, relationships. There's a *lot* of talk about relationships. We have women on the brain.

When guys ask me for relationship advice, I try to get a lot of details from them. It's hard to give advice without all the facts. Then I might say, "Look, you're inside the box. I'm outside the box. Things look different from out here." But I never tell them what they should do. I say, "Here's what *I* would do."

Not everything is black or white, you know. I tell guys that they have to do the right thing, but sometimes the right thing isn't always the honest thing. Sometimes you should confess. Sometimes you shouldn't.

I've been married since I was twenty-eight. Marriage is the best thing that ever happened to me. But I did something dumb once. One night, I'm hanging out with some friends. We're shootin' the breeze with some chicks at a bar named The Vibe. We're barhopping so eventually we decide to leave. I don't realize I've left my cell phone at the bar. Well, my wife calls and one of the chicks answers. Then my wife calls me on my buddy's phone. She says, "Where are you?" I say, "I, I, I . . . I'm in a bar." She says, "I just called your phone and a woman answered and she . . ." I panic. I realize that I don't know where my phone is so I start conjuring up a story. I say that this woman asked to use the phone and I

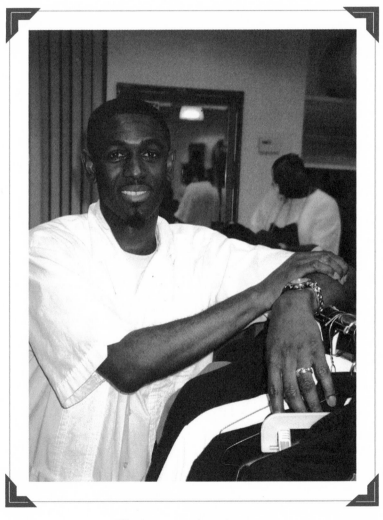

Fabian in the "dungeon"

forgot to get it back or some crazy story like that. I go back to The Vibe and the bartender has my phone.

When I get up in the morning, I realize that that was stupid. Why did I tell that lie? So I tell my wife, "Look, I was drinking last night, we met some chicks, I left and forgot my phone. That's all that happened." She said, "I know. The woman explained that you left your phone and she was going to leave it with the bartender, but then you created this *crazy* story." I told her I was wrong and I was sorry. I came clean and I think that helped strengthen our relationship.

Now, on the other hand, this client came in one day. He told me his fiancée said that she had a private detective following him around. He said, "I think she knows more than she's saying. Should I tell her about the affair?" I said, "Look, if she *had* the goods she'd put them on the table. She'd pull out surveillance photos and say, 'There you go with that little hoochie.' " I said, "Is it over?" He said, "Yes." I said, "Then if you confess, you'll be giving yourself up for nothing. She's casting the line out there and you're about to bite the hook. Swim away, my brother. Just swim away." There's nothing wrong with coming clean, but you should be prepared to lose something you love.

My wife has a Master's in psychology and she's working on her PhD. But I do more counseling than she does.

Robert Friday 22, Barber

I've never seen a barber steal another barber's customer. That's 'cause they do it when nobody's lookin'.

 Robert Friday

I've never seen a barber steal another barber's customer. That's 'cause they do it when nobody's lookin'. One of my customers told me he ran into a barber from my old shop one day. He said the barber told him I was chargin' him double, which I wasn't. But my customer told me he wouldn't sit in that barber's chair no way 'cause when he shook his hand the barber had cold fingers. More like sticky fingers.

Most barbers, we don't steal customers. But that same barber thought I was tryin' to steal his woman. Here's how it came down. I was cuttin' a guy's hair when this girl walked in. She had on baggy khakis and a blue shirt with a Wal Mart badge or somethin'. Her hair was straight and it was wrapped around her head, a little loosely . . . in a I'm-runnin'-late kind of style. I figured she wanted her eyebrows arched. I asked her if I could help her, and smiled. But I smile at everybody. She said she was waitin' on another barber.

So the girl went over to the candy machine. She put a quarter in and only two Hot Tamales came out. She said, "Dang, y'all tryin' to gyp people up in here." My boss shook the machine and two more dropped out. She said, "Shoot, this still ain't enough for a quarter." So I said, "Well, if you too upset, can I have 'em?" She looked at me crazy, but with a little smile. I said, "Naw, I'm just messin' with you."

Then I noticed her nails. The tips were two shades of purple . . . in a pattern that looked like flames. I said, "Can I see your nails?" She held her hands up. I said, "Yeah, those look nice." By that time, that barber, Cold

Fingers, he was gettin' upset over there. But I didn't know why. I seen his girlfriend and this wasn't her. I didn't know he was all messed up in the game. Either he was tryin' to be a pimp . . . or a sperm donor.

I had an application to fill out so I asked the other barbers for a pen. Nobody had one. I asked the girl for a pen. She didn't have one. So that barber said, "A *player* should *always* have a pen if he want the digits." I said, "Naw, these days a player can store numbers in his cell phone. But you wouldn't know that." So he was like, "If you don't have a pen or pencil, you must be illiterate." I was like, "No. You illiterate if you can't read or write. You also illiterate if you don't know what illiterate means." He wasn't gonna chump *me* down.

So the girl got in his chair and he arched her eyebrows. When she left, he was like, "Hey, that was my baby's mama." I said, "I didn't know that." Then he got all loud with it so I said, "I was just messin' with her about sharing her candy." He said, "You got dough. Get your *own* candy." I said, "Look, it ain't that serious . . ." He said, "*I'm* serious. You better not say nothin' to her." I was like, "I won't talk to her in that way again, but you can't tell me I can't talk to her at all. Come on, now. That ain't your wife. That ain't even your girlfriend. Why you blockin' in the first place? Only thing lookin' good about her was her nails."

I like peace in the barber shop. It doesn't have to be quiet, but it should be calm . . . no craziness. Best way to keep peace is to arch your baby's mama's eyebrows at home.

Robert raises eyebrows.

Kicks
of the Trade

Nathaniel "Cuz" Davis 62, Co-owner of a Barber School

A barber can't turn no business away. This man comes in. He says, "Cut me a Philly." I say, "A Philly? Okay, sit down." When I finish up he says, "Hey, this ain't no Philly." I say, "Well, Cuz, that's a Baltimore. That's as close as I could get."

— Nathaniel "Cuz" Davis

A barber can't turn no business away. This man comes in. He say, "Cut me a Philly." I say, "A Philly? Okay, sit down." When I finish up he say, "Hey, this ain't no Philly." I say, "Well, Cuz, that's a Baltimore. That's as close as I could get."

I call everybody "Cuz." Makes 'em feel good, like you best friends. I'll say, "Hey, Cuz, how you been?" But I don't bit more know 'em than I know Swahili.

Another thing a barber can't do. A barber can't let people take advantage. Parents will bring their sons in and say, "I'll be back." I say, "You'll *both* be back. We don't do no babysittin'." Man, they'll leave them children and won't come back till you put 'em through college.

This one guy tried to take advantage. I was halfway finished when he say, "Man, you know I ain't got no money." I say, "Cuz, what you mean you ain't got no money?" He say, "I ain't got no money." I say, "Why you sit in this chair if you ain't got no money?"

He say, "Well, I heard you had a program down here." See, me and my partner run a barber school. We're tryin' to educate these young guys.

*"Cuz" kicks it between classes
at his barber school.*

Some of our students have committed a felony. The government pays us to train 'em 'cause businesses don't hire felons. Slap some black on that and you can hang it up. So we teach 'em how to work for themselves. It's the students who do the free haircuts. So I tell the man, "Wait, you supposed to tell me before you get in the chair. I thought you were a regular customer." He knew the deal. Old as I look, how he gonna think I'm a student? I say, "Look, Cuz, you got to go." He looks in the mirror and sees I cut only one side. He say, "I can't leave lookin' like this." I say, "That's a new style. You heard of a Mohawk? Well, that's a *No* Mohawk. Don't come back No Mo'."

Here's the thing 'bout messin' up a head. Never admit it. Second you go, "Oops!," you busted. Woman came in for a Bob once. She had this long, long hair. I got so carried away that I gave her a Crew cut. But I say, "No, you ain't messed up. You in *style*. That's the look now." She say, "Oh? Good! I'm gonna tell *all* my girlfriends." I cut a gap out the back of a man's hair. Before he paid, he asked for a hand mirror so he could see the back. I say, "We don't believe in hand mirrors. Objects may be closer than they appear." It was a couple of days before he came back. He say, "Man, you messed me up." I say, "Cuz, you halfway to a full recovery. Take a couple aspirins and call me in the mornin'."

The barber students will take advantage, too. We had to stop 'em from usin' the phone. Man, these young jitterbugs, they do everything but make love on the phone. And maybe they do that, too, 'cause they fall asleep holdin' the receiver. I used to get all loud to make 'em hang up. I'd say, "Is that the girl that called a while ago?" They got hot, then. But they stopped messin' with that phone. I'd say, "Man, what you want to be . . . a barber or a lover?" I'd say, "I ain't sure, but I think Casanova paid his own phone bill."

I'm gonna school 'em yet.

Deborah Rondo 48, Barber

I asked the boy what happened to his head. He said, "Daddy said to say Mama did it."

 Deborah Rondo

Barbers have a secret language, a secret code. We have our way of talkin' to each other without the customer catchin' on. There's the turkey call, for example: *gobble, gobble, gobble.* When you hear that, you know a barber done messed up because they were in a rush or somethin'. We used to call it a Jackson. But "Jackson" sounded too close to the real thing: "Man, you *jacked* him up." So now we just gobble, and the customers don't have a clue.

Then there's the kiss: *smack, smack.* You make the kissin' sound when a barber keeps a customer in the chair too long. They're usually kissin' up to a customer who drops big tips. They're gonna trim his mustache. They're gonna pat him down with extra aftershave. They're gonna brush every stray hair off his shirt. That barber's gonna do whatever he can to keep those tips flowin'. I do it, too. We *all* do it. And we all give each other the kiss.

Now, if it's a Friday or a Saturday and we're really busy, you might get more than the kiss. Somebody might come out and say, "We got all these people waitin' and you took forty-five minutes on *one* customer? What were you doin'? Tryin' to make love?"

Another code we use is "two dollars." We say that when

"Daddy said to say Mama did it."

someone has gone to a bootleg barber or their mama done cut their hair. If you walk in here with a messed-up haircut you have to pay the regular fee, plus we tack on two dollars. That's the repair fee. So as soon as we notice a hack job come through the door, we say "two dollars" to each other. Customers think we're makin' bets.

A young man came in once. He said he had wanted a part down the middle of his head so he took his mother's clippers and tried to do it himself. But he had cut this wide, crooked gap. What can you do with that? Had to give him a bald head. Cut it right down to his thick skull, and charged him the extra two dollars.

Some customers don't realize how difficult it is to cut hair. You got some fathers who come in for a cut and they're watching you and the other

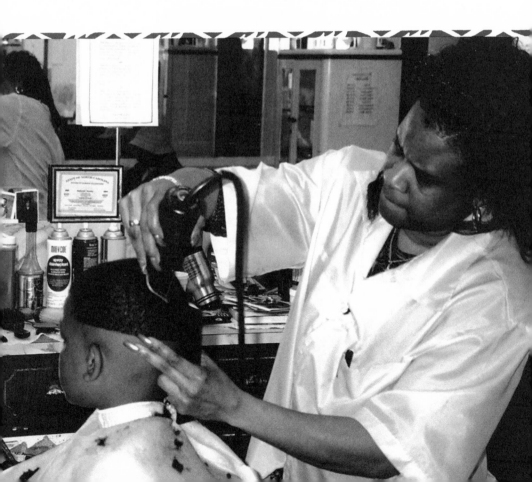

barbers the whole time. They're plannin' to go home and cut their sons' hair themselves. One time a customer asked me, "What's that cut called?" I said, "Oh, this is a Fade." Next thing you know he's draggin' his son in askin' me to fix his experiment. I asked the boy what happened to his head. He said, "Daddy said to say Mama did it."

Some of the fathers will wait till just before we close and smuggle the kid in the door with a hat pulled down on the boy's head, the poor thing. Either that or they're the first ones here in the morning. The father will whisper, "Can you do somethin' with his head?" When he takes the hat off the kid, you try not to laugh. Child's been traumatized enough, goin' to school with chunks of hair missin', lookin' like he got the tetters.

In barber school, they teach you the basics. But they don't teach you all you need to know to survive. You have to learn survival skills on the job. And you have to watch the older barbers and learn the codes.

Brian Butler 38, **Customer**

When I also started giving haircuts to MJ, my four-year-old son, my wife put her foot down. Cathy said she didn't want MJ's head looking all helter-skelter. But that's what baseball caps are for.

✂ Brian
Butler

Before you get a new barber, do your research. I learned that the hard way. For years, my regular barber here in Orlando was Willie Bradford. Everybody calls him Brad. Two years ago Brad closed his shop to undergo treatment for prostate cancer. He's fine now, but back then I started cutting my own hair. When I also started giving hair cuts to MJ, my four-year-old son, my wife put her foot down. Cathy said she didn't want MJ's head looking all helter-skelter. But that's what baseball caps are for.

When I found a new shop, I put MJ in the chair of a barber who had a good reputation. But then I made a bad decision. Instead of waiting for that same barber, I sat in the chair of a guy I knew nothing about. He was in his twenties and wore a little too much jewelry for me. The king of bling, as they say. His shoes were *GQ Magazine* meets *Jet*, not the plain-looking, comfortable shoes barbers usually wear. He just didn't look like the barber shop was where he belonged. He looked like a rapper with clippers for a microphone. His chair was open even though six or seven customers were waiting. That's always a bad sign. So I kept it simple. I told him, "Just shape it up."

A few minutes into the cut, I hear screeching tires. I look through the front window and see this man in fishing gear hop out of a Ford pickup

Brian and MJ hiding their cuts at the ballpark

truck. One of his front tires has jumped the curb. He flings open the door to the barber shop and proceeds to yell at the *GQ* barber.

He shouts, "Naw, you not gonna take *me*." The shop goes silent. The *GQ* barber says, "What?" The angry man says, "I'm no dumb nigga. You not gonna play me like a fool." The *GQ* barber says, "What you talkin' 'bout?" The angry man says, "You're skimmin' money from the register." The *GQ* barber says, "That's crazy." The angry man says, "And you're rippin' off the vending machine."

Okay, so now I figure that the angry man is the shopkeeper. But, mind you, the *GQ* barber is still cutting my hair through this whole argument.

As the fight intensifies, he scrapes my scalp harder and harder. Those clippers are hurting and I want to say something, but it's a bad time to complain. Poor MJ is looking confused. He's never seen two grown men arguing like children: "Yeah, you did." "No, I didn't." *"Yeah,* you did." *"No,* I didn't." Meanwhile, the other barbers look helpless. You can tell that they want to cool things down, but they don't want to get into it with their boss.

Then the angry man and the *GQ* barber *really* get into it. Four-letter words are flying and the guy is *still* cutting my hair. I don't know whether this is leading to fisticuffs or what. Sweat is pouring down my face and I'm wondering what my hair's gonna look like. Finally, the angry man says he's calling the police. When the *GQ* barber says he has nothing to hide, the angry man slings the phone in his direction, which is also in *my* direction. We both duck. Then the *GQ* barber grabs a container of talcum powder and throws it at the angry man. There's a big, white explosion.

"That's it!" the angry man shouts. "You're fired!" I'm probably more shocked than the *GQ* barber. I mean, I believe in taking care of business. But right in the middle of my haircut?

Kenneth Dodd 60, Barber Shop Owner

A tip is a courtesy. It's icing on the cake. But who don't like a little icing?

— Kenneth Dodd

I grew up in Mount Airy, North Carolina. That's where actor Andy Griffith is from. His old TV show was based on Mount Airy, but he called it Mayberry. Black people didn't know the Mayberry you see on the Andy Griffith Show. We wouldn't be able to eat at the diner or go to Floyd's barber shop. Mount Airy was segregated, so the TV show got that part right.

Blacks went to the Virginia Street Barber Shop. At harvesttime, I'd go on Saturdays, after priming tobacco all week. You sweat from sunup to sundown when you prime tobacco, snapping three or four leaves from each stalk and carrying them to the barn in loads for curing. It's all done by machines now, but when I was young it was all hands and back.

One time, when I was fifteen or sixteen, I was sitting in the Virginia Street Barber Shop, watching the guys cut hair. I was adding the money up as they went along. I saw one barber cut four heads in an hour's time, and he was getting seventy-five cents a head. I got paid seventy-five cents an *hour*. Right then and there I figured that hair was a better crop than tobacco. So I went to barber school.

The thing about working tobacco, it makes you appreciate little things. Like tips. Sometimes, tips are *real* little. Your average tip is a dollar. Sometimes you get two or three. The most you'll probably get is five dollars, and that's very seldom. And there are *plenty* of people who don't tip at all. Some people feel like, "Hey, I paid for my haircut. I don't owe you anything else." And that's true. A tip is a courtesy. It's icing on the cake. But who don't like a little icing?

There are little things you do to help customers tip. When they pay, we break their change down. We might break a five down to singles. Even then, some people will cram the singles in their pocket and say, "Thanks, man. See you next time." You have to be able to smile and say, "Okay, next time." I've been doing this a long time. If you don't bend, you break.

Every Thanksgiving season, we put shoeboxes on our stands. We cover the boxes in wrapping paper and cut a slit in the top. We don't put a label on the boxes, but people know they're for tips. That's been a tradition since

Kenneth chills in 1974.

before I started cutting in 1963. We have quite a few customers who will put a little something in every barber's box. It won't make you rich, but it's nice thank-you-ma'am money. That's what we used to say in Mount Airy when you got a little something extra: that's nice thank-you ma'am money.

Here's the lowdown on tipping. Customers are a little more giving around the holidays. Customers tip better after they get paid. When Social Security comes, tips are good then, too. Women are better tippers than men. Maybe they're nicer than men. Or maybe they just have more money. I don't know. When some men hit about fifty, they stop tipping. That's like church. You don't see too many old people in line to pay tithes, either. Maybe they feel like, "The Lord knows I've been tithin' a *long* time." A tip is something you appreciate, but it's not something you can count on. If you do, you'll wind up hungry.

Lennie Bosley 35, Barber

A good barber knows how to cut. A <u>smart</u> barber knows when to sleep. . . . You gotta intermission when you can.

✂ Lennie Bosley

A good barber knows how to cut. A *smart* barber knows when to sleep. We work six days a week, twelve hours a day. And we're on our feet the whole time. It ain't a easy job. You gotta intermission when you can.

We try not to sleep out there on the chairs 'cause it looks bad. If you want to take a ten-minute break, you're supposed to go back in the lounge. But I ain't gonna lie to you, those chairs are kinda comfortable. You start out just meanin' to get off your feet. But then you sit back in that soft leather and it kinda hugs you. Then your arms feel heavy, so you put them on the armrests. Then your head keeps noddin', so you rest it in your hand. Next thing you know, you've gone fishin'.

This ain't a regular nine to five. You gotta be in it, doin' it. Know what I'm sayin'? What you put out is what you get back. You put out nothin', you get back nothin'. But if you put out *everything*, you got nothin' to take home. And I'm a married man.

Having back-to-back appointments, that's a barber's dream. But it takes a while to build up that kind of clientele. I've been cuttin' hair since '82. But when me and my wife moved from Buffalo, New York, to Charlotte eight years ago, it was like startin' over. If customers don't know your face, they ain't jumpin' in your chair. So you try real hard.

When I first moved down here, I had this customer who still wore finger waves. I mean, Charlotte is growin', but it's still a decade behind. That guy would just be talkin' and talkin' and talkin'. I'd be like, "Un uh . . .

yeah . . . I know what you mean . . . for real?" But I *still* don't know what he be sayin'. He mumbles worse than James Brown . . . 'cause he mumbles with a Southern accent.

But you gotta be careful talkin' 'bout people down here. You never know who's in your chair. Everybody knows everybody. They're all related. You meet somebody and they say, "Oh, you know Leon? He's my cousin." I don't know how anyone can get married. They're all cousins. What kills me is people always ask, "What made you move from New York?" In Buffalo, there weren't a lot of jobs. So a lot of people sold drugs to get by. Some guys even sold drugs out the barber shop. And they carried guns. It was dangerous. But down here, they run a barber shop like a business. You can relax on the job. You can even take a nap.

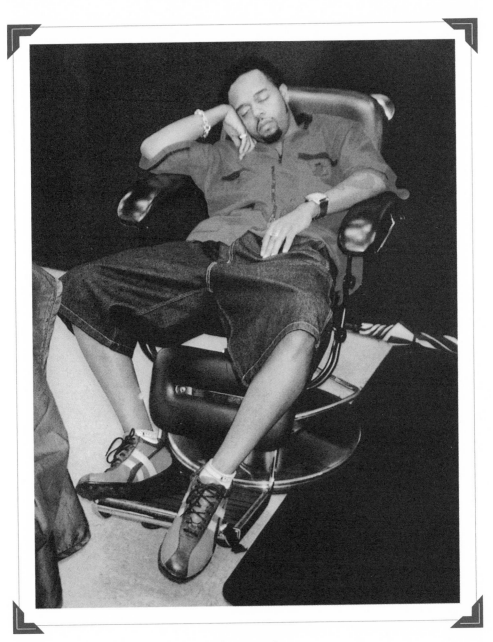

Gone fishin'

Acknowledgments

A collection of oral histories is only as captivating as its storytellers. My bottomless gratitude to the barbers and customers who shared their time and sentiments.

I would not have found many of the fascinating people in this book without leads from the following: Kim Anderson, Reginald Attucks, Aaron Bailey, Florence Brown, Rochelle Brown, David A. Butler, James Ford, Les High, Janet Grace Hill, Esther Levine, Teresa Morgan, Alexander Parker, Kevin Powell, Clara Powers, Bill Vaughn, and Chuck Wallington. Thanks, also, to Lenore Markowitz, who drove me to Dooney's barber shop in Dallas and waited with gracious patience.

Many thanks to Reginald Attucks, Taylor Blackwell, James Butler, Wheeler Parker, and Alexander Parker for use of photos from their private collections; to photographer Fabio Camara for his counsel; and to computer guru Jeff Lathery for extending his artistic talents, as well as his able family of couriers, Candi and Morgan. Thanks also to graphics designer Tim Love for dropping everything to pitch in. And to the legendary photographer Chester Higgins for the jacket image.

Special thanks to Molly Smith and Charles Randolph-Wright for picking this project out of the blue for a stage adaptation.

And thanks, too, to many others who helped in countless ways: Dan Bauer, Kim Cacho, Barbara Chavis, Susan Cochran, Dr. Marvin Curtis, Saint Paul Davis, Chuck Deggans, Mary Evans, Karen Goldman, Clarence Haynes, Yuko Ichioka, Mara Isaacs, Tracy Jacobs, Robert Johnson, Terry Karydes, Linda Fay McCord, Devin McIntyre, Joseph Onuoha, Cassandra Parker, Fleur Paysour, Vanessa Work Ramseur, Clara Schoffner, Lucy Sligh, Corey Smith, Rhonda Tankerson, Leonora D. Thompson, Anne Paine West, Babatunde Williams, Brent Williams, LaVon Stennis Williams, Miki Williams, and Dr. Frank Woods.

Last and foremost, for a book about black men I have a lot of black women to thank for guiding this book into finished form. My eternal appreciation to my dear friend Paula Robinson, who was first to critique the narratives and encouraged me throughout. To my marvelous agent, Tanya McKinnon, of Mary Evans, Inc., who has the singular talent of making her many clients feel as if they're the only one. And to Janet Hill, Doubleday executive editor and vice president, thank you for your energy, enthusiasm, and allegiance.

Photo Credits

Page 11: courtesy Alexander Parker; **Pages 12–13:** courtesy Taylor Blackwell, Blackwell Ink., Inc., from *David Played a Harp* by Ralph Johnson; **Page 15:** courtesy George Evans; **Page 21:** by Reginald Attucks; **Page 24:** courtesy Bruce Simms; **Page 26:** courtesy Robin Simmons-Blount; **Page 35:** courtesy Bernard Mathis; **Page 43:** courtesy James Butler; **Page 46:** courtesy Kenneth Norton; **Pages 48–49:** courtesy Wheeler Parker; **Page 57:** courtesy James Butler; **Pages 60–61:** by Reginald Attucks; **Page 71:** by Reginald Attucks; **Page 74:** courtesy Kwame Bandele; **Page 77:** courtesy Alexander Parker; **Page 102:** courtesy Rev. John C. McClurkin; **Page 105:** courtesy Damian Johnson; **Page 122:** courtesy Reginald Attucks; **Page 130:** by Reginald Attucks; **Page 164:** courtesy Brian Butler; **Page 167:** courtesy Kenneth Dodd. All other photos by author.

About the Author

Craig Marberry is author of *Crowns: Portraits of Black Women in Church Hats* and *Spirit of Harlem: A Portrait of America's Most Exciting Neighborhood.* A former television reporter, Marberry has written for the *Washington Post* and *Essence* magazine. He's a graduate of Morehouse College and earned his Master's from the Columbia University Graduate School of Journalism. His collection of oral histories in *Crowns* has been adapted into an award-winning play by Regina Taylor. Charles Randolph-Wright has adapted *Cuttin' Up* for the stage.

Marberry lives in Greensboro, North Carolina.

A portion of the proceeds from this book supports the Maya Angelou Research Center on Minority Health at Wake Forest University.